Athina Onassis
The Red File

By

Alexis Mantheakis

Fragments

"The key to an heiress's money is between her legs."
Gigolo, to an American reporter at the Carlton Bar, Cannes

"To live well you must live hidden (away)."
Industrialist and bon viveur Henri Roussel to his son, Thierry

"The only rule is that there are no rules."
Aristotle Onassis

"Rich people are not poor people with money."
The Author

©2018.Alexis Mantheakis

A Mistress for Hire in Belgium – A well kept secret 11
Escort, as in CALL GIRL! – Nicky's Story 13
A Soap Opera Wedding in Brazil 21
Nicky delivers the goods 27
Introduction 42
ONASSIS – That name! 42
The Brazilians 60
The English Detective Connection 63
Nicky's Choice – A Sex Cinema or a Swingers' Club 68
Nicky and the violin 70
The Split – 76
The Red File 86
The Bird has Flown 96
Athina Meets Doda 106
The Handsome Horseman and the Onassis heiress 111
Dividing the Onassis Fortune Spoils 117
The Billion Dollar Dispute 117
A Commando Kidnap Scenario 119
The Greek Administrators Accuse Thierry 131
The Onassis family beginnings 136
Interviewing Thierry at the Onassis mansion 138
Athina – the first sighting 139

Athina and the family arrive in Athens 145
Preparing the heiress to meet the media 150
On a yacht in Greece 153
Alone at the Boislande mansion 164
A fairytale Ibiza vacation with the family 169
First morning in Ibiza- 8 pools and SAS bodyguards 176
Goings on at Scorpios 190
The Orthodox Church reaches out to Onassis' granddaughter 192
A determined stalker and other admirers 205
Return with Athina to Scorpios, November 1998 218
A Romantic Onassis wedding by the sea 238
Christina's demons 256
"You were the best, Ari, and you were the worst!" 259
A Doll made of Steel 271
Thierry and Athina. A very expensive dispute 279
Cybele's suicide and the Onassis Curse 290
Cancer Ward 298
'Sharper than a serpent's tooth is a thankless child' (King Lear, William Shakespeare) 301
Epilogue 314

Sections of this book have previously been published under the title "Athina Onassis in the Eye of the Storm".

All rights reserved.

A Mistress for Hire in Belgium – A well kept secret

September, 2014. I had been scanning my email and social media messages, filtering out the usual spam, when I noticed a Facebook message from a woman called Suzy Suzon who said she had read my book on Athina Onassis and had something to tell me. This in itself was not unusual: admirers of Athina and would-be suitors contacted me regularly trying to gain access to the heiress for their projects – horse farms in Spain, hotels in Greece, stables in the US, charity events and school or municipal prize-givings, along with a steady list of long-lost Onassis relatives or former employees from Montevideo, Asia Minor or Athens wishing to establish contact with the elusive heiress to the Onassis fortune.

This message however was different. I wrote back to ask what she wanted, demanding to know her real name because the one she used for Facebook was that of a Thirties-era French actress, nor was there any personal information or any photos uploaded to her profile other than just one from a riding event. I wanted to know who she was. An hour later a message came to my mailbox. The woman had a story to tell Athina and would I please pass it on to her or her father Thierry Roussel? She asked for my phone number, which I gave, curious now to see what she had to say.

Around midday my home phone rang and I heard a woman's voice quietly addressing me in French.

"I had an affair with Athina Onassis' husband Doda for many years, and I want to tell my story to Athina."

I was surprised. I asked where she lived but the line was so bad and my school French so rusty that communication was difficult. I proposed she write to me in French and I would reply in English. This would make our exchanges easier and, more important, give me a record of what she had to say, if indeed she was not another storyteller or one more delusional Onassis celebrity fan, a fair share of whom stalked me after I became the family representative in 1998 and started appearing in media interviews or next to the heiress and her family on prime time TV news that their fame guaranteed. I told Suzy to explain how she had met Doda and to tell me anything more she had to say.

Escort, as in CALL GIRL! – Nicky's Story

The first message came in French soon afterwards.
"I will try and tell you a little about myself, without going into unnecessary detail. I am in fact Nicky T. The same person as Suzy Suzon, the divorced mother of a young girl who is 9 years old. I worked in a library for several years but have not held a regular job for a while.

I am the fifth daughter of six children in a family where my mother was a housewife and my father a general heading a well-known branch of the French military. A perfectly normal and ordinary life up until the month of January of 2006 when I met Doda, Athina's husband, who introduced himself to me as ROMEU.

I met him in my capacity as an escort. At that time I did not know who he was, but of course I had heard of the Onassis family, but nothing about Doda... It was only in 2011 when I was watching television, specifically an equestrian programme called Equidalive, that I recognised Doda along with some other Brazilian equestrians. (After this) I told him I had recognised him but assured him that nothing had changed for me.

As a result of this I started travelling. I went to Rio to attend the Athina Onassis Horse Show there with Doda. Bit by bit Doda started confiding family secrets to me, for example the reason why Athina was no longer talking to her father, Thierry. Could this have been because of an accident?[1] There

---

[1] There had been an accident in Ibiza where two East European girls riding a jet ski based at the Roussel Ibiza

were other small secrets which were not of significance to me at the time but later assumed importance. I continued seeing Doda until June of 2014 where we met at the Longines Athina Onassis Horse Show at St Tropez.

That was the last time I saw him. On our final evening together we were having a heated discussion in the car and something had happened that broke up our relationship. It was during this argument that he took his decision to finish with me. (I made it clear) I was no longer committed to being his plaything. I demanded that he be honest and sincere with me, as I had been with him. More so since he and I had something that would bind us together forever and he seemed to forget it very quickly.

It is because of this that I am so angry, and more so because he decided to send me his lawyers to protect the peace and quiet of his life."

I was intrigued. The woman, if she were telling the truth, had started an affair with Athina's husband just a month, or even less, after the high profile celebrity wedding of Athina and Doda in Brazil; Nicky had engaged in an affair with Athina's husband that had lasted for eight and a half years!

---

mansion belonging to Athina had been killed in a collision with a yacht owned by a German. Thierry had been implicated because he was entertaining eight young women at the time, according to an Italian press report. When I asked Yves Repiquet, Thierry's close friend and Paris-based lawyer, with whom I communicated regularly in the course of court cases we were both working on, he denied that Thierry was in Spain at the time.

The utter cynicism of Doda, if the story were true, was shocking. It put his whole much-vaunted fairytale love affair and marriage with the Golden Heiress, as Athina Onassis was usually referred to by the international media, into a totally different perspective, one that it transpired was rooted in cynicism, manipulation and deceit. Doda, according to Nicky's angry confession, had played Athina, his trusting, much younger, famous, and beautiful innocent wife on puppet strings for nearly a decade!

There were too many unanswered loose ends to the story at this stage. There was no proof, nothing had been heard about Nicky in the world's gossip columns, and it appeared unlikely that Athina had been so utterly in love and blinded by her handsome horseman Doda that she had noticed nothing in all this time. But they say that the wife is always the last to know, and Nicky, as she identified herself now, wanted her revenge on Doda by telling his wife to make that old adage, that she would be the last to know, come true.

I was cautious. I wanted proof if I were to warn Athina. Furthermore she was difficult to contact as Doda, Thierry had told me during our last meeting in Greece, would pick up her mobile phone and answer it himself if he were around.

Nicky said she realised the story would make Athina very sad, but that the trusting and generous heiress needed to know about her cheating husband. I told Nicky I would think about it and come back to her.

I spent a couple of days mulling over the story and its implications. If, as it appeared it were true, it would mean that the curse of the eternal love triangle that had haunted other Onassis women would have descended on the third generation, on Athina. The Onassis wives, starting with Ari Onassis' young, beautiful, and very bright wife Tina (Athina) Livanos, whose dowry of ships had put Onassis onto the front stage of the glamorous and high profile world of Greek ship-owners, had to contend with the humiliation of years of being one side of a love triangle involving Maria Callas, her husband Ari, and herself. Tina Onassis had responded by taking lovers for herself before finally divorcing Onassis to marry his arch-rival, ship-owner Stavros Niarchos, who had been her sister Eugenie's husband previously.

Onassis' own daughter Christina later was entangled in a long-term and emotionally destructive love triangle that involved herself, her French husband Thierry, and Thierry's long time mistress and later his wife, the Swedish model Gaby Landhage. Until Christina died, after Thierry had moved out to live with Gaby and have children by her, Christina maintained a civilised relationship with Gaby, taking Athina along to play with her half-siblings just half an hour's drive away in Switzerland by Lake Leman at Bois L' Essert at the villa Christina is said to have bought for Gaby to have Thierry nearby and the Roussel children for Athina to visit.

Athina, until Nicky contacted me, appeared to have escaped the Onassis love triangle syndrome that had dogged her mother and grandmother. The view was that Doda may have been fooling around from time to time but was not stupid or ungrateful enough to have had a long-term affair, and especially not one that had been indulged in in front of his Brazilian friends with whom Doda and Athina socialized and rode with in show jumping competitions.

Nicky's story shattered the image of domestic tranquility in the Onassis-de Miranda household. Athina had given Doda her youth, her trust, her money, and as a new "Mr. Onassis", the keys to the doors to high society and the plutocracy that opened wide for the South American equestrian. And this for a man, who according to Cybele Dorsa, the mother of his daughter, had previously lived in a small flat in Belgium with very little money - not even enough to buy a car for himself.

Doda had hit the jackpot. At first I found it difficult to understand why that was not enough for him. But there were things about Athina I did not know yet, nor had ever suspected. A darker side.

Doda de Miranda was older, had experience of life, and it was inconceivable that he would jeopardize everything to have another woman 'on the side' in a long term relationship. But it seemed he had.

After the weekend I wrote to Nicky about her statement that she met Doda 'as an escort'. I wanted to clarify this, to see what kind of escort she was talking about knowing that young people often are hired or volunteer to act as official event guides for visiting athletes, dignitaries and visitors. Something very different from sex escorts to be sure.

"What did you mean exactly by escort, Nicky?" I asked. Her answer was immediate and stunning in its forthrightness.

"What don't you understand? Escort, as in CALL GIRL! Doda paid me to have sex with him."

I had my answer.

Nicky deluged my private message box with details of her story. Dates, names, assignation venues, hotels and trips to meet him whenever he summoned her for himself, or for his friends. There were also stories about swingers' clubs and about other Brazilians whom she had seen there. Her story as it unfolded was a catalogue of events, venues and names that she had carefully documented. I needed hard proof I told her in order to pass on the story, but Nicky said she would only give the proof to Athina herself, something I could not risk because everything may have been made up and there was no guarantee she would provide anything at all in a meeting with Athina. Further, there was the obvious question of whether Athina would want to meet an ex-call girl who claimed to have been her husband's mistress for eight and a half years. It had been almost a decade of deception during which Athina had been the innocent victim of Nicky and Doda's clandestine affair.

"I can't do anything without proof, Nicky" I finally replied.

"I'm prepared to give some documents to Thierry if he meets me."

I thought about it and decided the best way to go about this would be to pass on some information to Thierry, stating my reservations. When I tried to contact him I was told he was in China, nothing unusual for Thierry who is never where you expect him to be. So I called Yves Repiquet at his office in Paris. Yves was Thierry's lawyer and childhood friend whom I knew well from our meetings in Athens, Geneva and Paris. I told him the story in a few words, emphasizing that I had no proof yet but that I felt the woman was telling the truth. I emailed him a photo of the Nicky showing off her mini skirt and long legs while sitting on the stairs of her two-story home, outside which was parked a white Porsche. I was not sure at the time if Thierry had any communication at all with Athina as there had been much bitterness between father and daughter following her moving in with Doda and after her not inviting him (or me either for that matter!) to her wedding in Brazil.

I heard nothing from Thierry after he returned from China three weeks later so I let the matter rest, telling Nicky that the family had shown no interest. I was not aware if Thierry had warned his daughter of her husband's reported shenanigans. Athina later confirmed to me over a lunch in Holland that Thierry had said nothing to her. There was the question of why a father would not warn his daughter of a cheating husband, especially when the husband was enjoying the benefits of a billionaire lifestyle paid for by his wife - mansions, a 1,100m2 penthouse in Sao Paolo, a Gulfstream jet, thoroughbred horse stables in Florida and Belgium, a Rolls Royce, Mercedes cars, chauffeurs, staff and bodyguards, entry into high society, his daughter living with the couple, and much more. Either Thierry did not want to get involved or he was so annoyed by his daughter's treatment of him and the public humiliation in 2005 of her not having invited him to the wedding that he had decided for her, as they say in Greece, to *"sleep as you have made your bed"*.

A Soap Opera Wedding in Brazil

December, 2005 - After several false starts by the media word came that Athina and Doda were getting married in Brazil. Speculation began immediately as to who would be the best man, would Archbishop Christodoulos of Greece marry the couple, what would happen with Athina's father with whom she had fallen out, which Greeks would be invited to the wedding, would the happy couple have their honeymoon on the Onassis island of Scorpios where Athina's grandfather, who had created the Onassis fortune, married Jackie Kennedy? The questions never stopped coming. Everything the international and Greek media asked boiled down to one issue - would the wedding be an Onassis affair in the grand family tradition or one dominated by Brazilian equestrians and local Sao Paolo celebrities. When details concerning the wedding became known it was clear that this wedding would be like no other.

The wedding was not to be held in a church like previous Onassis weddings but Hollywood-style under a marquee. There were no Greeks in the guest list when it became public except for the name of the best man Nikos Kotronakis and one young female relative of Athina. As soon as it was made known that there would be 750 guests attending the first question asked by the press was whether Thierry and the rest of the Roussel family had been invited. A string of calls followed from media organisations and well-known journalists from around the world and from Brazil to ask if I myself had received an invitation. As more information became known about the wedding arrangements the stranger the whole affair was beginning to look.

The only expected decision by the couple was to exclude the media from the wedding. At first it was leaked that the ceremony would take place in the presence of a photographer of Athina and Doda's choosing, something normal for celebrity weddings but still a far cry from Aristotle Onassis' and Jackie's wedding when Ari had gone outside the Panagitsa chapel on Scorpios and upon seeing the camera crews and paparazzi in a flotilla of hired fishing boats standing on decks in the rain he had waved to them to come ashore, some of them diving into the water fully clothed to get to the chapel first to photograph the wedding of the century for Greece. In Sao Paolo there was to be none of this spontaneity or Ari Onassis' empathy for those in the media doing their job. The press would be kept out of Doda and Athina's wedding. Other journalists were already on their way from the US and Europe in the hope of talking to the couple. It was to be a wild goose chase. After the wedding it was announced that no photographs would be released in keeping with the couple's wishes.

As more information surfaced it became plain that the wedding was to be an esoteric Brazilian gala with the equestrian Olympian Doda showing off his beautiful and very wealthy Greek young trophy wife to the domestic CARAS set.

The media had a lot to write about, Athina had ordered a Valentino wedding dress and there would be six best men. Athina's half-sister Sandrine was appointed to go to the nuptials as the Roussel family's representative. This token participation made it even more obvious to the world that the breach between the heiress and her husband with her family was deeply felt by the Roussels. I had expected Erik to be at the wedding. Erik was the Roussel child who had always been closest to Athina; they were of the same age and I had observed how proud he had always been of his dark-haired Greek half-sister. Sandrine who went to Brazil was Nordic in appearance, icily beautiful, serious, a Roussel through and through, and a truly gifted rider. I was surprised when I was informed that it was she who would represent the family because I had always felt that because she lived in the shadow of Athina that this bothered her. I had sensed as much during a paparazzi frenzy over Athina during our yacht visit to the island of Hydra when I had looked back from where I was walking next to Athina to see the then eleven year-old Sandrine take out a brush to once again comb her long, shiny natural blonde hair, trying to look her best in the crowd milling around us. In Brazil she would again be in the shade as all eyes and the spotlight would be, as always, inevitably on her wealthy and famous Greek half-sister.

Some of Aristotle Onassis' immediate relatives in Greece were invited but only Alexandra, the granddaughter of Aunt Kalliroi, Onassis' half-sister, attended.

According to people who were at the wedding a thousand bottles of the best champagne were opened for the guests, friends of Doda, and his family. Athina's friends, if there were indeed any at the wedding, were thin on the ground. None of her childhood friends from Switzerland, except Nathalie Jakobsson, were reported to have attended the event. Athina, cut off from her old friends and family was in a new world now.

The only international celebrity at the wedding was the Greek bride. After that it was Brazilian glitterati and local TV serial stars, businessmen, and athletes so driven by a desire to attend an Onassis wedding in Sao Paolo that, according to a report in Britain's Guardian newspaper they agreed to have their mobile phones and cameras banned and to be issued with photo ID's in order to enter a parking lot where they had to leave their cars to be ferried under escort in rented Audis to the reception area. Hundreds of Brazilians came dressed in their best clothes, curious to see the Onassis heiress at close quarters. Some of the guests wondered whether perhaps the bride's stated desire for privacy hid something deeper, that something was wrong. The gossip was not helped a few weeks later when a local magazine ran photos of a group of waiters from a Brazilian restaurant holding up a row of sheets outside the eatery so that Athina Onassis de Miranda, the new bride, could exit the restaurant where she had been dining with Doda and hurry to their waiting cars without being photographed by the paparazzi who were stationed across the street. Something like this had not been seen since the days when Howard Hughes, the eccentric billionaire, had forced British customs officers at Heathrow Airport in London to turn their faces to the wall in order not to see his face.

In Greece a television station invited a panel of guests to comment on the wedding as it was taking place. While the ceremony was in progress a helicopter hovering above the wedding tent managed to photograph the couple through a clear plastic section of the roof. Live footage of the ceremony showed a fair-haired man standing next to the bride. Immediately there was a media buzz since it appeared that Thierry had gone, after all, to Brazil to give his daughter away. I phoned Thierry to see where he was. He told me that he was in Morocco with Gaby and Erik. A photo published the next day confirmed this, showing a rather forlorn Roussel family standing together next to a Moroccan beach. It was a sad way for the Roussel family to celebrate her wedding.

The religious ceremony was unusual too. A Middle Eastern Orthodox priest without the traditional Greek Orthodox cassock and stove pipe hat read the wedding rites together with a Catholic priest. Six best men stood around the couple.

After the wedding the couple left to go on their honeymoon to Uruguay's Punta d 'Este resort. A long chapter in the Onassis family closed with the Sao Paolo wedding and a new one had opened in South America. The message to Greece and to Athina's Greek relatives and supporters was clear – there was a new sheriff in town. Doda was "in charge" now! And he would be for the next eleven years until Athena decided she had had enough of his ways and filed for a divorce.

Nicky delivers the goods

I kept in touch with Nicky for the next three years on and off. I found her to be disarmingly candid, always polite, and the overall impression I got was that she was telling the truth. Yes, she had an axe to grind, and after eight and a half years of a lifestyle where money from her lover was given to her generously she had become used to spending freely on designer clothes, expensive shoes and handbags and travelling to famous venues where she stayed at luxury hotels it had been a sudden shock to be cut off. Hundreds of thousands of Euros went through her fingers and it seemed that, in the words of the well known Mary Hopkin English pop song of the Sixties

"Those were the days my friend, I thought they'd never end!"

But end they did, suddenly, and unexpectedly. One night in St Tropez in a car outside the Longines Athina Horse Show venue Doda had told her it was over. I was never sure if she had signed a confidentiality agreement with Doda or not as she said she had no such contract in her hands. But in any event she was prepared to tell her story if Athina would agree to hear it.

In May of 2016 there was a television announcement that Athina and Alvaro de Miranda were divorcing! The fairytale marriage between the billionaire heiress and the handsome older Olympian equestrian from Brazil was over. I did not at first lend much credence to the story, so many celebrity break-ups were reported by the gossip programmes and magazines to be proved wrong later that I only decided to take any notice when I heard the foreign media describing how Athina Onassis had walked out of the home she shared with Doda, his daughter Vivienne and Doda's first companion Cybele Dorsa's son Fernando, after a bodyguard of Athina's had reported seeing Doda leaving with a blonde woman from the bedroom of the luxury mansion in Wellington, Florida, where the couple had their American stables. Previously images of Athina looking very thin and stressed had appeared in the press and it was obvious that something was seriously worrying her. She had abandoned her Belgian villa just days before the Longines Athina Onassis Horse Show in France where Doda was to attend too, as always. It must have been one of the most humiliating breakups of all time with Athina forced to ride and entertain at an event named after her, where she was the patron and owner, with her errant husband very prominently in attendance. The breakup had happened so suddenly that the website of the competition still mentioned Doda and how Athina had established the LAOHS with his help. He was everywhere, strutting about while his people stared down Athina's associates, one would not really call them friends, or stood close to her in what was considered by an observer to be a heavy-handed effort to spook her. Everyone there knew what had happened and gossip surged each time either one of the estranged couple walked by the stands or was competing. The utter chaos of the moment was 'in the details' with Athina's own name misspelled in the official Longines Athina Onassis Horse Show literature and in the online information for visitors.

I remember the date well when very soon after I decided to contact Athina to tell her Nicky's story because it was May 24th, one day before my birthday. As the marriage was over the information from Nicky could be of significant help to Athina in her divorce proceedings since Belgian law does not give alimony to partners who are unfaithful, abusive, or who misbehave. Nicky's story would help Athina to fight off any alimony claims that would follow as surely as day follows night since Belgian law provides for the richer spouse to provide for the poorer one when no adultery is involved. In this case, with Athina walking out of the home she shared with Doda, she would probably have to give him a large monthly sum in alimony in the absence of convincing evidence of her husband's infidelity.

I contacted Nicky first, telling her of my intentions and asking if she would provide proof and go to court if summoned by Athina. She agreed without hesitation. That was enough for me to go to Athina with the story. I decided this time not to contact Thierry who had not responded when I had first informed him about the Doda affair two years previously. Despite a meeting with Athina at her half-sister Sandrine's wedding in France there was no evidence of the chilly father-daughter relationship having thawed, so I wrote to Eric, Athina's half-brother whom I always liked and with whom I had always had a good relationship. We had occasional exchanges of emails, which were always very cordial. I wrote to tell him very briefly about the Nicky story, asking him to forward my email to Athina only if the marriage had indeed broken up and the split was not a media rumour.

    The next day I received a very cordial phone call from a Netherlands number from a man who identified himself as Athina's Dutch lawyer. He said Athina wanted me to update him about what I knew. I emailed him back saying I could help, but since I had done a lot of unpaid work as well as helping pivotally with the recovery of a multimillion Euro asset for Athina without pay, and having been let down over a promise to assume the management of Scorpios (where I had lost ten years of potential salaries as a result, a sum approaching $800,000) as a reward for supporting Athina and her father in numerous multi-million dollar civil court cases as their witness, plus sitting in court for four years in Greece, accused falsely of perjury, as it was unanimously proven, by the Onassis Foundation, of having influenced a court decision in favour of Thierry in a $15,000,000 case, I now wanted a fee for bringing the witness and the evidence to court. The lawyer said he would respond after talking to Athina. That night I thought more about the issue and decided to give her the story anyway, verbally, and not demand a fee if that would be enough for her. The only stipulation was that Athina must call me herself in which case I would give her the basic details over the phone without it becoming a contractual arrangement; just the story basics that she could follow up on. I sent an email to this effect to the lawyer the next morning.

Within an hour or so Athina called me on my mobile. It was like old days to hear her childlike high-pitched voice again! It immediately brought back memories of being together with her and her family on the family yacht, the *Pickwick*, off Ibiza, or the *Ariadne* two-mast schooner in Greece, holidays with her family, sharing outdoor meals under the star-studded Balearic skies, her coming to my daughter's 22nd birthday dinner in Athens with all her Onassis and Roussel relatives. It sounded like the old Athina I had known before the Doda wedding! The same unmistakable voice, a little more mature, but still high pitched and friendly. But we had serious business.

"Athina, what I have to say will upset you. It is worse than you can imagine. Are you sure you want me to tell you?" I asked before continuing, "It's not a nice story. What do you want?"

Her answer came without hesitation, "The truth, Alexis, all the truth".

And so we talked, and I lost track of time. Once the line crashed, and we picked up again from where we had left off. I could hear her gasp once or twice, and once she said '*Oh, NO!*' when I mentioned something very personal that had to do with Doda and Nicky. We discussed what I had heard from Nicky and Athina told me things of her own that cannot be written here.

"Talk to M. and send him anything you can," she said finally, referring to her lawyer whose contacts I already had. And so I started to send copies of Nicky's correspondence which had been arriving on a daily basis since news of the divorce had become public. I asked Nicky more and more questions and also those that the lawyer himself wanted answered. What surprised me was that Athina appeared to have little hard evidence of Doda's unfaithfulness. She had walked out of the house in Belgium after the Florida incident, but that in itself was only based on a report by a bodyguard, a person who was in her employ, and therefore not a credible witness whose testimony would stand up in court without further corroboration. It was very shaky if it were the only evidence she had of his unfaithfulness, and she clearly needed more with which to confront Doda.

We spoke several more times. In the meantime Doda had started his social media defence, saying that he loved Athina "very much", posting images of the Virgin Mary on his Instagram page while his best man, Kotronakis, the former honorary consul of Greece at Recife in Brazil, who was a friend of Doda's[2], stated to a journalist that it was only a passing hurdle that he was sure the couple, who were "very much in love", he assured the journalist, would soon overcome.

I passed Nicky's messages to me on to Eindhoven to a voraciously keen for information law office. A few days later M asked if I could fly to

---

[2] Surprisingly, when I mentioned Kotronakis, Athina seemed to have no recollection of who he was, even though he had been one of her and Doda's six Best Men at the wedding in Brazil. Athina showed a similar lapse of memory when I referred to two incidents, one that had taken place when I was staying with her and her family in Ibiza, and the other on a yacht cruise in Greece when we were sailing from Lagonissi, where her Aunt Kalliroi Onassis Patronikola lived, to the island of Hydra.

Belgium or Holland to meet Athina after I mentioned there were other things, not from Nicky, that I did not want to discuss over the phone. My previous experience with a document sent between Thierry's lawyers in Switzerland ending up in the hands of the Onassis Foundation and in a court had convinced me that there was no such thing as safety of cyber communications.

    A little while later my ticket and accommodation in the Netherlands was arranged, so I flew to Amsterdam, was picked up by a driver and taken to the Park Hotel in central Eindhoven, a quiet scenic Dutch town with canals and scenery that is often depicted in Dutch masters' works. The Park Hotel was a somewhat impersonal but immaculately clean and modern businessman's hotel designed to service the numerous visitors who come to Eindhoven on business, primarily with the Philips conglomerate that has its headquarters there. I was booked into a high-tech suite decorated in the now current trend of smoke grey fittings offset by white everywhere. After unpacking I had a call from reception from M, Athina's lawyer, who was waiting to take me to dinner and to discuss initial details of how the Nicky story was unfolding before us meeting up with Athina the next day for lunch. Over a quiet dinner at a corner restaurant overlooking a square lined by two-story houses with drawn lace curtains and brown and grey facades we sat down to discuss Nicky and Doda and to see whether the story had any value with what I had provided him. After dinner we went to M's house in a quiet residential area nearby where I felt a little uncomfortable to barge in on his slightly flustered at our invasion, but very hospitable wife, and their charming blonde two year old daughter who was being fed by a nanny when we arrived. A young female colleague from M's law office was already there. A rather sombre looking Belgian arrived soon after carrying a box of sorts, introducing himself as a former police officer who now had his own company specialising in cyber forensics. He downloaded my written exchanges with Nicky from my laptop to validate for the court that they were genuine and not doctored. Genuine they were and shocking in their candidness, for sure. It had after all been a sexual relationship between a married man and a call girl, but there were also more players and variants involved. This was only the beginning. After two or three hours of intense discussions with everyone poring over the message texts between Nicky and myself the lawyers and former detective had what they wanted, and I had been primed as to what to expect the next day when Athina was to meet me and M for lunch. It had been almost twelve years since I had last seen her and fourteen since we had spent time together in Athens when she and I, along with the Roussel family, had been invited to attend an Onassis family wedding at Lagonissi at the seaside estate of Aunt Kalliroi Onassis, Athina's favourite aunt, the half-sister of Ari Onassis.

  The driver picked me up at 12.30 the next day and dropped me off at a restaurant called *Lugar*, located in a small building on the corner of a large tree-lined square, neither urban nor country, just

Dutch, with traditional houses, canals, trees and flowers.

I was the only guest when I arrived at the restaurant. I had noticed a man in a suit sitting alone at an outside table, despite the cool weather, and realised that he must be an advance security party belonging to Athina's bodyguards. Soon after M arrived and ten minutes later he said "That's her!" pointing out through the plate glass front window of the restaurant to a dark blue Mercedes that was maneuvering to park. I immediately recognised the driver, Guy Merat, Athina's trusted chief bodyguard who had come to Athens with the heiress and Gaby, her step-mother, some years before.

When Athina entered the restaurant it seemed like old days again, but of course she was now 32 and grown up. She was very tall and very slim, but unmistakably Athina, with the expressive eyes and high pitched little girl's voice with its slightly accented but totally fluent English. She told me she was taking a break from her training nearby and had just thrown on a jacket over her riding clothes to meet me for lunch.

For Greeks it is customary for guests to bring a present to their hostess when invited for a meal. What could one give the richest girl in the world I wondered in Athens before leaving? Scorpios island had given me the answer. When on vacation there with my wife and daughter in 2002 at the Pink House on the island I had been pouring myself a glass of water thinking back on the hundred million dollar yachts that had anchored at Christina Dock near us, the fifty million dollar Gulfstream jets that brought guest from jet setters' playgrounds, the solid silver cutlery, the bespoke porcelain plates with the *Christina* yacht name on them, the two hundred million dollar island we were on, and wondered what a two Euro bottle of water was doing there, its PET PVC bottle half emerged in a three thousand dollar silver ice bucket!

What water would Onassis have chosen to serve his guests I asked myself, and then the idea, almost in fun, came to me. Water from the purest origins on earth, with 24 carat gold flakes in a designer bottle with real gold lettering, and in a glamorous black and gold embossed box. I told an old ex-East Africa school friend living in Auckland, Alan Smith, of my concept of what was missing on Scorpios, something that would fit in with the Onassis billionaire lifestyle. After four years of looking for and finding the purest ancient artesian aquifer of rain water that had been filtered naturally through rock and shale of the Southern Alps after being blown in from Antarctica, then locating a centuries-old European supplier of edible gold flakes, and rejecting design after design before creating the right bottle, New Zealand GOLD artesian water was born. Its gold flakes sparkled in the light and the water was naturally sweet, and it came in its own malt whiskey type pack, so we made it available for richies and celebs, and before long NZGold was being poured for state guests in the Al Bateen royal palace in Abu Dhabi, in the Trump Tower and Hotel in Chicago, listed in their Famous Waters Library, on a couple of Russian oligarchs superyachts, at the home of a black rapper in LA and in a luxury tented safari camp at Lake Natron in Tanzania. I had my present for Athina and presented it to her when we sat down at the lunch table in the inside private room at *Lugar* restaurant. She looked at it quizzically, and thanked me.

It seemed for a few moments that not a day had passed since we had last met when as we settled into conversation about things in general and people from the past, before locking onto the serious topic of Doda. I noticed she got up three or four times to go towards the kitchen to talk on her mobile but always came back to pick up from where we had left off. M sat by quietly, without interrupting.

Our conversation at lunch was sombre, the subject being Doda. I had brought a large file that had to do with a family issue of several years previously, while the rest of the lunch was taken up by our exchanging information. I updated her about what I had discussed with Nicky, and spoke about much more intimate issues concerning people associated with Doda when M left the room to take a phone call in the front room of the *Lugar*.

I always remembered Athina in the past enjoying salads and fruit and today was no exception. Her lunch was light, with still water, beef carpaccio and a chocolate sweet afterwards. I had a shrimp and pasta dish and we joked when I asked her what was her favourite sweet. She answered with a chuckle "Chocolate, Alexis!"

"Dark chocolate, Athina?"

"Yes!" she responded enthusiastically, with the delight of a young child. It was mine too.

There were issues that former servants of the couple had told me about that I did not want to put in writing and things that she too wanted to tell me. It was sad for me at the time to see how hurt this tall thin young woman was, but carried away by this I had missed the undercurrent of something that in time would reveal itself to be more sinister and closer to an observation I had made on a chilly November day when we were having lunch at the Main House on Scorpios island. It happened when Thierry, Athina then just 14, and I were in conversation when I observed an argument developing with her father. I had soon after in an interview said that she wasn't at all the timid girl that the media described her as, but a doll made of steel.

Athina had lived through much with the spotlight of the world on her when she was growing up, however much her Roussel family tried to a treat her as just one of the children, but she had always been a girl in a fishbowl - "the Richest Girl in the World". Her unusual circumstances and the behaviour of people around her had over the years traumatized her severely. There was no doubt about this.

That day at *Lugar* we spoke in quiet tones not to be heard by the attendant waitress a couple of metres away as we discussed her divorce, Doda's character, and his vanities. It was to be a high profile divorce and already the media covering it were thirsting for information. Very little was forthcoming as the court proceedings were *in camera*. Documents were presented to the judges by both sides, explanations were demanded and given by the lawyers, and there were to be many delays as more papers and injunctions were to complicate the split.

Doda was still playing the role of the abandoned and innocent husband who wanted a second chance, according to his Instagram posts where he continued to speak of his great love for Athina, insisting on his faithfulness. We had Nicky's written statements and messages to me, and it was agreed that though this would be useful to the court, hard evidence was the key to establishing guilt on his part as he changed stance to ask for a huge amount of money in more recent court actions. I never asked about the pre-nup which I believe was a million dollars for every year the marriage had lasted, eleven in total.

When Doda saw that she was determined to divorce him he put in an alimony claim for a reputed ten thousand dollars a day; three million six hundred and fifty dollars a year in perpetuity, as long as he was single. It was less than his soon to be ex-father in law Thierry was getting every year from Christina's estate according to her will where she had specified he receive $2,450,000 a year for life. A sum that was adjusted for inflation and was for sure more than Doda was asking. But Thierry was the member of a famous and historic French industrial family and an aristocrat with chateaux in France, and estates in Marbella, Kenya and elsewhere. Alvaro Affonso de Miranda Neto, despite the string of names and his cool bearing was but the son of a middle class family that was not even a part of the Brazilian plutocracy. He had done well nonetheless, and the divorce was his opportunity to do even better.

Athina's lawyer in New York, known as "Toxic Cohen", well known for his high profile clients, among whom had been Ivana Trump, one day put out a press release, unexpected and normally forbidden by the heiress for those representing her, stating "Mrs. Athina Onassis was surprised by the exceedingly high financial demands of her estranged husband, Mr. de Miranda".

There were to be no more press statements from Athina's American, Belgian or Dutch lawyers, in keeping with their reclusive client's demand for privacy.

We agreed that it was important for me to gain possession of the Nicky said she had with proof of the affair. So far we had seen none except for what she had claimed. There was no question of paying for her to testify because Belgian criminal law stipulates it is an offence to remunerate a witness. Under the circumstances it would be a Herculean task for me to convince Nicky to give up any documents to Athina that she had squirreled away, with no benefit to her now that Doda had dumped her and she was without any means of support for herself and her daughter whose father Nicky claimed did not give any financial support to them either.

Nicky was in a difficult financial position and was no longer turning tricks, something she had given up sometime after hooking up with Doda. She was working as a nurse, back to a day job again. It would not be easy to convince her to cooperate by releasing the file without payment, but Athina's hands were tied. I promised Athina and M I would give the matter all my attention as soon as I was back in Athens.

Athina paid for our lunch with a credit card, kissed me on both cheeks, Greek style, broke into her familiar smile and wished me a good trip back to Athens. It was a magnificent performance. As I was being dropped off by the driver at Schiphol airport I received an sms from Athina asking if I was leaving that day. I called M to see what she wanted and he asked if I could I stay on for another day, but it was already too late, my flight I told him was leaving soon but promised to come back if I were needed.

Back home, four hours later, I stretched out on my bed, tired but happy to see that I was once again in touch with Athina after her marriage to Doda had driven a wedge between her and her Greek family, as well as estranging Athina to a great degree from her immediate Roussel relatives and those close to them. My interpretation of Athina's friendliness would be proved totally off target before many months had gone past.

Introduction

ONASSIS – That name!

Aristotle, Tina, Christina, Alexander and Athina all bore the legendary Greek surname that has been handed down from generation to generation. Today it is used only by the last surviving member of the dynasty; but all is never what it seems in the Onassis family, as indeed it never was even with the founder of the dynasty.

Athina Onassis, the attractive, on occasion borderline anorexic heiress, is a world class equestrian who is obsessively reclusive to the frustration of her admirers and the media. The last of the line of a family that is said to carry a curse from the days they lived in Asia Minor when a dastardly act of an ancestor prompted a curse to be put on the family forever, according to Greek folklore.

Athina today bears the legendary Onassis name only after legally adopting it in Athens by applying to the Attica area prefecture. Her real registered name was Athena Helene Roussel, a name she used until she married her faithless Brazilian husband. She dropped the name Roussel following a bitter rift with her former playboy father, Thierry Roussel, who had, not unreasonably, objected to his then 17 year old daughter leaving home to share bed, board, and soon her money with the much older Brazilian Olympian horseman who had been living with a Brazilian model, Cybele Dorsa, the mother of his three year old daughter. The dispute between Thierry and Athina and her decision to hire one of London's most expensive law firms cost father and daughter a rumoured thirty million dollars. Additionally Athina had paid Thierry to resign his seat on the board running her trust, a package for Thierry estimated to have cost his daughter in excess of eighty five million dollars!

Technically Athena was not an Onassis at all. A member of the family, yes, but not a legal bearer of the name until that day in Athens at the Prefect's office when she applied to adopt the famous Greek name for herself for reasons we shall see. In fact whenever I accompanied the Roussel family and we were met by journalists or others who addressed her as Miss Onassis, she would cold shoulder them, or respond "Roussel". A chauffeur at the Roussel family home in Lussy-sur-Morges where Athina lived with her father, her Swedish stepmother Gaby Landhage, and her three half-siblings, Sandrine, Joanna and Erik, told me that the local village post office had been instructed to delegate all letters addressed to Athena Onassis – and there was a constant stream from Greeks who worshipped the historic family name and others - to the post office's wastebasket. When Athina came to Athens in 1998 with her family a couple of months after Thierry asked me to become the family spokesman and to help him with the lawyers who were handling a difficult set of law cases he was involved in, the visit of the heiress to Greece was a huge press deal, a "media frenzy" as the Associated Press correspondent present described the tsunami of reporters and TV crews waiting to meet the granddaughter of Ari Onassis at Athens Hellinikon airport.

It was in March of 1998 that we introduced the heiress and the Roussels to the Greek public and the media. The next day, surrounded by bemused ex-SAS and Greek bodyguards trying to hold back the crush of reporters and fans, she signed autograph hunters' proffered slips of paper at the Acropolis and at other venues for Onassis admirers of all ages. She responded to autograph requests to "Miss Onassis" by signing, correctly, as "A. Roussel". That was it. Of course she was right. That was the name on her passport and her birth certificate. Anyone calling her Athina Onassis would get at best, a brief pointed glance, or be ignored. How life and financial-professional interest changes us all though.

After she moved in with her Brazilian lover she progressed before long to what was one of the most glamorous lifestyle weddings Brazil had ever seen soon after which the public was informed that the eldest daughter of the Roussel family was now to be called "Athina Onassis". It was official, and what was more, something many in Greece lauded, she was riding in international and domestic show jumping events as a Greek team athlete. Many like me were not surprised when she and Doda, as her husband Alvaro Affonso de Miranda Neto liked to be addressed, organised the first of what was to become a series of world class equestrian events that would take place every year in a different international venue.

It started off as the Christina Onassis Horse Show, but after a bungle up in Athens where it was held at the Markopoulo Olympic Equestrian Center, a couple of kilometres from where I live, unsuspecting

Doda ran into the hardly hidden hostility of certain Greek politicians who were associated with the administrators of the Alexander Onassis Foundation, an entity locked into numerous court cases, civil and criminal, with Athina's father over money, of course, and with the heiress herself, at other venues. She and Doda wisely moved the event to Rio where it was renamed the Athina Onassis Horse Show. It was an event established under the guidance and international equestrian experience of Olympian champion Doda, together with Athina's Dutch chubby-faced coach and mentor, Jan Tops, who set up the Global Champions Tour at around the same time, and some say, with the financial help of Athina. Thierry, Tops and Doda were the three men of influence in the Onassis heiress's life, and this was to continue for several years until she broke free of her father, paying him over 80 million dollars to resign from the five member board of trustees managing her fortune. Doda in 2016 was given the boot by a distressed Athina who had had enough of his wanderings, and he too was rewarded well financially, though with much less than he had claimed at one time. The heiress retired to her paddocks in Holland and her communications were primarily with her lawyers in New York, Brussels, and Eindhoven, and of course with her four-legged friends who received the best of the best in training, board and equine lodging - as long as they too performed well. A broken leg at a competition or in training for the high jumps was dealt with in a businesslike manner; the horse was dispatched by a vet by lethal injection or, possibly with a bullet to the brain. No expensive and complicated long hours of surgery and a future in a grassy paddock for the injured four-legged companion that had been so lovingly looked after when it had been able to perform at the jumps and deliver the goods.

The story of AD Camille, the beautiful white championship mare with the plaited mane, a star of the A+D stables, is salutary. After the magnificent horse broke a leg at a qualifying jump in Geneva, throwing Athina to the ground, the animal was taken away by crane and put to death soon after, with its owner's consent.

The heiress's newly acquired surname, Onassis, attracted big-name sponsors, and, again, knowing Athina's previous antipathy to being addressed as Onassis, a name she did not have, it was a source of wonder for us that she was now parading before the world as an Onassis, and had named her horse show with the legendary family name. Doda had no doubt impressed on his young and innocent rich wife the importance and drawing power that the Onassis name had, and he was right. The normally secretive and publicity shy Julius Baer, the largest private asset managers in Switzerland and bankers to the plutocracy who were on the board of trustees of the heiresses' trust, became sponsors, followed by others like Audi who had sponsored Doda in Belgium. More came on board after Athina became the proud and fully fledged bearer of the Onassis name. Before long Longines Watches of Switzerland took over as master sponsor and the games were renamed the Longines Athina Onassis Horse Show, or LAOHS for short. No one suspected the scandal that would be associated with the event later.

Athina's publicity team flooded her events with her logo; her name was on every prize, banner, and horse blanket, on cutlery, crockery, entrance tickets, reservation forms and menus; in fact everywhere, except on the luxury venue's toilet paper.

She had realised the value of the Onassis brand that her tycoon grandfather had built during his life when he became the first of the post war big spenders, but to a purpose. Onassis understood human weakness where one could impress others by the clever use of status symbols, and so Post World War II Conspicuous Consumption was born. Spend, Spend, Spend, was his motto, but only where it could be seen. He created the impression of being far wealthier than he actually was. Impressed conservative bankers opened up generous credit lines for him, shipyards fell over themselves to receive his new vessel orders while women, of course, seeing the diminutive man with the deep set dark eyes and heavy accent, identified a generous ticket provider to a better life via a glamorous evening and the chance to be bedded on Onassis' 300 foot yacht, the *Christina,* one of the first super yachts of its day. He was generous to his female lovers, and women of all nationalities, ages and professions fell at his feet. He, along with film producer and tycoon Howard Hughes (in his pre-microbe phobia phase), competed with one another as to who would seduce the most female stars and sexy starlets. Onassis was cynical, never falling for the self-deception of many rich or famous people, that the women were throwing themselves at their benefactors for their good looks or charm. He knew why they were after him. When his son Alexander was 16, and still a virgin, he took him to his favourite trysting house, the high-class brothel of Madame Claude in Paris. A bevy of starlets, models, stunning moonlighting housewives and down-at-luck society beauties were on call. Entering the gilded mansion with the heavy velvet curtains and antique furniture Ari Onassis and his son Alexander were greeted by the affable Madame Claude who summoned a lineup of available half-undressed beauties to walk past the Greek magnate and his son. Alexander was not happy. He turned to his father and said "Dad, I don't want it to be like this my first time... to have to pay the woman."

World-wise Ari put his arm around his uncomfortable son's shoulders and replied, 'Son, with women, one way or another, you always pay!"

And so his resigned son let himself be led to a luxury suite by a stunning young girl who initiated him into the art of love. Or paid sex, if you prefer.

The Onassis name grew in drawing power and mystique as the years passed. Partly because of the great wealth and lifestyle associated with the family, partly because of a series of tragedies that were to befall the family; some put it down to the Gods being angry at the hubris of Onassis – his penchant for ignoring everything and everyone except money, women and business. Onassis and his socialite wife Tina Livanos who married him when she was just 17, the daughter of one of the richest Greek ship-owners in the world, and he 47, invested little in family. There was none of the doting attention that normal parents give to their children to establish an environment of love and a safety net of emotions as they discover life growing up.

Tina Onassis, soon fed up with Onassis' philandering ways, took lovers of her own, most notably a South American polo rider, and never tried to hide her disappointment and aversion when her daughter Christina was born with heavily downwardly slanted eyes, the swarthy looks of Onassis and puffy bags under her eyes. Tina wanted only beautiful things around her while Onassis was too busy with travelling, making money and entertaining to give his children the attention they craved. Christina withdrew into herself and was not helped when her mother, with the capacity to have nannies and governesses to make her parenting easier instead shunted Christina off to a private English boarding school where Christina felt she had been parked out of the way, and so it was. Alexander in the meantime reacted by becoming aggressive and would at a very young age tear around in speedboats putting himself and others at mortal risk. A letter the wife of the chief mechanic of the Onassis' yacht gave me written by her husband recounted his being driven in a speedboat by Alexander, then around 11 or 12, at full speed towards some rocks at Glyfada.

"That crazy brat wouldn't listen to me; I swore at him and saved our lives at the last minute by grabbing the steering wheel!" And so it went on. Alexander a few years later drove his Ferrari at breakneck speed round the winding roads of the Cannes-Nice coastal highway, crashing it into and totally destroying an old car belonging to an impecunious Frenchman who had been quietly coming round one of the Riviera bends. The result was that instead of an apology and the gift of a new car the shocked man was harangued by Alexander and his driving companion, and was later sued by the Onassis' family lawyers. Alexander fared better than Christina. Though unable to stand up to Ari's overbearing personality and to live up to his father's expectations of him academically, he began a small air taxi operation called Olympic Aviation at Athens Glyfada airport. It was a start-up that was under the wing of the five-continent modern Olympic Airways that his father had created after buying the small state airline, TAE that operated a few ancient Dakota DC3's. The air taxi business went well with Alexander appearing to have found his role as a pilot and business executive. He was known for unhesitatingly taking the small charter planes out in heavy weather when there was a flying doctor call from one of Greece's isolated islands; flights that other pilots liked to avoid, but Alexander saved many lives and gained the respect of his father's employees and of the mechanics at Athens airport. He was however obsessed with the issue of overall flight safety and kept pestering his father to replace the ageing Piaggio amphibious plane they owned and used to fly with to the Onassis island of Scorpios, with a new helicopter. Onassis did not agree. Generous to his women and his friends, always quick to flash his money, boats and Olympic plane ownership and to entertain celebrities, richies and politicians on his yacht and private island, he balked at spending when he could avoid it, or when it would not be in the public eye.

On occasion he was notoriously tight with his own children. When Christina walked across Syntagma Square from the Olympic Airways head office of her father to Vourakis Jewellers next to the Grande Bretagne Hotel, where she bought a simple gold ring for 1500 dollars, the bill, as was the custom for the family shopping, was sent to the Onassis offices the next day for payment. The accountant took it to Onassis for approval but he refused to pay and told Christina to take it back. A few days later Maria Callas who had been Onassis lover for a while saw Onassis in a paparazzi photo with another woman at a private dinner during one of his recent trips abroad. Callas, true to style, exploded in a fit of anger and jealously and harangued Onassis in the most vocal and theatrical manner. To calm her down Onassis took her shopping. He bought her an $800,000 emerald necklace with matching earrings from Cartier. It was sufficient at the time for a down payment on a new tanker, but that was Onassis. In the meantime poor Christina learned of her father's generosity to Callas and reacted by engaging in another of the provocative acts that she knew enraged her father.

Alexander was not much luckier as far as money was concerned. He had pestered his father for a smart sports car; he was after all the son of Aristotle Onassis, the richest man in the world, and Onassis agreed, buying him an E-Type Jaguar - a used one. "Nothing wrong with it", he told his son, who was happy to get even that.

One characteristic example of Onassis' fits of parsimony was when Alexander asked his father for some pocket money.

"What do you want it for?" Onassis gruffly replied.

"I need new socks, Dad, mine are worn out!"

The reply was typical. "Go to the chest of drawers in my bedroom. Take a pair from there. They will fit you!"

The family was feasted and feted around the world. The rivalry between Onassis and Stavros Niarchos, Tina Onassis sister's husband, was soap opera fare for magazine and newspaper articles. The two shipping rivals, boosted by huge dowries from their wives, who were sisters, and the daughters of the patriarch of the Greek ship-owners, Livanos, burst onto the world shipping scene determined to outdo each other. Stavros Niarchos, from a village near Sparta, was a Prince Philip lookalike, hobnobbed with the aristocracy and had a patrician way about him with his Harris tweeds, his elegant sailing yacht, the *Creole* with its characteristic black sails, while Onassis was a man of more plebeian pleasures who could spend all night drinking with sailors and workers in dives in Piraeus, enjoying the load music and dancing. No opera fan he, but with Callas, the finest soprano in the world in his cage, he went to all her performances and enjoyed the reflected glory of her fame. Christina said of her father "Some people collect things, my father likes to collect famous names" and so it was.

Onassis, because he genuinely liked to hang out in *bouzouki* clubs and to drink all night in the company of people who amused him, took breaks from his famous friends to be one of the people and his exploits, dancing and drinking and breaking plates were enthusiastically recorded by the paparazzi and hangers-on reporters who followed him around, knowing that they were offering him a service and that he would, when in a good mood after some successful money making deal had been concluded, often invite them on board the *Christina* or to his night club table. And so the myth of Onassis as a modern day *Zorba the Greek* grew around him, and this persona, in contrast to Niarchos' racing stable activities and aristocratic grouse hunts, made him a popular icon among the Greeks.

The Onassis name and its association with great wealth and an envied lifestyle became firmly established. Christina tried to follow in her father's footsteps but was seriously troubled by inadequate marriages and problems with weight after binging on Coca Cola and chocolates. This was exacerbated by her erratic consumption of prescription drugs. She, however, despite her timidity in front of audiences and crowds, after Ari's death became president of the Alexander S. Onassis Foundation that was established through his will by Onassis after he lost Alexander in a plane accident, the result, in part, of Ari not having listened to his son's appeals for a helicopter to replace their aging sea plane. Onassis never got over his guilt feelings, knowing that his son would have been alive if he, Onassis, had not been so tight with his money and insisting Alexander fly in the old Piaggio in which he was killed at Athens airport on 1974 at the age of 24.

After Alexander's death Onassis would have his staff lay out a table at his son's marble tomb at the Panayitsa chapel on Scorpios where he was buried, and stay up all night eating and drinking and talking to the ghost of his dead son that only he saw. A year later he too, struck down by Mysathenia Gravis, the debilitating auto-immune disease, and betrayed by a diseased liver, the result of a lifetime of drinking, died in Paris at the hospital where his granddaughter Athena Helen Roussel was to first see the light of day eleven years later. But the Onassis name did not die with him. Christina kept it alive, partly with her charity work, and partly by the publicity buzz her famous parties on Scorpios created. Scorpios was where she showed her extreme generosity to a circle of layabouts and hangers-on to whom she offered the best of the best in hospitality, often sending her pilot to fetch a friend from Paris or London in her Lear Jet and then taking them to St Moritz to the Onassis family chalet, Villa Crystal, in a desperate round of parties and disco hopping, looking for the happiness and security that her family had denied her. The death of her mother, Tina Livanos Blandford Onassis (who had in the meantime married her father's arch rival and brother-in-law, Stavros Niarchos) from an overdose of sleeping pills, and that previously of her aunt Eugenie, Niarchos' first wife, in very murky circumstances on their private island of Spetsopoula, further shattered Christina's self-confidence. The goings on in her private life and the wild parties were the nectar that gossip columns fed off, but her fourth husband, Thierry Roussel, the French pharmaceutical empire heir, taking the domestic reins, immediately booted out the large group of Christina's friends from Scorpios, thus putting an end to the Saturnalia that had become associated with Onassis' daughter. The Frenchman, tall, with highlighted dyed blond streaks of hair and mesmerizing blue eyes, was strikingly handsome, but soon brought unhappiness to a totally besotted Christina because of his continuing penchant for other women. But he sired a daughter for Christina, Athena, whom Christina adored and spoiled to the point of kitsch, buying her a miniature Ferrari when she was two, Dior baby clothes, a flock of sheep when her daughter first recited the poem *Ba Ba Black Sheep*, and stocked a miniature zoo for the infant at their Gingins mansion *Boislande* near Geneva, a sprawling 1,200 m2 mansion in ten acres of gentle rolling countryside, a property bought from the kaftan-wearing playboy Gunter Sachs, the Opel automobile empire heir.

Christina doted on Athina, but her own life was to be snuffed out in a bathtub at her friend Marina Dodero's house in Buenos Aires before three years had gone by following the birth of Athena. Another tragedy in the Onassis family, another layer of publicity to add to the myth, as the world looked on as a cortege of women dressed in black, like the chorus of a Greek tragedy, comprised of her aunts and Jackie Kennedy Onassis, Onassis last wife, followed the coffin to where Christina was laid to rest in Panagitsa Chapel, next to the white marble tombs of Ari, his sister Artemis, and Alexander. Only little Athena Helene Roussel was left to carry on the dreams and hopes and ambitions of the family and of a doting Greek public for whom the name Onassis was a word of respect, awe, and on a par perhaps with that of the ancient Gods. The name was firmly riveted into the psyche of the Greeks and instantly recognisable by a majority of people around the world.

The interested public waited to see how little Athena Roussel, the three year old orphaned daughter of tragic Christina, would turn out. They had great expectations of her. She had fame, unlimited money with which to do good when she came of age, a billion dollar family funded charitable foundation named after her late uncle Alexander whose share of the fortune was earmarked to fund the foundation. There was no indication at the time of the change that would come over her regarding her attitude to helping other people and how little interest she would have in running the foundation that her family had created specifically as a public benefit vehicle to help those in need and to give others, individuals and organizations, support for their projects.

Athena blossomed in the bosom of the Roussel family and her dark good looks drew people's attention as she grew into a tall slender girl with doe-like eyes and a sweet, shy manner. There were however from time to time, disquieting signals that this was perhaps not the angel that her polite manner indicated: that a Doll of Steel was forming behind the sweet smile that masked a streak of ruthlessness that would shock those who got to know her well.

As *The Last Onassis* it would be her responsibility to either assume the public function that the responsibility of the now legendary name and fortune came with, or to retire from public life, from doing good works for the world community, and to limit herself to only what she needed personally, in other words to turn her back on her public role and live her life only for herself with the money that her family had bequeathed so generously to her.

By the summer of 2014 her father Thierry had divorced his second wife Gaby. She now sold the Californian style ranch bungalow overlooking the Lausanne-Geneva motorway, the adjacent green fields and Lake Leman at Bois L'Essert where she had raised Athina, Eric, Sandrine and Johanna.

Thierry in the meantime had moved his offices to Nyon on Lake Leman, keeping the Boislande estate as a sort of bolthole where he could get away from family and the world and be attended to at the mansion with its gym, inside and outside swimming pools, residential wing and beautifully landscaped gardens. When he left Gaby, she sold the Lussy house to an Italian and moved back to her native Sweden.

Thierry was rumoured to have already moved in a former Miss Senegal to *Boislande* after setting up a Fund of Funds investment vehicle that he ran with the advice of top investment bankers, including Rothschild's. Eric, after completing a banking internship in Geneva, set up a LED light sales company at his father's offices at Nyon, but unlike Athina, he was gregarious and his Instagram posts alone were witness to a partying lifestyle where he appeared at society venues, ski resorts, nightclubs and at the family states is Sologne and Ibiza with a large group of raucous friends, among whom were several young society beauties with famous names. A constant stream of selfies with the group having fun or sticking their tongues out in classic social media style charted the travels of the gilded group following the handsome half-brother of Athina, to whom she had been so close until she met Doda. In Belgium it was Eric who occupied the middle floor of the house Thierry and Athina moved to when Athina registered at the Nelson Pessoa Riding School.

Thierry had by 2014 taken over the iconic Avenue Foch apartments of Onassis, the Ibiza La Jondal fairytale estate with its 8 pools, while Athina Onassis, as she now was known, had entered the ninth year of her marriage to Alvaro Affonso "Doda" de Miranda Neto, her Olympian horseman husband under whose supervision and guidance she blossomed as a world class show jumper and established the Longines Athina Onassis Horse Show.

Doda was often seen around good looking young women and rumour was rife that he went out with his Brazilian pals to enjoy themselves while his young rich wife sat home watching DVD's before retiring early, to be up at five or six the next morning to resume training at the A+D Horses company stables the couple owned near the Belgian-Dutch border. The stables were just a few minutes from their luxury villa and not far from the Valkenswaard stables set up by Jan Tops, Athina's old coach and mentor. Recently, Athina had been photographed at various riding events looking frighteningly thin, with dark circles under sunken eyes, and to all intents and purposes she was, if not anorexic, then just a hairsbreadth away.

The Brazilians

Nicky, the former call girl had told me she had met most of the Brazilian horsemen and those around Doda in the years they had been together, and slept with some. They had of course known Athina too as several of them competed in the LAOHS events as well as being with Doda and Athina at other Global Champions Tour equestrian competitions they all took part in.

Athina spent years around the Brazilians without an inkling of the charades being played behind her back, or in fact right in front of her. Those same Brazilian friends Doda had were the ones who were part of a conspiracy of silence woven around the heiress who was financing her husband's billion dollar lifestyle. Athina was the chump in the circle. *Nudge nudge, wink wink*, was the order of the day. Whether their wives were in on the charade I don't know. Nicky told me she had never met any of the Brazilian women. Her presence though was known to the men, of course. She had stayed at the same hotel as them, the 5 star Windsor Atlantica during the Athina Onassis Horse Show in Rio in 2012 and knew them well.

Doda liked to have his women under the same roof it appeared; with Nicky telling me that her luxury room was a couple of floors below that of her lover, Doda, and his wife Athina. A photo of Nicky, her daughter, and Rodrigo Pessoa at the fateful last event she attended with Doda, the LAOHS at Ramatuelle, St Tropez, shows a smiling Rodrigo in full riding kit with his arm around Nicky's daughter's shoulder in a photo taken by Pedro Costa, another of Doda's friends.

Nicky showed me the photo of a souvenir from the games, a Longines Athina Onassis Horse show riding cap, signed by Rodrigo Pessoa. Among those she hung out with Doda were Flavio Abreu, Felipe Ramos and Pedro Costa. She mentioned two (not the above) in a revealing message to me -

"Comme j'ai egalement vu XXXXXX et XXXXXX dans les clubs libertins!" ("I had seen XXXXXXX and had met XXXXXX at Swingers' Clubs!)

She described having sex with one of the Brazilians in a car while another watched. She also said that she went to Brazil, because some of the Brazilians wanted to have sex with her there. They never paid her themselves she said. The money was given to her by someone else. Most of the sex with the Brazilians was in Belgium and Holland, according to her correspondence with me, while a friend of hers, Marie-G, who states among other things in a signed statement that *"I clarify that at the time I was practising the profession of an escort"*. The call girl continues by stating that Nicky and she met in front of a hotel in Liege called Le Lys Blanc where they were joined by a man whom she recognised later as being Doda in a photograph Nicky showed her where he was dressed in riding kit. The girl was surprised she wrote, at the large amount of money Nicky gave her, 1,000 Euros, for the one hour that the three of them stayed at the hotel and added that she understood that the client had paid 3,000 Euros to

Nicky. She states that from what she saw he and Nicky were very close.

In all Nicky said that she had sex with a total of 15 men from Brazil, whom she does not name. In 2016 she had been in contact with Doda again when their lawyers had taken over for issues the estranged couple had. When Nicky wrote to some of Doda's Brazilian friends to have them verify an event regarding her relationship with Doda she was subjected to a barrage of very threatening emails from the Brazilians' European lawyers. She responded by saying that she demanded nothing except for them to verify what she said they knew regarding her and Doda. It was her alone against what seemed like half the Brazilian male population. Not the best odds, and by her a gross miscalculation as to how men react to women who sell themselves for sex. Once out of the door men do not want to know, and if they haven't had sex, then even less so, especially if something looks like getting messy and there are married people involved.

The English Detective Connection

When I mentioned the name Ken Lodge to Athina during our first meeting in 2016 in Holland she immediately responded "I know who he is!"

Yes, indeed she did. Lodge was the head of S.I.P., a specialized company of those we used to call a private detective agency; companies that now are generally referred to with the grander sounding title of Security and Risk Consultants. They usually have a list of services on their websites such as investigations, asset recovery, close protection (a fancy name for body guarding), international corporate and private security, and, occasionally, private intelligence gathering. Often the more fancy ones set up by former detectives or members of the secret services out to make a buck in the commercial world will say that they work closely with law enforcement and intelligence agencies.

Mr. Lodge's company was based in Canary Wharf at the time Nicky first mentioned him to me, close to a gym where many phone calls appear to have originated to Belgium. He lists international investigations and domestic disputes among the services he offers, and he certainly does offer those services though not always successfully, cloak and dagger ops being a tricky business at the best of times as a story leaked to the press some years ago implicated the Englishman in a surveillance operation that went horribly wrong. The client, according to the article, was a suspicious and wealthy wife who hired Ken Lodge to spy on her husband and his new girlfriend. So far there was nothing unusual, but it turned out to be very risky and some would say foolhardy venture because the country where the wandering husband had taken his paramour was Fidel Castro's communist Cuba! It was a place where a bunch of pink-skinned Brits hiding in the bushes on a surveillance mission was not the sort of thing that the swarthy cigar smoking jungle warfare and urban fighting veterans of the Communist state's security services took well to. The Englishmen working for Lodge were arrested and put in jail. The Cubans were not amused but soon realised this was not the capitalist British Empire in cahoots with the Arch-Enemy, the gringos from the US, practicing espionage and other mischief among the frangipani bushes and palm trees, but a group of very foolhardy Englishmen, whom they quickly deported, no doubt after much mirth, *chingars,* chewing on Cohiba cigars and backslapping as they watched the humiliated Brits go.

If it had been industrial or military espionage the Lodge group would no doubt have spent a couple of decades in moldy tropical prisons in damp cells, treated to regular beatings and encouragement, aided by kicks and electric wire therapy, to identify their capitalist collaborators and details of their spying mission. But seeing that all the fuss was because some macho male had taken off to Cuba on a romantic interlude of sex, sun, palm trees and mariachi music with a tight-skinned big breasted *chiquita,* away from his demanding wife, well, that they could understand and forgive. Lodge's humiliated colleagues were soon back in the United Kingdom to attend to less dangerous assignments. Dealing with Nicky, the Belgian call girl, for instance.

I asked her about Mr. Lodge and how she knew him. She explained that he worked for Doda and had popped over to Belgium to give her a package of money from him on one occasion. Another time he had sent her two I-Phones on behalf of Doda so that he and Nicky could communicate more easily without his young wife stumbling over a series of long telephone calls to a nearby Belgian number in the monthly bill. Lodge, according to the invoices and shipping slips from Sleaford that Nicky provided, had sent her a package with a commercial value of GBP 1150 containing 2 I-Phones, a USB stick "with data" (only God knows what that was), and three I-Phone covers that he purchased in Sleaford and sent by courier to her in Belgium. Interestingly this package's contents were described as a 'gift' in the document signed by a K. Lodge of Grantham Road. Now why a private investigator in the UK would be buying, privately, and sending two expensive cell phones as a gift to a call girl in Belgium, unless for his client and lover of the woman, would be interesting to know.

Nicky's insists that the phones were from Lodge's client Doda. The fact that she has produced a bill of sale and a related shipping document adds credence to her version that Athina's husband was the common denominator that linked the British investigator and her. Another document, a bank one this time showing a transfer for a similar amount listed as the value on the phone's bill of sale, indicates a sender, K. Lodge, but with a corporate address in

London for S.I.P., Mr. Lodge's company, and a certain NT (her full name is listed, it is Nicky's) at a Belgian address, as the recipient.

This was not the only reference to Ken Lodge by Nicky. In 2014 in December she sent me a rather panicked message saying that Ken Lodge would be coming to her house with Doda's lawyer Maitre Haouideg, who despite the exotic sounding North African name was described by Nicky as working at the law offices of a respected English law company called FieldFisher Waterhouse of l'Arsenal, Boulevard Louis Schmidt, whose British head branch was awarded the Law Office of the Year on Dec 1st 2017. Haouideg, whose expertise is intellectual property law, was coming, Nicky wrote, on the Thursday to have her sign a document. I understood the visit was related to an agreement between the ex-lover husband of Athina Onassis and Nicky and to apparently allow Ken Lodge to collect documents and other papers relating to Doda. It will have been interesting to hear Hakim Haouideg's side of the story, if indeed he did go to Nicky's house, and to illuminate what the connection with Nicky, the mistress of Doda, was with his field of legal expertise, intellectual property, and whether it was customary for lawyers in Belgium to visit client's mistresses at their residences with private detectives from another country in tow.

There were always so many loose ends in the Onassis story. Plus ca change.

To double-check Nicky's references to Ken Lodge I wrote telling him about the documents and asking whether he had visited Nicky's house in

Belgium with Hakim Haouideg, and if so what was he doing there with the lawyer. Nicky, methodical always, had kept a photograph of a BMW outside her house the day she said Haouideg and the British private eye had visited. The number plates of the car are clearly visible in the photo she had later given to her Belgian lawyer, Professor Thierry Moreau.

I asked the detective the obvious question. Why had Mr. Lodge sent a very expensive present to a call girl living in Belgium?

There was no answer from him, either to confirm or to deny Nicky's story, or to deny knowing her. For a professional gatherer and purveyor of information with a website describing a wide range of activities and his international presence he was unusually taciturn where his own name and that of his celebrity client Alvaro Affonso de Miranda Neto, aka "Doda", the Olympian Equestrian Bronze medalist, were involved.

Nicky's Choice – A Sex Cinema or a Swingers' Club

Nicky had a very organised section of her email correspondence as Princess Charlotte with her lover Romeu who had special orders and requests for her. She would in another more romantic world be labeled perhaps as a social secretary.

He told her where he wanted to enjoy himself and she was the one to *find* the locations for the meetings that would follow as well as arranging the times of the rendezvous.

A short series of excerpts gives an idea of the relationship between Romeu and his Princess Charlotte.

Friday, 4th April, 2014 14.49.45
Princess Charlotte01 to romeu01
I have no idea! Where is this Lichtaart?

He responds to clarify - *Max Follies*
Princess Charlotte
I have looked for a club. There is the Bornedries at st.trop, one has already been down there.

Or there is a new one called the croxx club in Limbourg

Friday 4th April
Princess Charlotte to romeu
Yes, it still exists. It's in Liege or Brussels. Open every day from 11.00 until midnight.

Romeu asks her if there is one where he is.
Princess Charlotte replies
The choice is up to you! It's a long time since I was last in a sex cinema. I'll check to see if it is still there. It's much more discreet for you!

At 11.23 romeu asks her - *sex cinema or a club?*

In another email Princess Charlotte writes to confirm that she has made arrangements to book an apartment.

Wednesday May 16th 2014 11.32.36
Princess Charlotte to romeu
Just to confirm that the reservation has been made for the event!

I have found a small apartment not far away! Actually there wasn't much choice!

Nicky and the violin

Doda was particularly attentive to his body, vain to a point unusual for a man of his years. In this he was not unlike Athina's father, Thierry Roussel, who is always on a diet, works out constantly, and is a keen sportsman. Doda as a professional athlete had to watch his physical condition of course, but people who know him well describe how he likes looking down and commenting on his trim waistline with satisfaction, even when sitting at table in a restaurant or when walking past his reflection in a shop window.

There were other similarities between father-in-law and son-in-law. Both Doda and Thierry married Onassis heiresses, though Thierry got a worse bargain as he was saddled with a psychologically erratic, older and dumpy Christina Onassis, addicted to prescription drugs; an heiress who came with the unwelcome appendage of four aging Greek administrators of her fortune. They were middle class Greeks who despised the handsome aristocratic Frenchman and were permanently locked into disputes, both in court and in the media, with Christina's husband. It was a situation that continued after Athina inherited Christina's fortune and that of her grandmother Tina Livanos Onassis when Christina's millions passed to the three year-old Athina under the management of a five member board where the four Greeks' votes outnumbered that of the fifth member, Thierry.

Doda was far better off. He had a tall, slim and very attractive-looking younger wife who also had a five member board of trustees managing her fortune, but they were far better disposed to the new husband, seeing their involvement merely as an administrative one. Apart from Thierry who was on the trust board, and who did have negative feelings towards his son-in-law, seeing perhaps too much of himself in the handsome Brazilian, the other members of the trust handling Athina's money were from Citibank, Rothschild's, Julius Baer and the international banking giant HSBC. Doda had the better deal all around, but with one proviso, unlike Thierry he had to be careful of his extra marital activities. Christina had been aware that she had latched on to one of the most handsome playboys in the world and that he could not be kept on a leash, so she put up with his affairs, forgave him much, including the news that he had a permanent mistress in Gaby, while Doda could not take the risk of having his wife discover his other life, so he kept Nicky's presence carefully hidden from Athina, but not from the Brazilians since he wanted Nicky to be out with him and his friends when his wife was at home watching DVDs and having her customary early night.

Athina was not totally in the dark about Doda, but she did not know about Nicky. She had her suspicions, but no proof of Doda's wandering, which made it worse. Nicky told me that when Doda was with her on several occasions Athina called him on his phone, crying, something that annoyed Doda who would look up at the ceiling and exhale as if to say *"Oh, shit, it's her again."*

Nicky told me that she felt bad for Athina whenever it happened, but that is how it was.

Nicky's relationship developed into something more than just a sexual one when Doda spent more time with her, taking her to various venues and to other countries where he and Athina and the Brazilians would be. He grew close to her daughter and in 2013, knowing the little girl was taking music lessons he bought her an expensive violin for Christmas. Nicky's daughter, wearing a Santa cap is seen in a photo delightedly holding her violin, playing it in front of a Christmas tree with several wrapped presents under it. Nicky uploaded the photo to Instagram with a note -

"Thank you Santa Claus for having made my princess so happy with this violin! Happy Xmas. @dodamiranda"

Among the likes under the photo is one that reads **dodamiranda**. It was indeed a Happy Christmas for Nicky and her daughter, as it was for Athina a few kilometers away celebrating a quiet Xmas with Doda and his daughter Vivienne who had settled in well with the new lifestyle she had at her step-mother's mansions with the attendant staff, the Rolls Royce and Mercedes cars with their chauffeurs at her service 24/7, and of course the expensive private school to which her unhappy model mother Cybele, now dead after jumping from the seventh floor balcony of her apartment, could not have afforded to send her. Doda's parents too were happy with the way things had turned out for their son, now married to the most famous heiress in the world. Their Greek daughter-in-law, who apart from being dizzyingly rich, had not used her inherited money to tie him to her apron strings as other heiresses such as

Barbara Hutton, the American Woolworth's heiress, had done with their husbands, demanding they attend dinner parties every night to be with the rich wife's large circle of friends. Doda was lucky that his wife did not like the social gatherings and parties of the jet setters. Athina was happy to stay in or see a movie, and then go to bed early. It was the perfect arrangement where he had a good excuse to go out to join his friends for a drink or dinner, while Nicky was waiting for him with some of his riding companions. Athina stayed home, as she had done when Doda went with a group of local partygoers in Athens to dinner with some attendant girls when Athina was still in Belgium deciding whether to come to Athens for the Olympics or not. To be sure, his young wife was wealthy, healthy and devoted, and in the first years of their marriage she was like a puppy dog following him around while he strode ahead of her. Puppy dog or sheep, the comments varied, and they were not too kind.

  She was always generous to him, once buying him a prize cow, Esmeralda, for more than $200,000, something that caused much mirth and sniggers among the Brazilian and international jet set and among the equestrian elite with whom they regularly rubbed shoulders. His family of course was proud of their son who was now much more famous than he had been as an equestrian. Their daughter-in-law was also generous to them despite her reputation for being tight with money. Her parsimoniousness is central to a well known story leaked by Doda's entourage recounting how she had been asked about a restaurant in Brazil, and according to the press report, she had complained on leaving that it was "very expensive"!

Her own clothes, apart from the stunning $70,000 Valentino wedding gown, runs to off-the-peg Timberland sorts apparel, while her hair is generally held back in a pony tail or a knot. It is rare for her to be seen well groomed and in elegant clothes while she was rarely, if ever seen wearing any of her mother's striking family jewels until she sold the lot one day, much to the shock of the general public in Greece who were amazed that she would dispose of such personal items; those that had belonged to her dead mother -so casually - for the money.

She had the money not to give a toss about anyone's opinion, and she lived the way she wanted, with hundreds of millions in the bank, but spending as little as possible on luxuries that her husband had not demanded. The Rolls, the Gulfstream jet, and other toys of the super-rich had been of no interest to her before Doda entered her life. He now had a billionaire lifestyle financed by his wife, but it was not enough, he wanted more and by the eleventh year of his marriage he had become careless, caught by Athina's bodyguard in the now notorious incident in the house in Florida, with a woman who was to be the catalyst in forcing the heiress to walk out of the marriage.

The Split –

Days after the media reported that the couple had split up, her Greek best man Kotronakis[3]'s wife, a pleasant looking young woman who had tried to be hospitable to an offhand towards her in front of the cameras Athina, when the heiress and Doda had come to Greece for the Christina Onassis Horse Show [4] told the press that she had been 'speaking to Athina regularly' and that Athina was definitely divorcing Doda, but she would let Athina give the details.

    The press was having a field day with Doda who was using his Instagram account to declare his "great love" for Athina, no doubt not believing that she had finally woken up and was showing him the door in no uncertain terms. I saw a post on his page that in my loose Google translation said "God hates lying and dishonesty"!

Wow! Don't you really *love* those Brazilians!

    After the first meeting in Holland with Athina and with her Eindhoven lawyers who were passing on the sudden and unexpected windfall of documents, primarily Nicky's written messages to me, and my updates to M, I was in almost daily contact with Nicky.

    During which time there was some discussion as to whether Athina would summon her as a witness

---

[3] The Honorary Greek Consul and best man at her wedding that Athina said she could not remember.
[4] The precursor of the LAOHS

to the divorce proceedings, something that was complicated and could have unpredictable consequences. Nicky had been, after all, the "other woman" in the marriage, the mistress of Athina's husband, and not exactly the kind of person a wife would normally summon to court for support in a divorce case! Secondly the fact that she was, by her own admission, a prostitute when she started having relations with Doda was problematic too. We may have had every reason to believe she was being honest, and indeed that was the impression she gave to me over the years I have been in contact with her, but a call girl on the witness stand was an invitation for her to be savaged by the other side's lawyers in what was already becoming a very hostile confrontation between the two former partners. Things were made worse by Athina being reported as blocking all the assets she could and stopping Doda from visiting his beloved Olympian partner horse Cornetto, forbidding him to even pet the horse in the stables. Photographs of the horse looking out of its box morosely did not help. Athina's use of the A+D stable animals to deprive Doda of his horse did not go down very well with the public even though many were angry at his betrayal of the young heiress. Athina had briefly also displayed her killer streak when she went for the jugular and turned against Doda's daughter; Athina reported to have applied to the Belgian courts to have Vivienne's school fees stopped and to repossess even the child's pet rabbits! The court rejected this and ordered Athina to keep paying the girl's school and living expenses until a final ruling was issued. This action was a rare and brief glimpse as to the Doll of Steel soul that the Onassis heiress had hidden so well from those who did not know her well, or indeed from those who knew her like me. The chinks in the affable, shy, soft-spoken girl image were starting to show as they had some years previously when she had cut off, for a while, an aunt's income, forcing her to forage in garbage cans and stand in church charity soup lines in Athens in order to physically survive. Doda no doubt who knew Athina in her most intimate moments may not have been surprised after the split when she let loose all the dogs of war on him and his daughter.

I had a second meeting in Holland with Athina, again over lunch, at my request, where we discussed an issue that had arisen as a result of my defending her right to sell Scorpios to Dmitri Rybolovlev, an appearance on TV that had brought to the surface a campaign by certain politicians and ministers in Greece to dispute the legality of the sale, while a panel on a very hostile TV programme had promoted the idea of the island being given to the Onassis Foundation so it could hold concerts and other events there. The taped interview I gave of my speaking of the right, that she had, to sell the island, Athina's personal property via a company created by Onassis, resulted in a full scale attack on me, Thierry and Athina, for which I sued the channel. It was also an opportunity to explain to Athina the circumstances regarding another issue of Scorpios in which I had become involved when the vice-president of the Onassis Foundation, Pavlos Ioannides, Onassis former personal pilot, refused me entry to the island at the time I was working for the family. I had let the media know about this when Stelios Papadimitriou, who was on the board of Athina's administrators, declared that "Athina does not own Scorpios, she only has the use of the island!" A patent falsehood, and as expected a big scandal broke out in the Greek media. The Foundation members attacked me personally, disputing my official role with the Roussels as well as disputing Thierry's signature on the letter of authorization I carried. I conferred with Thierry and told him I felt we should investigate the Scorpios company records to see what was happening. After my wife Dimitra volunteered to help me she discovered in state archives that neither Athina's father, nor any Onassis relative, nor a member of the Swiss Juvenile authority had been placed on the board of the Scorpios company by Stelios Papadimitriou and his three associates.

I discovered also that on several recent occasions there had been unexplained changes in the published statutes of the company. Strangest of all was the fact that company board had passed a resolution saying that *"the shareholder (Athina) will have no right in the future to question any decisions or actions taken by the board of directors."* This was an unusual way of protecting Athina's interests. It meant that neither Athina nor her father, as long as she was still a minor, could veto or question the management of her island, even if potentially damaging, but legal, decisions were taken or personal use made by the Greek administrators of the island as a place to entertain and feed their guests or the media, something that happened several times without the prior knowledge or the approval of the owner. Obviously any board resolution limiting an owner's rights over his own property must be invalid, and even more so when this is taken by the administrators of a minor's estate, administrators who later illegally voted to exclude Athina's father from the board meetings of her patrimony. It should not have surprised us then when some years later the Onassis Foundation board took a decision to change, in violation of the written statutes of the Foundation, the article which referred to the Onassis descendant's right to be Foundation President without the need of election.

Even more strange was the fact that a special resolution was passed saying that the Scorpios company was no longer a real estate company but a company authorized to carry out commercial ventures. More unusual for us was the phrase "the company may open shops and commercial premises all around the world". The intention for this change in the statutes of a private island was unclear. Why had the board felt it necessary to make special changes to the status of the island? From the above it seemed we were missing something.

I called Nuot Saratz, Thierry's and Athina's lawyer in Switzerland. He was the lawyer responsible for contacts with the Tutelle, the Swiss authority overseeing administration of minors' patrimonies. I explained the situation to him, and he was not pleased by what we were discovering in Greece. He agreed that we should look further into the matter.

I then tried to get access to the board minutes of the Scorpios company – Mykinai SA - but the Greek authorities said that beyond what was published in the company registers I would need the authorization of the company board in order to read the minutes in the copy of the board sessions deposited with the Ministry of Commerce. I could imagine the look on Ioannides' or Papadimitriou's face if I called them with such a request. It was out of the question.

I sent a fax to Thierry and his lawyers. Thierry instructed Saratz to bring the matter before the Tutelle and petition them to order that all safe deposit boxes containing shares and financial instruments belonging to Athina be opened and an inventory of company shares be taken.

It was certainly a risk, because if the Swiss authorities, bank officers, the lawyers on both sides and the Greek administrators were involved in what was to be a major operation, and everything was in order, then I would have egg on my face. Additionally Thierry would be compromised before the Swiss authorities for having shown so little faith in the Greek administrators and forcing them to go to Switzerland on a wild goose chase. Thierry nevertheless went ahead and applied to the Tutelle to summon the Greek administrators to open the safe deposit boxes in Geneva. The administrators replied to the Tutelle that there was no reason for the effort and expense such a venture would entail. These objections were overridden by the Swiss judicial authority who ordered them to go to Switzerland and make a new inventory of Athina's shares and companies.

In January of 1998, for several hours a Greek patrimony administrator, his lawyer, the Roussel lawyer, a representative of the Tutelle, and a bank officer carefully itemized the contents of two large safe deposit boxes registered in the name of Athina Roussel. There, at the offices of Credit Suisse in Geneva, the shares of more than one hundred and twenty companies were carefully inspected, counted, and a new inventory taken. At the end of the second day the shares of all the companies were accounted for, except for those of Mykinai SA and Agamemnon SA. These were the companies that owned the twin islands of Scorpios and Sparti.

There was a silence when this fact was discovered and the Swiss confronted the Greek administrator present, asking for an explanation. This was immediately forthcoming.

The shares belonging to Athina, he said "*sont dans les mains de la justice grecque*". The Swiss, hearing that the shares were in the hands of the Greek judiciary ordered the return of the other company stock to the safe deposit boxes. These were duly sealed and the inventory signed by all the members present.

Marc Bonnant, the Roussel lawyer and later head of a Swiss Bar Association, who had been present when the safe deposit boxes were opened, informed me of what had happened. I was still not convinced, and told Thierry so. There was little though at that stage that we could do and the matter of Scorpios went onto the back burner now since there were more pressing matters which took priority.

Papadimitriou gave us the chance we were looking for with his court action against Thierry for defamation two months later. One morning Thierry changed the direction of the questioning and asked one of the administrators "Where are my daughter's shares of the Scorpios company?"

"They are in a safe deposit box at the Citibank Branch of Piraeus," came the reply.

They had not told the truth to the Swiss authorities in Geneva and now they gave yet another explanation as to the whereabouts of the Scorpios company shares. Previously there had been an explanation that Athina's shares were not in Switzerland because this category of shares by Greek law was not allowed to leave the country.

We waited for the case to end and then I called Nuot Saratz and Thierry in Geneva, suggesting that the time had come to appoint a specialized corporate lawyer here in Greece. Thierry agreed and asked me to find him one.

"Alexis, I have paid millions in legal fees, but I am fed up with this story with the Scorpios shares. Get your expert."

I contacted an old friend, Professor Costas Katsigeras, a respected lawyer and college professor who was the legal adviser to a string of embassies and corporations. Katsigeras in his turn introduced me to Drilerakis Associates, a specialized Greek firm of lawyers used to solving the most esoteric problems for international clients and companies doing business in Greece. Three days after New Year of 1999 when everything in Athens was shut down and those Athenians who had not escaped to the snow-covered slopes of Gstaadt and St Moritz were sleeping off the excesses of their previous nights' revels, I received a fax from the law firm of John Drilerakis. He informed me that since 1992 there were NO restrictions on the movement of shares of commercial or real estate companies from Greece within the European Union. A photocopy of the presidential decree and its subsections were included in the fax. Once again someone among the administrators had been caught out not telling the truth, either to Athina's father, to the Swiss Authorities, or to the Greek courts regarding the whereabouts of Athina's Scorpios shares.

The Swiss were not amused. They summoned the Greek administrators to come immediately and hand over the shares to them. A few days later a Greek member of the patrimony board arranged for the shares to be delivered to Switzerland. Athina's Scorpios shares were placed in her safe deposit box. Two months later the Swiss Tutelle fired the management board appointed by Christina Onassis to manage her daughter's patrimony. The 4 Greek members protested and appealed. At the end of the summer a higher Swiss court rejected their appeal and ratified their firing. The Swiss court decision stated that the *"Greek administrators had acted in ways that were unacceptable for trustees of a minor's patrimony"* and appointed KPMG, the multinational accounting corporation, to assume responsibility for the management of Athina's considerable assets. What was sure was that the family was much happier after this decision. Additionally no-one would now have access to Scorpios without the family knowing or approving the visit.

This then was the story I told Athina, giving her the file with the steps I had taken at the time to secure her ownership, something that allowed her in

2012 to sell the island to the Russian oligarch Ribolovlev's daughter Ekaterina for a sum estimated to have been in excess of $100,000,000 though foreign press reports previously had said that she had refused to sell to the Emir of Qatar who had been interested in the island, for less than $200,000,000. In any case she had the Mykinai SA and Agamemnon SA shares and had been able to transfer the use on a long lease, if not the title of the island, to the Russian, and of course to get a huge cash injection into her bank accounts. Athina told me she had not been aware of the share dispute and in fact was skeptical when it was first mentioned, but after reading the details she had the complete picture of how she was able to legally dispose of the island.

I had reason to discuss this successful asset recovery with her a year later, in the autumn of 2017 when it was my turn to request support...

The Red File

From June until October of 2016 there was a flurry of mutual court actions by Doda and Athina while I was busy collecting information from Nicky describing her affair with Doda. Soon it become clear that she had been very much a part of his life, more so than anyone had suspected.

She described going to the Rio AOHS games and having VIP entry clearance and tags, mingling freely with the sponsors and the VIP guests. It was not unusual for the rich to have expensive call girls in their lives but it was not every day that a call girl was invited to mingle with them in public, as in Nicky's case, and be near the host's wife and friends. By this time the Brazilian riders and those accompanying them knew Nicky. Some had slept with her with Doda's knowledge. For her it was an entry into the world of the plutocracy. She reveled in the new-found luxury of the surroundings and the free spending of the rich around Athina and Doda. Another call girl who signed a witness statement she gave to Nicky and she in turn to her lawyer professor Thierry Moreau, stated that Nicky spoke of the luxurious surroundings she found herself in for the first time. She became a regular at equestrian events where Doda and Athina were present.

My main task for Athina was to convince a very edgy and mercurial in her moods Nicky to agree to give us the Moreau file where she said she had hard evidence to back up her claims regarding Doda and her. It was what the lawyers of Athina wanted but the problem was that Nicky was having issues with Doda again and was in the middle of a divorce herself.

In one messenger exchange I wanted to understand the parameters of her relationship with Doda, was he possessive, jealous, or uninterested?

"Did Doda want exclusivity over you?"

"Au contraire,' she replied. "He was happy for me to go with his friends, in fact he ██████ ████ █████ ██████ She had more to tell, giving detailed descriptions, dates, and place names.

After the spilt with Doda Nicky wrote to his friends for them to confirm certain details about the relationship with Nicky, as he was being elusive. The response was a barrage of threatening lawyer's letters sent to Nicky accusing her of blackmail. She responded that blackmail was not her intention since she was asking for nothing from the; at this point she wrote to one of them who knew Athina very well, reminding him of the *club exchangiste*, the swingers club called ONLY 4 YOU, telling the Brazilian that she had been there frequently with Doda and had sex with several of his friends there, including the recipient's brother, and in a move to deflate their macho Latin egos Nicky wrote that for the sexual encounters with them in the swingers club she had been paid, making it clear that she had not engaged with them because of their good looks. A woman scorned!

I was in contact with Athina who was competing regularly in the Global Champions Tour organised by her close friend and mentor Jan Tops whose home base was the state-of-the-art equestrian facility at Valkenswaard in Holland near the Belgian border, close to both where the De Miranda couple lived, and to Nicky.

One day when Nicky realised that the divorce was on its way she sent me a note to say that she was prepared to give the Doda file to me to take to Athina. The news was received with much joy by the heiress's lawyer M in Eindhoven who said we should act quickly before Nicky changed her mind again. Nicky was having some issues with her professor lawyer who was in continuous contact with Doda's lawyers. The only way for her to get her file and the evidence back was to terminate his services and legal representation of her. A letter was duly prepared that she emailed to Professor Moreau asking what she owed him and that she wanted an appointment to come to his office to pick up her file. I had in the meantime some reservations as to how she would handle this and asked her if she wanted me to accompany her to the Professor's office near the Belgian capital, about two hours drive from Nicky's mother's apartment into which she had moved with her daughter after Doda cut off any financial support he had been giving her. She liked the idea and responded that it would be an honour for her to meet and to have me accompany her there.

Moreau told her that we would have to see him on the Wednesday because his brother had died and he would be leaving the office the next day to go and meet his family. After that it would be days until a new meeting could be arranged, with the risk for us that Nicky would change her mind again. So I told her to go ahead with the appointment. M's office booked me a flight on Wednesday morning from Athens to Brussels. I had the same driver with the 6.3 AMG Mercedes waiting for me. I gave him our schedule – to drive to Nicky's apartment building, pick her up from there and go to the Professor's law office, get the file, and after going to my hotel in Brussels with the file, to give it to the driver who would then drive Nicky back and go to Holland to deliver the goods for Athina. I planned to take an evening flight back to Athens. Mission accomplished.

After the usual flurry of sms and other messages and phone calls following my arrival I arranged to meet Nicky at 2.30 p.m. after she got off her nursing shift at the hospital. We needed to then get back to Brussels in afternoon traffic and meet Moreau who would be at his office until around 5pm after which "the bird would have flown"!

I had seen photos of Nicky that indicated she was tall, with a very good well exercised body and what looked like endless legs! What a surprise then when I saw her come out of the apartment building to meet us further down the street as she did not want her mother to see the large car with a strange man and a chauffeur and to have to explain who we were and why she was meeting us. Nicky was shorter than I had expected, of medium height, very conservatively dressed in dark clothes, black leggings and a three quarter coat over her dress. She was wearing glasses and looked more like a primary school teacher or the nurse that she now was than the *femme fatale* I expected. Pleasant, soft spoken and happy, as it turned out, to see me. There was some excitement when she needed to go to a bank and the branch she used was closed that Wednesday afternoon because of a strike at the specific branch. We drove around looking for an open branch of the bank in question some miles away with one eye on the clock since Moreau would be leaving his office before long and we had a long way to go in afternoon traffic. But after a stop at a helpful shopping centre bank branch we were on our way to Moreau's office. An hour and a half later we entered a leafy affluent suburb of Brussels with free standing large houses surrounded by carefully kept gardens with mature trees lining the street. Nicky pointed out Number 17 on the left, saying it was the professor's law office. It looked just like any of the other houses on the street, certainly nothing gave away that it was an office building. We had the chauffeur park further down the street and I followed Nicky to the front door where she rang the bell and gave her name over the intercom. The door opened via a buzzer and Nicky and I walked into an empty hall, then we turned right and left again to enter a room where a receptionist asked us to wait, saying Professor Moreau would see us in a few minutes. A little later she beckoned to us to follow her through a door on the left and ushered us into a room with a wall lined with books, some artwork, and sitting at a large desk was a good looking man of around 65 with long silverish hair. The whole wall of the room on my right was of glass, with a view over a garden to a row of large trees lining what appeared to be a brook or a canal. It was a deceptively peaceful setting. The professor looked at me for a moment, without any sign of welcome, gave me a handshake, neither friendly nor weak, and asked us to sit down. I had told Nicky that she should introduce me as a friend who had undertaken to bring her to the professor's office, and had indicated to her that I would not take part in any conversation, but just be there to give her confidence in what was not the easiest of situations as she was collecting her personal files from the famous law professor whom she had just fired. Moreau engaged in conversation with her regarding discussions that he had recently had with Doda's lawyers and then gave her a thick red file. He explained that legal convention did not allow him to give her the file of his communications with Doda's lawyers as these were protected by legal deontology and could only be passed directly to her new lawyers after she had named them. She thanked Moreau, wished him a safe trip the next day and we left through the narrow winding mazelike passage and out through the front door where our driver was now parked on the street waiting for us.

"Well, that's done, Nicky!" I said, seeing her expression of relief. Our next stop was for the lunch that we had missed since it was now around four thirty. We decided to stop somewhere along the route to taking Nicky back and take pot luck. Nicky and I settled into the back of the car to continue the update she was giving me about her eight and a half years with Doda.

The red file was now safely locked in the boot of the Mercedes. I phoned M to give the good news to Athina. He was overjoyed, an unusually expressive man I thought for a Dutchman, but we had in the course of several months of communication and meetings arrived at a very open modus of communication. I was aware that his professional loyalty lay with Athina as did my personal feelings, so we were on the same side, and his emails were more like those of an old friend than of a lawyer collecting information for the divorce proceedings of the most famous of international heiresses.

We stopped at village after village and found nowhere to eat, finally after visiting several eateries that were either not open or had no food, just coffee and cakes, I told Nicky that I was famished, having got up at five that morning in Athens and eaten nothing all day apart from one of those fidgety airline breakfasts on a plastic tray with infant size helpings – I would eat anywhere that was open. The driver pointed to a Pizza Hut. I told him to stop there. It was perhaps the most miserable American franchise hole-in-the-wall corner eatery I had ever seen, all in all with just one table for four, a take away counter, and no toilet, with Pizza Hut posters as the main decor in its 15 m2 total area. But it was at that moment the answer to our search so we ordered pizzas, a beer and some sparkling water. I celebrated the acquisition of the file that possibly held the most important evidence that could be key for the celebrity heiress to use against her husband who was demanding millions from her, and to all intents, if there was no other evidence to make him retreat, he looked like coming out ahead as the injured and abandoned husband dumped by the fickleness of a young billionaire wife who it appeared had tired of him. In the boot of the hired blue Mercedes parked outside next to a sleepy railway station lay the dossier with hundreds of documents meticulously collected by the former mistress of Athina Onassis' husband.

After the chauffeur, Nicky, and I were done, we set off once more to go south to leave Nicky at her apartment. M in the meantime had indicated he would be very happy if I could bring the file to his house, so I asked him to change the booking from the five star hotel in Brussels to the Park Hotel in Eindhoven where I had stayed on one of my previous trips. He agreed it was a good idea and so I left Nicky at her mother's after she and I took the mandatory selfies, each for our own reasons, and the driver and I entered the late afternoon traffic crawl across the Dutch border, continuing to M's house where we arrived after dark. I apologised to his long suffering wife who had once again had me dumped into her dining room with hardly any notice as M, I, and his colleague Jill, who had been at the previous meeting at M's house sat at the table where we spread out the contents of the red file, each document going from one to the other, with brief exclamations of delight, surprise and approval as document after document backed up with evidence the incredible story of the eight and a half year relationship between Nicky and Athina's errant Olympian horseman husband. M's wife ordered Thai food as there was no way she could cope with the influx of visitors from her husband's law practice who took over the long wooden dining table and the cozy living room a few steps down to the side overlooking the now partially illuminated and well tended garden beyond the bay window.

Athina had been informed that the much sought after file with her husband's misdeeds was now in Eindhoven at her lawyer's house and at that moment we were inspecting the documents. Jill then asked if she could leave with the file to take it to the new offices that M had moved his practice and partners to, in order to scan them, promising she would email me all the contents of my dossier by the next morning. I agreed. After dinner M drove me back to the hotel where I went up to my suite overlooking the square. I took a quick shower, feeling the fatigue of the day being washed away by the hot water, and soon after I lay down on the crisp starched sheets, switched off the side light and fell asleep almost immediately.

It appeared that the prediction of the Greek press who had often written that "when Athina grows up she will have her old family friend at her side to help her through difficult situations" was coming true. I was convinced that things would pick up from where they had been the last time we met when I was a guest at her Ibiza mansion with its magnificent Moorish style gardens with waterfalls and palm trees overlooking the azure Mediterranean. Athina appeared very appreciative, recently sending me several warm sms *Thank You* messages.

But I, carried away by the euphoria of recent events, had missed the warning signs that there was a very different person inside the smiling, welcoming shell of the heiress and old friend I had once again met up with.

    The next day when I arrived in Athens two emails came from M asking if I had recovered from all the travelling of the previous day, indeed I had been in total in four different countries, had covered the length of Belgium by car twice in an afternoon and had then gone to Holland, and the next day I flew from Amsterdam to Strasbourg and then to Athens.

The Bird has Flown

During the course of my working for the Roussel family and with Athina's lawyers in Greece, France and Switzerland, the lawyers updated me on the progress of each of the cases, from those of Dr Nuot Saratz in Switzerland who was responsible for Athina's patrimony issues, to those of Marc Bonnant of Zurich, who became the president of the Swiss Law Association, Yves Repiquet in Paris, who in turn was voted as president of the Paris Bar Association, a frequent visitor to Athens and Geneva where we had meetings with all the lawyers at Thierry's company offices in the Boislande mansion at GinsGins, meetings that had also been attended by professors Kourakis and Karras from Greece, and of course numerous meetings in the law offices of Professor Katsandonis, the most respected senior criminal law professor in Athens, Professor Takis Papanikolaou, a civil law expert whom I hired for Thierry and Athina to try and untangle the web of numerous complicated cases by and against the Greek administrators of Athina's patrimony and members of the Onassis Foundation boards. Additionally with Thierry's authorization and approval I had hired, along with the other Greek lawyers, my friends and personal lawyers Yannis Aletras and Eliza Wosenberg, now a Greek member of the European parliament. The amount of cases was staggering as was the necessity to efficiently coordinate all the legal offices, sixteen in all, that were involved at one time or another with Athina and Thierry's cases. The result of this, the numerous court appearances as Athina or Thierry's witness in court and declarations to the press outside the courtrooms, or when travelling with Thierry and Athina resulted in the media confusing me for a legal professional. From a day in December 1998 when a reporter erroneously referred to me as a lawyer I have been dogged by this false label to this day, despite numerous denials I have made on camera, on Facebook, in articles, to no avail. Most recently HOLA! of Spain, CARAS of Brazil and others wrote about the Greek *abogado, avocat, advogado*, lawyer of Athina! Anyway, the point is that during the difficult days when the court cases were at fever pitch over the Onassis fortune I was called to sit in at meetings with the lawyers of the family and to bring investigation results, suggestions and proposals to the table. It had been like that in the five months from when I first contacted Athina with the Nicky/Doda story – until the day I delivered the Doda-Nicky red file.

I was sure we were back again to the good days judging from the heiress' easygoing friendliness, her numerous sms thanking me for "your support" and her willingness to pay for me to fly back and forth from Athens to Holland and Belgium, with hotel suites generously provided by her, along with the Mercedes and its multilingual driver. Every effort was taken to make sure I was comfortable, that I was well cared for - the hospitality was exceptional – classic Onassis and Roussel hospitality that I had experienced in Paris, Geneva, Ibiza, Scorpios, and Athens along with the invitations to go skiing with Gaby and the family in the past. This stream of hospitality continued until October 27th 2016 when I handed over the file to an ecstatic M and a delighted Athina.

Back in Athens at my house I stretched out and waited for an update as to the progress of the divorce now that the file with the collection of damning documents and correspondence was in the hands of Athina's divorce lawyers, a very big stick to wave at Doda to make him accept that the game was up, that he had been discovered. M wrote more than once about the great help the file and the previous documents in it had been, and that one of the incidents described by Nicky, and backed up by the written and signed statements by another call girl were, in the words of M, "great leverage".

I mentioned I was pleased to provide evidence that would undermine Doda's alimony claim and save Athina millions if he was confronted with incontrovertible proof of having been systematically unfaithful and disrespectful to his younger wealthy and innocent bride. Belgium does not give alimony to adulterers, but it DOES give alimony to the poorer of the two parties divorcing, irrespective of their sex, if the divorce is a No Fault one. The hope had been that Doda would back off in face of the evidence and reduce his claims, coming to an agreement to receive an agreed pre-nup amount, not the millions he was claiming in damages to his professional career and for alimony. In this case the best result would be Athina and Doda signing a No Fault divorce after Doda dropped his substantial financial claims, in which case neither party would reveal detrimental things about the other and the court would grant a divorce based on mutual consent.

But the phone calls and emails from M did not materialise, only very friendly non-committal responses to my enquiries, and nothing about the course of the file, how it was being used, what the Brussels and New York lawyers were doing with it, and the general progress of the divorce. Once or twice when I mentioned an update the answer from M was that "nothing much" was happening except for papers being taken to the court for the judges to see. Absolutely nothing of a legal nature, or a detailed, as had been the habit in the past, update on progress was sent to me. Athina, whom I had expected to follow up after her gushing thanks and repeated friendly messages while I was in the process of the complicated and drawn out negotiations with a very jumpy Nicky, who changed opinion from one week to the next, was quiet! From Athina there was radio silence - I was mystified. Never thinking that sweet Athina had taken what she had wanted and that all the lunches, drivers, limousines, lunches and charm had been anything but a genuine expression of friendliness and renewed friendship, and not a cynical ploy to feed me with hay until I had taken her over the last hurdle that she could not negotiate herself even with the most expensive lawyers in the world, the NY ones and her Belgian team.

At first it was a little niggly feeling, a doubt, an idea that flitted into and out of my consciousness. It could not surely be that all this had been a carefully staged masterful operation done with the cooperation of her effervescently cordial and charming young

Dutch lawyer M who signed off each email "with a big hug" (and he was not gay, being happily married with a very beautiful, talented wife and a charming two years old daughter!)

Another month passed, and another one and another one. My sms to Athina, not wanting to swamp her, were spaced apart, usually when she was about to start or had just finished a riding competition, to congratulate or encourage her and to see how she was. She did not reply to two or three messages and I asked M if something had gone wrong for her, but he assured me she had "a lot of issues on her mind". That was all!

When I mentioned in an sms to her that she had not replied to some messages, asking if everything was in order, she answered to assure me she had been busy, to wish me well, and for me to pass on her greetings to my family.

There was nothing more of substance from any of her lawyers, no more invitations from her, and no phone calls. More months went by and by now it was clear that I had been used, stripped of what was to be useful to her - essentially taken for a ride, cynically, by boosting my vanity to knock down my defences, my Greek *filotimo* flattered by the great hospitality offered by Athina, iconic Onassis' granddaughter , when she needed the file to learn what I knew of Doda from various parties, primarily from Nicky, but also from other people I knew in the equestrian circuit, and last, but not least, from her former servants in Belgium and Switzerland who had anything but flattering things to say about her husband and his Brazilian friends. Some of what I told her had shocked her, some things she had suspected, while all the while, directly or through M she appeared very keen to suck up every scrap of information that I had collected and of course to know the progress of my contacts with Nicky and if she would give up the file with the proof of Doda's adultery over the eight and a half years Nicky had referred to.

By March of 2017, five months after I had delivered the red file Doda realised there was no point in defending his innocence any more. According to a Brazilian magazine he now admitted being unfaithful from the second year on, something that tied in with Nicky's story of the beginning of their affair. He justified himself by saying that his wife had been problematic in her mental behaviour and had been unwilling to discharge her marital obligations, in other words to have sex with him, so he had been forced by circumstances to look elsewhere for companionship. He added he would bring a top Brazilian woman psychologist, who was named in the article, to court, to verify Athina's mental instability.

This surprising interview did not go down well with the general public that adored the once again blameless female victim of male exploitation. First it had been her father Thierry Roussel after the Onassis Foundation had accused him of acting against his daughters interests, then there was the Foundation itself with a series of claims by them for fees and a huge claim by a Swiss lawyer working with them, a Maitre Augustin, from the patrimony of the formerly underage heiress; a claim of close to twenty million dollars for supposedly unpaid due legal fees.

Athina had always been portrayed as the victim, the poor little rich girl who had been left an orphan after her tragic and cuckolded mother Christina Onassis had died in unexplained circumstances in a bathroom at the villa of her close friend Marina Dodero in Argentina. Athina, then just three years old, without a mother and with her hundreds of millions and a playboy father depicted as a money grabber by his enemies, became a figure of great pity and a tsunami of sympathy was directed at her wherever she was seen over the years. This was nurtured by the heiress' own shy behaviour and excellent breeding, never acting like the spoiled rich brats that people had seen so much of in the gossips magazines and on reality TV shows. Athina was the shy, retiring princess, and we all adored her, and those close to her, as I had been on and off whenever she needed help, were always there for her. And it was not for the money.

Sweet, tragic, doe-eyed, retiring, publicity-shy, equine lover Athina Helene Roussel de Miranda Onassis had the world and the media eating out of her palm. And we of the media and those around her supported this image, of our own volition.

All was not well, however, in the Kingdom of Denmark.

The term Doll of Steel that I had first used to describe her in an interview with Ta Nea newspaper those many years ago when we were at Scorpios with her father for the tenth anniversary memorial service of her mother Christina's passing was prophetic, as time would show.

Doda now had spoken about her mental condition, breaking ranks with the hordes that adored his young wife. His former companion Cybele's, son, Fernando, had given an interview that was very badly received as it appeared he was ungrateful for the billionaire lifestyle Athina had offered him to move in with Doda's daughter Vivienne to her Belgian mansion. Fernando told the interviewing television journalist that Athina had been acting strangely ever since her fall in Geneva when she had ordered her favourite Horse A+D Camille to be killed after the horse broke its leg while trying to carry Athina over a jump.

Doda's mother chimed in, saying that she did not recognise Athina as the daughter-in-law she had known in Brazil because of the way she had been acting lately. It looked like a de Miranda family hatchet job on the innocent and wealthy bride of Doda, an attempt to justify the unjustifiable, but very soon I was to find out it was not exactly so. Doda's ex-wife was not the Athina we all were convinced we knew and whose image I and the media had been, to a great degree, responsible for creating by meeting criticism of her or anything negative in the press by offering a convincing, hopefully, justification for her actions. In more extreme cases I had flatly denied the truth of the media reports, looking for a plausible justification to protect her.

A Greek paparazzo had written a preface to a book on Onassis saying "You lived the myth that we reporters and journalists created for you, and that legacy has followed you long after your death". And so it is with Athina, the taciturn Snow White of the international show jumping world with its sheiks, princesses, counts, Olympic Games Gold medalists, dashing riders and athletic daughters of the plutocracy and pop stars, who ride magnificent phenomenally expensive shiny horses with 5 star event hairdresser-styled and plaited manes. Glitzy advertising draws ordinary people with their children to line up for tickets for the public stands to see the privileged and wealthy equestrians going over the hurdles in a race against the clock, with a very few riders winning money prizes that often do not pay even for the cost of bringing the horse to the venue. Nicky's story and her observations give a different perspective to those she rubbed shoulders with or had sex with for money, in the sequestered VIP section of the Athina Onassis Horse Shows with their gourmet 5 star oyster and champagne menus, silver service and the glamorous mix of corporate sponsors like Bentley and Longines, billionaires, high class call girls, society names, business and show business luminaries. As the story unfolds the reader will see that the fairytale world of Snow White and her dashing Olympian husband will unravel to reveal a Doll of Steel, and Romeu driven by a years' long desire for the body of a call girl, his very own Princess Charlotte, whom he took to share the events with him, a whisker's distance away from his unsuspecting wife at circuits where glamour mixes with sleaze and the prize steeds, often worth between ten and twenty million dollars, have the Damocles' Sword of their trainer's revolver ready to shoot them in the brain or the lethal injection in the waiting vet's medical bag should they make a mistake, slip, and break a leg while carrying their rider/owners over a hurdle.

Such is the harsh and glamorous world of the Longines Athina Onassis Horse Show and the other equestrian competitions that Doda and Athina have made their home.

Athina Meets Doda

Athina had been pestering Thierry for a long time to allow her to go to Belgium where she wanted to enroll in the Nelson Pessoa riding academy. Athina was obsessed with horses and show jumping and what had started as a hobby in her spare time now took precedence over all her other extracurricular activities. Thierry liked horses and the family had theirs at a nearby stable. Athina, Thierry and Sandrine were the riders in the family. Erik, Athina's half-brother was allergic to them and kept well away from the equine companions that his sisters admired so much.

    Thierry had seen changes in Athina recently. After her sixteenth birthday tensions were building up in the family. Athina was changing from the docile, cheerful and shy teenager seen hanging onto her father's arm whenever they were in public together, into a brooding, introverted girl with many things on her mind. The conflict with the Onassis Foundation, public scrutiny and criticism of the heiress and her lifestyle, tensions created by the court cases, her father's five year prison sentence in Greece and a kidnapping scenario in Switzerland, plus the pressures of being the last bearer of the Onassis name made Athina look for something that would keep her away from public attention and allow her time on her own. She found refuge in the privacy of her stables and the freedom she felt when she was riding one of her favourite animals. Here she could have a sense of achievement as she coaxed her steeds over ever higher jumps.

Thierry was not an easy man to get on with. I had observed him at home and knew that his family was expected to do what he said. The extent of this control and his view that he would always be in charge of Athina, and by extension of her affairs, financial and social, were apparent to those close to the family. An incident at Athens airport made it even clearer that Thierry was not prepared to let go. He still saw Athina as the little girl she no longer was. When Thierry stepped out of the arrivals lounge where I had been waiting for him two Greek television reporters approached us and started asking about Athina. Thierry's answers were well rehearsed and expected until one of the reporters asked him "Does Athina have a boyfriend?"

Thierry thought for a moment. "No, of course not, she is only fifteen."

The answer took the reporters by surprise. It was clear that he was unaware or unwilling to accept that his daughter was now a young woman and that it was the most normal thing in the world for her to have an interest in boys of her own age.

As the pressures of puberty and of growing up as an Onassis started closing in on Athina she began losing her former interest in her lessons and turned her attention to her horses. The ghost of Christina Onassis with all the accompanying stories of sexual excess, emotional instability, drug use and incapacity to forge lasting and meaningful relationships hung heavy in the Roussel family home. The situation was made more complicated by the realization that no matter how fairly Gaby, Athina's Swedish stepmother, treated the children Athina was always going to be something different. She could not escape the fact that she was the child of a tragic Greek shipping heiress who had willed her whole fortune to Athina and Thierry, allowing the Roussels and Athina to have a lifestyle of luxury that was the envy of the world and the secret jealousy of their friends. Athina had to cope with the rumours and gossip she heard and read about her mother and her grandmother Tina whom Truman Capote had called 'a whore', and also with the knowledge that Gaby had stolen Thierry from Christina. Christina's death and the repeated news items referring to it as part of an Onassis 'curse' must have weighed heavily too on young Athina as she prepared to make her way into adulthood. For Athina the situation was not made easier by statements in the press that Thierry had cynically married an overweight Greek heiress for her money. Christina Onassis became an object of love but also of shame for her teenage daughter. Christina's photos were one day taken down from the mansion outside Geneva that she had given to Athina. Things came to a head one evening at the dinner table in Lussy when Athina asked for another piece of bread and Thierry exploded, saying "You are just like your mother, putting on weight all the time with chocolates and food!"

As time passed Athina demanded to go to Belgium to train at the Pessoa Riding School. This time Thierry realised that he could not continue refusing his daughter because in a year's time she would be in charge of her multi-million dollar Onassis patrimony and Thierry wanted to continue managing the money for her. It stood to reason that if he caused a rift with his daughter she would in all likelihood take her money and leave the day she turned 18. The Onassis women were known for their rebelliousness and Thierry could not take the risk. One day Thierry summoned Athina and announced to her and the family that he was going to send her to Belgium to become a professional standard show jumper. Athina put her arms round her father's neck and kissed him, beaming with happiness. But there were conditions, Thierry said. They would rent a house in Brussels where Athina would have her own apartment with her maid, Erik would be on the middle floor and Thierry would be living on the ground floor apartment to be able to keep and eye on who came and went in order to protect Athina. Thierry was also adamant that Athina should not abandon her studies and would have to enroll in a school in Belgium to get her Baccalaureate.

Athina was ecstatic. After arrangements were made and a suitable house was found in the Belgian capital for Thierry, Athina and Erik, they left with her personal maid and other staff for Brussels, leaving behind Gaby, Johanna and Sandrine at Lussy.

When they arrived in Brussels Thierry took Athina outside the capital to Nelson Pessoa's country riding school and enrolled her there.

It was a decision he was to bitterly regret for years to come. Unknown to Thierry Roussel a tall, good-looking, unsmiling Brazilian Olympic silver medalist show jumper named Affonso Alvaro de Miranda Neto who was also enrolled at the riding school was to steal and later deeply wound Thierry's daughter's heart and redirect the Onassis fortune for a while.

The Handsome Horseman and the Onassis heiress

Three men were of pivotal influence in Athina's life, all older than herself - her French father Thierry, her Dutch riding coach and co-founder of the Global Champions/Athina Onassis International Horse Show, Jan Tops, and her Brazilian husband Alvaro "Doda" de Miranda. Each had a special place in Athina's life and each was to put his stamp on the Onassis story.

When Athina moved to Belgium with Thierry, he confided to me that he was unhappy with Athina's passion for show-jumping because he considered it a dangerous sport. Athina was so passionate with riding and dedicated to her training at the Pessoa Riding School that all Thierry could do was to keep an eye on her and to accompany her to the riding academy whenever he was not travelling. What he did not know was that Athina was starting to get emotionally involved with her fellow rider Alvaro Affonso "Doda" de Miranda Neto. De Miranda was 12 years older than the teenage heiress and had been living with a Brazilian model, Cybele Dorsa, with whom he had a young daughter, Vivienne, in Sao Paolo.

Athina was struck by the tall, dark, Olympic medalist who lavished attention on her and before long the impressionable 17 year old heiress and her fellow rider were a couple. They initially kept their affair a secret from Thierry. Athina knew her father would have objections when he found out, but for her the man in her life was now Doda. It was a repetition of the Onassis story where in every generation the heiress took up with an older man and their first marriage had as much to do with getting their own way as it did with love.

Athina's grandmother Athina 'Tina' Livanos, the daughter of one of the richest Greek ship-owners shocked her family when she declared that she would be marrying the brash shipping upstart Aristotle Socrates Onassis. Tina was 17, Onassis 47. Tina and Onassis own daughter Christina ran off to marry a grey-haired middle aged American real estate man she met at a hotel swimming pool in the Riviera when she was 19. It was a marriage that was to infuriate Onassis who did everything he could to end it. Now it was the turn of another Onassis heiress to declare her love for an older man. Doda was 30 and a man of the world. When Thierry got wind of the affair he was incensed, but knew he would have to handle the situation carefully. He was nonetheless shocked by his daughter's decision to leave home and stop her studies in order to be with Doda. At the same time Roussel was concerned, knowing very well how susceptible young heiresses were to good-looking men. Thierry knew it from his own relationship with Christina who had been a plaything in his hands and would do almost anything Thierry wanted of her. He knew nothing of Doda and understandably had fatherly concerns that his daughter's new lover could be a fortune hunter. It was a label that he himself had had to endure after his marriage with the inordinately richer daughter of Onassis. Thierry knew that it would be a matter of time before the media caught onto the story and he wanted to protect Athina and his family from what would follow. He also wanted to see how serious Athina was about her new boyfriend and above all he wanted information about who Doda was, what his financial situation was and anything else that would help him meet the challenge from the newcomer. His lawyer in Paris sent letters to request copies of all press articles referring to Doda and Athina. Thierry wanted to know what was happening with Cybele, who had learned of the affair and was about to go to the media. Athina put her foot down. It would be Doda, whatever Thierry or anyone else said. She did not care if Doda had money or not, if he had children or not, it was he she was in love with and she would follow him to Brazil or to the end of the world.

    I was driving along the newly opened Attiki Odos motorway in Athens to the new airport of the capital near where I was building a house when my mobile phone rang. It was a journalist who worked for one of the Athenian tabloids wanting to know if I knew anything about an affair or about Athina getting married in Thailand because a wedding invitation had circulated that afternoon in the Greek media. I denied knowing anything about the story and said I would call Thierry to see if it was true. I knew it would soon be in the public domain and there would be a lot of misinformation and probably attacks on Athina and her new beau if answers were not readily forthcoming to put the record straight. Thierry confirmed the liaison and we agreed not to say anything yet to the press. The affair suddenly became public when Athina left with Doda to go to Thailand and the couple was photographed by a Greek tourist who recognised her. Soon journalists from around the world were calling anyone they thought could confirm the Onassis heiress sighting in Bangkok with an unknown man.

Not long afterwards Doda's companion, a Brazilian beauty called Cybele Dorsa – it was unclear if she was in fact married to him - gave a scathing interview about Doda and Athina. She said that Doda was only interested in the Onassis money because he himself had none, he did not even own a car, she said, and quoted Doda as having said in the past that there was nothing going on between him and Athina who was "like an elephant". Thierry and his family were distressed at the turn things had taken. They were in contact with Athina but the relationship with Thierry was becoming more strained by the day. There was another cause of concern for Thierry. Athina in a couple of months would be 18 and half the Onassis fortune would be under her total control with Doda at her side. The idea was not appealing to Thierry who had other plans and who considered his daughter unready to handle the huge fortune without his help. It did not take much imagination to guess what Thierry's felt. He had brought up his daughter over the years in a very protected environment, had endured endless battles and attacks from his Greek fellow administrators of Athina's fortune, had seen his family humiliated and had sat accused in a criminal court in Greece for months as a result of actions he took to protect, as he felt, Athina and her Onassis Foundation legacy. A whole office in GinsGins in Switzerland was filled with dossiers of court documents and media articles referring to the Onassis fortune battle between Thierry, who was Athina's guardian, and the Four Greeks, his co-administrators of Athina's fortune. Another office, in Upper Engaddin in Switzerland, belonging to Athina's lawyer, Nuot Saratz, was wall-to-wall with Athina Roussel's Swiss case files, while more than thirty large dossiers packed with media articles and press releases, court documents and property deeds and Onassis wills from Swiss, French and Greek jurisdictions took up a ceiling-high bookcase in my study in Athens. After millions of dollars spent and years of conflict having elapsed where Thierry had stood up as Athina's champion, aided by his legal teams and the Athens office, it appeared that everything he had fought for, including his daughter, was slipping through his fingers. He was not without blame.

Cybele's statements about Doda's lifestyle in Brussels where he had been for several years did not reflect the presence of money despite the stories that were circulating about the de Mirandas being a wealthy family with insurance companies in Brazil. Public records showed that Doda's father Ricardo Lima de Miranda and two business partners had problems stemming from a violation of Social Security law no. 95 that resulted in their receiving summons from the prosecutor regarding a company called Pamcary Administracao de Servicos. What was surprising was that the amount in question was quite small, equivalent to around 20,000 CHF in 1995. This raised even more questions about the reported wealth of the Brazilian family.

Doda had made his personal choice and would have to live from now on with constant suspicion and public distrust regarding the difference in his and Athina's financial situation. Thierry himself, though from a much wealthier family than the de Mirandas of Brazil, and an aristocratic one at that, had never been able to totally free himself of accusations that he himself had been a fortune hunter too. Few men indeed have turned down the chance to marry a woman with more money than themselves because of pride and ego, and neither Doda nor Thierry had said no to a bride with the Onassis millions.

After Athina returned from Thailand with Doda she left for Brazil where she bought a 1,100m2 duplex penthouse overlooking Ibirapuera Park in São Paulo where the couple set up their love nest, dividing their time between Brazil and Belgium.

Dividing the Onassis Fortune Spoils

The Onassis fortune after Ari's death was divided into two parts, his son Alexander's share went for the founding of the Onassis Foundation, with Christina as its president. The other half of Ari's fortune went to Christina. After her death in 1988, it passed in its entirety to a trust to be held for her daughter Athina until her majority at 18. It was these two successions in the fortune that were to cause the bitterly fought battle between the family and four Onassis employees, one of whom – Stelios Papadimitriou - had been entrusted by Ari as a co-executor of his will. The rest of the executors were almost all members of the family.

The Billion Dollar Dispute

Christina, Athina's mother, in her last will specified that Athina's inheritance would be managed by a board of five people. First on the list was the name of Athina's father, Thierry Roussel, followed by those of Stelios Papadimitriou, Pavlos Ioannides (Onassis former pilot), Apostolos Zambellas and Theodore Gavrielides, an Onassis Foundation lawyer.

After a series of confrontations between the Greeks and Thierry, the four Greeks voted to eject Thierry from the patrimony board. They also added a clause doubling their own salaries to 800,000 dollars a year in total. Additionally they voted to hire an accountant at 150,000 dollars a year to help out with the extra work made necessary "because of the actions of Roussel".

In the meantime the Swiss juvenile authority, the Authorite Tutelle, alarmed by what the deluge of recriminations in the press was doing to Athina who was distressed by what she was hearing at school and elsewhere, forbade all involved parties from making statements to the press. Roussel complied. Papadimitriou, as Roussel told me, knew that the law applied only to Swiss residents and ignored the ban. He continued with his press statements against Roussel.

There was more to come in the media. Papadimitriou was quoted several times as saying that Christina did not trust Thierry and that he was after her money. "Athina is a hostage," said Papadimitriou to the press going on to accuse Roussel of purposely isolating her from her Greek roots. This accusation was one that was accepted by many over the years when they saw how rarely Athina came to Greece and how little interest she and her Brazilian horseman husband Alvaro de Miranda subsequently showed for Scorpios. More was to follow. In an interview with the Greek gossip magazine "Hai" Papadimitriou said that Roussel was a "Mafioso" and that he had dealings with the underworld!

A Commando Kidnap Scenario

The minivan with its 'Green Wheels' stickers stopped on the side of the Swiss country lane in Ginsgins, a hamlet populated mainly by affluent businessmen and a concentration of diplomats working at the various international missions in Geneva, 30 minutes to the south.

Three athletically-built young men and a girl wearing cycling gear climbed out of the van. They unloaded their mountain bikes and conferred briefly among themselves. A fourth associate stepped out of the front of the vehicle and joined them, showing them a map. The leader of the group, who called themselves the Green Wheels, looked up and pointed to a distant group of houses. The cyclists put on their helmets, mounted their bicycles and set off in the direction of the mountains looming like a grey wall five kilometres to the north. They rode their bikes at a steady pace, leaving behind them the man in the minivan and the sound of traffic on the busy Geneva-Lausanne highway.

It was cold that day: the weak winter sun was unsuccessfully trying to take the chill off the thin air to coax the first reluctant buds of spring from the dormant fields. The group rode in single file past flat fields and parallel to the hardy hedges that shielded the occasional grey mansion in the bleak winter landscape.

The cyclists stopped at several houses on their way, telling the residents that they were a group of environmentalists called the Green Wheels, and that they had come from far away to learn more about the environment of the village and about its residents. The Swiss whom they talked to were pleased to see these four well-behaved young foreigners who showed such sensitivity to the environment and had an interest in the local inhabitants.

Some of the village residents were happy to contribute money when the cyclists asked them for a donation. One old lady who lived in a cottage outside the village found the young men and the girl particularly affable and feeling sympathy for them gave them five hundred francs. The group had shown such an interest in Gingins, and seemed very impressed that the home just up the road from the old lady belonged to Athina Roussel, the 12 year old daughter of Christina Onassis and Thierry Roussel.

The cyclists wanted to know all about the Roussel family, when were they at the house, what did they do, did they have guards and where did the bodyguards sleep. The old lady, proud of her famous neighbours, told the Green Wheels everything she knew. She told them, when they asked, that Athina was not seen often here, but that she could be spotted quite often roller-skating in the village of Lussy-sur-Morges, twenty minutes further north, near Lausanne, where the Roussel family had another home.

The cyclists mounted their mountain bikes again and made off up the gentle slope towards the Onassis mansion with its extensive grounds nestling behind large trees. The environmentalists took a left turn onto a narrow uphill lane, passing a field and a grey house on their left. At the next turn they came to a low wooden gate bordered by hedges surrounding the Onassis property. From where they stopped, in front of the gate, by stretching up on their toes they could see a winding drive inside the wooded setting.

On the left of the drive was a small guard house, just as the old lady had described it, and on the opposite side, partly concealed by a mass of bushes was a two-story mansion with a sloping shingle roof. The house had been designed by its architect to blend tastefully into the country setting. It was in keeping with the absence of any external ostentatious features of the homes in this wealthy neighbourhood.

On the wooden gate there was a nameplate which identified the mansion as *Boislande*, the famous last home of Christina Onassis. It was where she had lived with her husband Thierry and Athina before she died. It was here on a stormy winter night that she had summoned Stelios Papadimitriou and his three associates as well as the manager of her shipping office in Monte Carlo, David Banfield, for a hurried meeting.

It was said that the day she summoned them Christina had had a row with Thierry who had previously divorced her and gone off to live with Gaby Landhage, the Swedish beauty with an MBA, a soft-spoken and charming former model and multinational company executive who later married Thierry. Thierry's fiery outburst against Christina that day was to cost him millions of dollars and trapped him in a web of court cases and a public squabble with Papadimitriou and three Greek colleagues from the Onassis Foundation that would take up the best part of five years.

Christina had originally "stolen" Thierry from Gaby, and now that he was again with her Christina had tried desperately to get Thierry back, offering him financial and other inducements. He refused. She lowered her sights and asked him if at least he would agree to give her another child. Thierry was adamant, it was over.

It was after this row that the four Greeks had found Christina in a desperate mood, and they quickly and - according to an unsuspecting Banfield whom they left behind at their hotel - secretly went to Boislande. There they met a distraught Christina, who rewrote her will in haste in their presence. It was a will of just four pages. Strangely there was nothing in it about her daughter, except that she was to get the bulk of the estate. Nothing about any last wishes, only some brief financial instructions which would cause problems for everybody in the coming years. Problems for Thierry, for the Swiss authorities, even for the 4 Greeks , and most important it would be the document that launched years of unhappiness and insecurity for Christina's daughter Athina, making her the centre of a worldwide publicity and legal battle that seriously affected her happiness and curtailed her freedom.

The Green Wheels cyclists rode around the boundary of Boislande that afternoon, taking photos, making a video of the mansion and its surrounding approaches, and later they went back again for a second look. There was no sign that the family were there. What they did not seem to know was that

Boislande was being used as offices by Thierry and that Athina was not there.

They hid their van and entered the grounds carefully. The cyclists were not what they claimed to be. These polite young men and the girl were part of a hardened Israeli team comprised mainly of former Mossad and Shin Beit agents carrying out reconnaissance for a mission which was scheduled to take part in June that year. One of the men, Rafi Pridan, was an electronics expert who boasted that he had laser equipment capable of eavesdropping on the family conversations inside if he could have access to a window pane from which to bounce off his laser beams. Christina Primsit, who accompanied the team later, revealed that she worked for a security company, the ISC group that had offices in Athens, Tel Aviv, Geneva, and in Columbia. ISC was headed by Moshe Lan, a former general in the Mossad.

Another member of the Green Wheels group was Benny Bayl, an independent security consultant in civilian life. He was engaged by ISC to take part in the mission against Athina and her father.

The Green Wheels group spent several days in Switzerland. They went to the residences of the Roussel family trying to locate Athina and Thierry to find out what their daily schedules were. Their main contact in Switzerland was the ISC representative, Ronen Ballulu. It was Ballulu who was instrumental in coordinating what was to be known as plan A of the operation. The proposal for Plan A was detailed in a contract sent to the financiers of the operation.

Plan B, the main object of the operation was to take place in June, but was never committed to paper.

The activities of the group came to the notice of the Swiss police. An arrest order was put out for them. Some were apprehended in Switzerland, one in Milan and the rest in Israel. When word leaked out that the object of their operation was Athina Roussel and her father, the press and wire services went into high gear.

A media frenzy followed as stories leaked to the press of a possible kidnapping operation. Some accounts identified the father as the object of the group, yet others said it was the daughter who was to be "lifted". For some days there was no information from the police. Then Juge Delieutraz, the investigating magistrate, subjected in the meantime to enormous pressure by journalists, called a press conference.

"Certain foreign nationals have been arrested for planning an illegal operation on Swiss soil. The operation in question was a planned kidnapping, though at this moment we do not yet know whether the victim of the kidnapping was to be Athina Onassis-Roussel or her father."

The statement was a bombshell and was transmitted worldwide by Associated Press. It was picked up by hundreds of newspapers, radio and television stations, all of which clamoured for more information.

The Onassis name once again was a magnet which attracted the public's interest. Journalists and

TV reporters besieged the Roussels and the Swiss police for a follow-up. There was nothing at this point to reveal who was behind the attempt, if indeed it was a kidnapping attempt.

A second bombshell dropped only hours later. Stelios Papadimitriou, president of the Onassis Foundation and his three associates, all co-administrators of Athina's patrimony, made a public announcement that the Israeli commandos were working for them. It was not a kidnapping, they insisted, but a security operation demanded by Lloyd's for the protection of the little girl.

It was a mess. Athina and her family were terrified. Her security staff – former SAS commandos - was put on extra alert and the moves of the family were restricted for safety reasons. Erik, Athina's half-brother, began having nightmares and Sandrine, Athina's half-sister shook with fear at every sound. Only little Joanna, the youngest of the Roussel children, was oblivious to all the activity going on around her. The house of the family in the village of Lussy-sur-Morges became a fort. Because it was located on the edge of a forest the guards were exceptionally vigilant. Every few minutes one of the guards would scour the tree line with his binoculars to look for signs of any suspicious activity.

Athina attending a public high school in keeping with her father's wishes for her to grow up in normal surroundings with normal everyday friends was for a while not allowed to skate to school or take the bus, but was driven by an armed chauffeur and accompanied by her bodyguards.

As the investigation proceeded the Israelis admitted under questioning to being part of an operation against Thierry Roussel. In a sworn statement to the Israeli police, the leader of the group said:

"Our company head in Athens, Moshe Peri, called us to meet one of his clients, the president of the Onassis Foundation for whom ISC was already engaged in doing security work. We were summoned to the Onassis Foundation headquarters in a Neo-Classical building opposite a Roman arch in Athens; there we were met by Mr. Stelios Papadimitriou, a Mr. Ioannides, and a lawyer called Theodore Gavrielides. Papadimitriou explained in detail that under the terms of Onassis's will half his money went to his daughter and this would in turn go to his granddaughter Athina Roussel. Papadimitriou explained that Roussel had been appointed as one of five co-administrators in Christina's will, and also received personal money due to him according to the will. It was Papadimitriou's intention to withhold any payments due to Roussel, and to have him lose custody of his daughter, over whom Roussel had a strong influence."

Those interrogated gave versions of the above. They also said that Papadimitriou wanted in the first instance for them to follow Roussel, investigate his private life and the suspicions that Roussel was a drug dealer who held orgies in the presence of his 10 year old daughter and there was even worse to come in one of the depositions, where it was implied, without proof, that Roussel had done more. Papadimitriou wanted information about Roussel's businesses and financial affairs. He wanted the Roussel family investigated in Switzerland,

France, Spain, Portugal, England and the US. Everywhere they had homes or contacts.

The Israelis would admit to no more under questioning. The Swiss police did not give up so easily. There were too many loose ends for them. Also the reputation of Switzerland as a safe haven for rich foreigners was in doubt if rumours persisted that the authorities could not guarantee the safety of those in the financial bracket of the granddaughter of Onassis. The Swiss government sent investigating officers to Italy, England and Greece as well as to Israel to follow leads and speak to witnesses. Security inspectors Pahud and Mottet interviewed suspect after suspect and followed every lead that came up. The family was told to increase their security after the police interviewed a witness called Patrick Chastagnier.

In February 1998, when the investigation was in full swing I was sitting in the VIP lounge of Athens Airport with the Roussel family. Athina was very quiet and introspective. The lack of noise in the private lounge was in startling contrast to the media stampede that she had been exposed to for the duration of her two-day stay in Athens. Athina was sitting just opposite me, still holding an olive branch given to her on the Acropolis by a young girl admirer. Four bodyguards hovered a few feet away. Outside the door of the VIP lounge there was a group of anti-terrorist police ordered by the Greek government to guard Onassis' granddaughter and her family.

Thierry was sitting next to me when I leaned over and asked him "Has there been anything new in this kidnap story from Switzerland? Papadimitriou and his people say it was a Lloyd's mandated security check and that you are making it all up." I spoke quietly so that Athina would not realise what we were talking about. Thierry looked concerned.

"It seems worse than just a kidnapping. A man called Chastagnier, if he is to be believed, confessed scary things to the Swiss police".

Hearing the word police, Athina who had been petrified since the kidnap story had broken, looked up at me and her father with an expression of concern. We halted the conversation and only took it up later after Athina, her brother and sisters and Gaby had boarded their plane for Geneva. Thierry had stayed behind to wait for the departure of the flight to Zurich fifty minutes later. As I sat with him, the two of us alone in the lounge, he let me know that there was new information from the police who had questioned Chastagnier.

The following document is an extract of that deposition -

Canton of Geneva,
11th December, 1997

POLICE DEPT – SECURITY 105

<u>Declaration made to Inspectors Mottet and Pahud</u>
"My name is Patrick Chastagnier, I was born on 25.10.1953 at Angouleme, France, and I am a hotel employee and married.
... I recognize the photo you are showing me of the man you call Ronen Ballulu. Three weeks after our first

meeting he asked me if I knew people in the Belgian "milieu". I know a bar in Belgium where mercenaries gather. He then asked me if I knew of anyone who could neutralize a person. I asked him to explain what he meant by "neutralize". He told me that he was looking for a "killer" (he said the word in English).

Three days later he (Ballulu) asked me whether I had thought about his request. It was then that he told me that he was part of a team of agents from Mossad, the Israeli secret service. He explained to me that they intended to kidnap Athina Roussel, and kill her, because in the event that the minor disappeared her father could not inherit (her fortune) and that the Onassis Foundation, which was managing her fortune, would become the beneficiary.

He asked me where the best place to hide a hostage in Switzerland was, and if I was able to locate a hideaway. I answered that a farm in the canton of Fribourg would do best for this purpose.

I had children of my own and replied that I had no intention of getting involved in this operation.
In order to convince me he said that if I found an assassin I would personally receive $400,000.
I have nothing further to add.

Signed,
Patrick Chastagnier.

Ballulu was Papadimitriou's personal security chief in Switzerland and a member of the ISC group in Athens which worked for the Onassis Foundation. The testimony as it appeared at that moment was chilling and naturally terrified the family. There was more to come before the matter finally cleared up and the Swiss authorities put the matter to rest.

The Greek Administrators Accuse Thierry

The Greek administrators said that ISC and its agents were hired to do a standard security check for Lloyd's. The kidnapping story had another side to it. On the one hand Israeli News Service quoted a police official in Tel Aviv who said that there was no kidnapping planned by the Green Wheels and their employers at the Onassis Foundation. The official explained that according to the arrested operatives there had been an operation designed to make Thierry lose custody of Athina. This, if it had been successful meant that she would have been deprived of the happy home in which she had grown up with her half-brother and sisters.

As the Swiss police investigators dug deep into the kidnap scenario Juge Delieutraz went to Israel to interrogate the arrested Israelis. No further evidence was forthcoming regarding an illegal operation.

While the former agents were in prison, the Onassis Foundation presidency - Papadimitriou, Ioannides, Gavrielides and Zambellas - called a press conference at the neo-classical mansion which houses the Onassis Foundation at 56, Amalias St. opposite Hadrian's Arch, on a busy street junction. The Foundation building decorated with Onassis family paintings and bric-a-brac housed the so-called "Onassis Museum", a couple of rooms with furniture and items belonging to the heiress.

Representatives of the domestic and international press now crowded into a wood-paneled room with floor-to-ceiling curtains. At one end there was a long table for the speakers. Blinding klieg lights illuminated the room while a jumble of cables lay across the floors, tripping up careless reporters who sought somewhere to sit in the rows of folding chairs brought in to accommodate them. A bank of cameras was set in the second row of seats. There was a buzz of anticipation in the air as the Foundation Four filed in and took their seats with Stelios Papadimitriou, always the protagonist, nodding to familiar faces in the crowd and making joke asides to reporters closest to the podium. I watched the screen as the Foundation Four took their seats and shuffled papers in front of them

At the center sat Stelios Papadimitriou, a short rotund man with a loud tie and a thin mustache. His brown eyes were large and darted back and forth, while his heavily gelled ginger-and-white hair was slicked sideways in tightly scalloped waves. He reminded me of a well-to-do Levantine businessman and I expected him at any moment to pluck a set of worry beads from his pocket and start fiddling with them. At that moment I did not suspect what was to follow would drag me into the monumental conflict between these four people and the heirs of Aristotle Onassis. In coming months I would come to know a wealth of detail about the Foundation directors, their characters and the way they functioned.

On Papadimitriou's right sat a man who introduced himself as Pavlos Ioannides, he was the only tall man among them. Thin, bald and narrow-shouldered, with a white military-style moustache, he was smartly dressed in the passé manner of ex-India Army British colonial planters. He sat ramrod straight in his chair and moved his head and torso simultaneously when he wanted to look round, swiveling from the waist upwards as if he had a stiff neck. Ioannides was clearly the 'aristocrat' of the group. Later I found out that despite his lack of a university education he was the son of two upper middle class Athenian doctors and had grown up in the wealthy Athens diplomatic suburb of Psychico before becoming a pilot.

The crowd of journalists at the press conference could not decide when the press conference should start. There was banter about what language would be used. The foreign correspondents preferred English. The Greek TV crews wanted to go out live on the 8 o'clock news and wanted the interview in Greek. A compromise was reached as we watched the discussion. A third member of the Onassis Foundation Four at the press conference was Apostolos Zambellas who some years before had been responsible for the Onassis Cardiac Surgery Hospital tenders. He was some years later to turn against his colleagues when internal disputes in the Foundation came to a head.

On Papadimitriou's left sat Theodore Gavrielides, a pale, bespectacled man. He was the newcomer to the group, a lawyer who had entered the Onassis Foundation stable after the others. I later got to know him and found he was an affable and decent man who had had a successful career as legal adviser to some of Greece's largest companies.

"Gentlemen of the Press," announced Papadimitriou, "We are here to give you details about a situation which I will describe as 'The

Announcement of a Pre-Decided Entrapment Conspiracy'. I will describe this to you."

Papadimitriou went on to say that Thierry Roussel's lawyers in Switzerland Maitres Bonnant and Saratz had conspired with two Swiss judges, Messrs. Joos and Delieutraz to arrest the Greeks by linking them falsely with a supposed attempt to kidnap Athina Roussel. As proof he produced two letters sent by a Roussel lawyer to a colleague saying that they should be ready with their media reply for when the arrest of the Greeks was to take place.

Papadimitriou did not say how he received these confidential communication letters between two lawyers. He said only that the letters were the originals. He then went on to describe how much he respected Switzerland which is "a big country", but that he was going to sue some corrupt judges and lawyers there.

The whole story of the kidnapping was a fabrication, he said. What had happened was that the four, as part of the administrative group for Athina's fortune (the fifth member was the father), had an obligation to protect her patrimony. Because of this an insurance policy against kidnapping was taken out on the child. It had been a requirement of the policy that security checks had to be done.

"For this purpose," continued Papadimitriou, "we contacted a respected company, ISC, serious people, with many clients and offices in Greece and in other countries. It was not a kidnapping. This story about a kidnapping was a fabrication by the father who wanted to discredit us, to have us thrown off the board of his daughter's administration so that he could get his hands on the money."

"Who were these Israeli commandos, and how long did your check take place?" asked a French reporter.

"They were not commandos, this is Roussel's nonsense. They were employees of ISC, serious people. The security check took place over a period of three months," Papadimitriou replied.

"Who would have an interest for Athina to be kidnapped or to be killed" asked a reporter close to the Foundation.
"Roussel," he continued, "was a man who had financial problems; he was always asking for money, he had lost large amounts in two business ventures. He would be the beneficiary."
We were stunned. A father setting up his daughter up to be killed?

"You see," said Papadimitriou, "we were worried about the little girl's security. There had been stories of Roussel taking her on his motorbike, and getting away from the guards. Also there was a story in the New York Post that Athina had a premonition of dying. That she would be writing a will to make him the beneficiary. All these stories made us worry."

Papadimitriou continued, demonizing Roussel, driving a wedge between him and his daughter's interests, negating him as a father. Papadimitriou described himself and his three colleagues as close and trusted confidants of Onassis

The Onassis family beginnings

In 1922 when my father had escaped the slaughter of Greeks and Armenians in Asia Minor another ambitious young refugee, Aristotle Onassis, embarked on a journey to South America. Onassis' daring character and unique ability to spot a business opportunity helped him make a vast fortune, while his jet-setting lifestyle, his legendary luxury yacht *Christina* in Monte Carlo and his numerous affairs with glamorous and famous women later made him into a twentieth century legend.

The media clamoured after Onassis and begged for details of his extravagant lifestyle. The Onassis legend took root and the tragic family events that followed made the Onassis myth even stronger. One after another the members of the golden family died or were killed by hands unknown. Of all the Onassis family only one person survived - Athina - the daughter of Christina Onassis and Thierry Roussel, Christina's French fourth husband.

On the morning of the 29th of January of 2003 Christina's reclusive 18 year old daughter Athina Roussel inherited half the Onassis fortune while trying to ignore the crowds of journalists, international television crews and paparazzi waiting outside to report on the handover of one of the world's great fortunes.

Interviewing Thierry at the Onassis mansion

I had not read good things in the press about the former husband of Christina Onassis. The media had repeated accusations made by the Onassis Public Benefit Foundation presidency that Athina, the heiress, was growing up as a virtual hostage. There was much more. The accusations were so intense that I was now sceptical and was curious to meet the man and his daughter. I suspected that things were not as they had been presented by their opponents. I accepted the invitation to go to Switzerland and at five thirty the next afternoon I was looking out of the window of a Swissair plane as it banked over thick woods and small, pristine patchwork fields with red-roofed matchbox-like farmhouses as we approached Geneva airport. I did not know what I would find in Switzerland but I was excited at the prospect of my first contact with the legendary family of Aristotle Onassis. It was January of 1998 and the beginning of my association with the Roussel- Onassis family.

. I was excited by the prospect of meeting Christina's former husband and visiting the Onassis mansion at Boislande. It was a place of popular legend for us Greeks because of its association with the ship-owners family. I left on a Swissair flight for Geneva, carrying a detailed schedule faxed to me in Athens by Pascale Luscher, Thierry Roussel's personal assistant.

Athina – the first sighting

When I returned to Athens I phoned several papers to say I had an exclusive story with revelations both about Roussel and the Foundation. I was surprised to find I was up against a blank wall. I discovered an unofficial embargo of news against Roussel was in force. It was clear that interests that I could not identify wanted neither Roussel nor the granddaughter of Onassis to gain sympathy or a new family foothold in Greece. The same enmity became apparent some years later when despite the millions that the Onassis family had given to Greece Athina's husband, the Olympic medallist horseman Alvaro de Miranda was refused Greek citizenship to ride for the Greek Olympic team by the Minister of the Interior.

Thierry Roussel and I later discussed the matter of the battle with the Onassis Foundation members. I had studied all the documents at the hotel and at our new meeting at Boislande I told Thierry that in order for him to win what was a very difficult fight he would have to organise a two-pronged attack. Media and lawyers. We needed the additional support of a legal team with heavy media clout and we needed a concerted information campaign to let the media first of all know what was happening and secondly to let the public know the truth.

Thierry agreed. He asked me to take responsibility for the two sectors and to write a plan for him. Thierry asked me out of the blue if I would like to interview him and Gaby for television at the family home in Lussy-sur- Morges. I was delighted of course, but told him I had no camera crew.

"I shall get one for you," he said, and picked up a phone calling Gaby to be prepared. He then called Paris where he had his personal cameraman, Felix.
"He will fly here from Paris in two hours" said Thierry, smiling. Thierry and I went outside where his driver was waiting to take us to the Roussel family villa at Lussy-sur-Morges, just outside Lausanne. This was the house that Christina Onassis had bought for Gaby so that Thierry's children with their two mothers could be near one another and Athina would have her half siblings to play with.
While waiting for the cameraman to arrive from France Thierry conducted me around the villa and its grounds while we were discretely watched by members of Athina's personal bodyguard contingent. The house itself was surprisingly modest. It was a one-story bungalow of around 400 m2, with what I estimated to be a half-acre garden. The villa was not unlike a California ranch house, finished externally in pale pink stucco while inside the rooms were in light beige colours. Thierry's study had bleached-blonde wood paneling. In the kitchen there was a long rectangular dining table with a metal top – supremely practical when there were so many people to feed, while high up in the living room there was a riveting painting depicting three Moroccan warriors on camels. It was a haunting painting with exceptional use of light which emphasised their features and the movement of the riders in their white burnouses waving their rifles. Thierry took me outside to a

cobbled patio forecourt for the cars. We walked in the garden and he took me across the lawn to a small house filled with children's toys, next to which was an enclosure containing two very white and woolly sheep. Thierry opened the door and the sheep came out to greet us. We now talked about his home at Kilifi Creek near Mombasa and his fishing experiences there.

A little later when we went back inside the house Roussel took me to see the children's' rooms. I was surprised to notice how "normal" they were and how modest in size. Athina' room had white furniture and next door there was a triangular room with a computer, a white desk, a photo of Christina Onassis, various teddy bears, the head of a Greek statue, I do not remember whether it was of Apollo or the Goddess Athina, the ancient Greek Goddess of wisdom. There was a bookshelf and various decorative items. What particularly impressed me was that the children shared bathrooms and how ordinary yet practical their rooms were. They were rooms for school children. It reflected the ordinariness of old money that had no reason to show off. How unlike the palatial marble palace suites of the children of the nouveau-riche in Athens with their ensuite bathrooms, Jacuzzis and room sized walk in-closets filled with rows of colour matched clothes and dozens of pairs of shoes. One thing that drew my attention was that in every child's bedroom there was a wire cage containing a live rabbit. I could not explain this, especially since there was a health risk, and wondered whether the rabbits had been imposed as a calming foil because of the kidnap scare's effect on the children or whether this was in fact some unusual way for the children to not feel alone in their individual bedrooms.

We went back into the living room where I met Gaby. The crackling of walkie talkies signalled the preparation for the departure of Athina for afternoon activities. The Roussel children came in for a brief moment to kiss their father goodbye. Erik was the most curious and immediately approached me to introduce himself before leaving. I was charmed by his good manners and his openness. He was a nice boy and I could see Thierry beaming with pride as the door closed behind his only son.

The cameraman had arrived a few minutes ago from Paris so we did a quick session of on-camera questions and answers with Gaby who had to leave for an appointment. She spoke of how much anguish the family had been through because of the media attacks by the Foundation and how the story with the arrested Israelis had shaken and terrified the children. Thierry was a "wonderful father" she said who never missed any of his children's birthdays and would always come back from wherever he was travelling to be with the family on these occasions. She told me off camera that the stories about Thierry and other women that were lately in the press had put a strain on the family but she said that they were united and were coping. It was not to last forever as a few years later Thierry moved out and blog articles reported that he was living with a black girl. I never got confirmation of this and never asked, as it was not my business, but I was saddened to see that a family that had been closely woven together had loosened their close bonds with one another, with Thierry living separately.

The interview with Thierry was conducted in a race against the setting sun. The last shots were taken as a shadow cast by the setting sun crept up on Thierry who was sitting in a chair in the garden. The final scene showed Thierry's face weakly illuminated while from the neck down his body was in almost total darkness!

Thierry at this time had been sued by the Foundation Four for defamation arising from a complaint which his lawyer, Professor Nestor Kourakis, had lodged some months before to the Greek prosecutor. As the case approached Papadimitriou appeared to hold all the aces. Most Greeks felt that the Foundation had the judiciary and the political parties on their side. Influential people were saying that the Foundation Four were the last Greek bastion against the Frenchman who would take over the Foundation. The Four were Greeks and the Foundation owned a Greek fortune claimed those supporting the attacks against Athina's father. Thierry also had to contend with a large hostile wedge of Greek society – middle-aged women who were passionately and vociferously against him for their own reasons. Roussel was a man known to have had many women in his life and had indulged in the now much-publicized concurrent love affair with two women, Gaby and Christina, impregnating both. He had also had children by "the other woman" while still married to Christina Onassis, something that was anathema to insecure middle-aged Greek housewives who saw in Thierry a dark mirror image of their wandering husbands.

Perhaps he reminded some of the man who had left them in middle age for another woman. Thierry's court case would be an occasion for a general catharsis for the frustrations and humiliations of those thousands of women who had suffered at the hands of faithless husbands. Roussel had unwittingly struck a raw nerve in Greek society. In the general climate of hostility I found that eminent lawyers I approached would not undertake to represent the client when they heard that the person I came to talk to them about was Thierry Roussel.

Thierry, in an attempt to counter negative and often untrue media reports had recently opened up his home in Switzerland to journalists in the hope that they would report some of the facts and restore his family's reputation. The reporters came and went, and articles appeared about the Roussel family's clothes, their horses, Athina's hairstyle, but almost not one word was printed about the positions put forward in his defence by Roussel.

It was a difficult situation to say the least.

Athina and the family arrive in Athens

Saturday, 21st March 1998

The kidnapping story concerning Athina kept cropping up in the press in 1997 and 1998. Conflicting statements were made by both sides and the matter became more and more confused as the Swiss police investigation went on. The information I received from Thierry was disturbing. The public in the meantime became more and more curious about the teenage Onassis heiress who had only been seen in some television telephoto footage when she had made a brief appearance in Greece four years earlier to Scorpios Island.

Just after midday on Saturday 21st March, 1998 the rumour of the impending and unannounced arrival of a 13 year-old girl at the East Airport terminal of Athens sent television station owners and managing editors scrambling for their mobile phones while journalists desperately tried to get return bookings on ferry boats or planes in order to get back to their studios and newspaper offices in the capital.

After years of absence from Greece, Athina Roussel, or Athina Onassis as the press and public called her, the granddaughter heiress and only surviving descendant of Aristotle Onassis was due to land at Hellinikon airport in Athens at 2.55 p.m. aboard a Swissair flight.

I had been at the airport since 1.15p.m and was one of the few people who had no doubt about whether Athina and her family were coming to Athens since I had made the arrangements for their visit. As I approached the arrivals gate I saw a frustrated policeman engaged in an agitated discussion with a group of noisy reporters who had blocked the exit of the arrivals lounge.

The milling crowd of journalists and television camera crews had quickly formed themselves into an impenetrable wall of bodies, tripods and camera equipment outside the glass exit doors of the luggage claim lounge. Some of the reporters were now trying to barge into the arrivals area. The exasperated policeman was unsuccessfully trying to clear a passage for exiting passengers and their loaded baggage trolleys. The confused new arrivals brought to a halt by the mass of reporters and blinded by a bank of klieg lights tried to comprehend what the huge fuss was all about.

Careful not to get caught in the tangle of black electric camera cables I pushed my way through the group of jostling journalists and forced my airport pass into the hands of the policeman. The reporters assailed me with a staccato barrage of questions. Hands, seemingly out of nowhere, clamped themselves firmly onto my coat sleeves in an effort to keep me from getting away before I had confirmed whether the rumour that had brought them hurriedly to the airport was true.

"Will Athina Onassis be here?", "Are the Roussel's really coming?", "Where are they staying?" I noticed the red light on two of the television cameras light up, indicating that I was being filmed. "Why are they coming?", "Will all the family be with Thierry?", "Is Thierry alone?", "Why is Athina coming?"

A TV anchorwoman who is a household name in Greece asked me why I was going into the ordinary arrivals area and not into the VIP lounge. "Are you misleading us so that Athina can leave through the VIP exit?" she asked suspiciously.

With the help of the policeman who had in the meantime been joined by two more colleagues I managed to disentangle myself from the octopus-like mass of arms. I told the reporters that I would answer all their questions later and quickly went through the glass doors into the cavernous passenger arrivals and baggage claim area beyond.

Two planes had landed within minutes of each other and the lounge was full of passengers pushing trolleys or waiting by the luggage carousels. In contrast to the cacophony outside the hall, inside there was only the hum of hushed conversation and the squeak of wheels of loaded baggage carts. As I went forward I was startled by the sudden grunt and squeak of carousel Number Four as it began turning its scuffed black rubber scales to receive and deliver neatly labeled cases removed from the belly of an Airbus that had arrived from Frankfurt a few minutes previously.

The overhead display confirmed that Swissair flight number 333 from Zurich had just landed. I made my way to a vantage point at the far end of the lounge next to the staircase leading up from passport control on the lower level. I knew that in a few minutes the normal weekend calm in Greece was about to be shattered, at least for the media.

A group of Swiss tourists and Greek businessmen were now coming up the escalator. At the back of the ascending line a tall blond man in a blue suit stood out. He was looking around somewhat anxiously. When he reached the top of the steps he saw me and smiled in recognition, extending his hand to me. It was Thierry Roussel. I ushered him to a row of PVC bucket seats opposite the carousel to wait for the rest of the family while the four Greek bodyguards I had hired waited at a discreet distance, scanning the room and checking the faces of the passengers in the lounge.

Thierry and I talked, catching up on recent events and filling in time as we waited for Gaby, his Swedish second wife, to arrive on the flight from Zurich with Athina and the three other Roussel children, Erik, Sandrine and Johanna. The Roussels, for security reasons travelled on separate flights. There have been too many premature deaths in the Onassis and Roussel family for Thierry to tempt either fate or his enemies by flying with Athina in the same plane.

I took the opportunity now to inform Thierry about the arrangements I had made for the family stay in Athens and to ask how Athina viewed the trip.

"Athina hates the media. You know how they badger her," he said and continued "Everyone was against this visit, Alexis, but I trust you and I took the decision for us to come."

Athina and Thierry had not come to Greece for several years owing to the acrimonious and very public battle which was taking place with the Greek members of the Alexander Onassis Foundation. Because it was the Onassis fortune that was involved and the accusations on both sides so bitter in the ensuing fight for control of the fortune, the international and domestic press was following every twist and turn of the battle with immense interest, happy to feed a voracious public interest in the Onassis family saga.

On Wednesday, February 11th, 1998 I had received a phone call late in the evening. It was Thierry.

"I am coming, Alexis. With the children. On Saturday. Make all the arrangements and send me a schedule. I will also speak to selected media."

The next three days were busy. I needed to organize the visit with the precision of a military operation. Cars, bodyguards, hotel rooms, schedules and visits had to be booked and arranged. For security I planned alternate travel routes and fallback plans. It was my responsibility to see that what I had promised would be done. All without any leaks to the press.

On Saturday as I was getting ready to leave for the airport I got a call from a reporter from a television station. Someone had broken the news to him of the arrival of Thierry, though nobody as yet knew that Athina would be coming. By the time I reached the airport the reporters were already there.

Preparing the heiress to meet the media

'There they are" said Thierry, standing up. I leaned over the banister to see four middle aged SAS bodyguards standing in front of, and behind the family group. The slim, tall, dark-haired figure of Athina stood out among the four blonde members of her family. I knew Gaby, a great beauty and former model in Paris from Switzerland, where I had interviewed her at her home in Lussy-sur-Morges for a television station. Standing at her side was Erik, Athina's half-brother, dressed in a blue blazer and tie, like a British public schoolboy. He turned to whisper to Sandrine, his blonde sister. The youngest of the group was Johanna, the 6 year old charmer of the Roussel family. A very reserved Athina, dressed in a beige trouser suit, stepped forward and shook my hand. I showed them where to sit while the bodyguards went off to claim the suitcases.
Gaby was nervous, her blue eyes betraying a tension which lined her face with worry. I could see that she was making an effort to make small talk but her mind was elsewhere. Only Johanna was carefree as she eagerly opened a package her father had given her. As the minutes passed there was an exponential increase in the conversation noise emanating from the other passengers in the now crowded arrivals lounge. Heads turned when people recognised Athina. The Greeks in the room stared incredulously, and when they were sure Athina Roussel Onassis was the girl sitting with us they smiled and pointed to us. For them the sudden appearance of Onassis' granddaughter in their midst was an exciting and

unforeseen event. Even more so that she and her famous family should have chosen to arrive in the public arrivals lounge and wait patiently for their luggage with everybody else rather than demanding the privacy and convenience of the independent VIP facilities at the end of the terminal building.

Those in the room were startled by the presence of the reclusive Onassis heiress among them because the name Onassis and anything to do with it was magical, a part of the very consciousness of every Greek family. Here then, right in front of them, was Ari Onassis' only surviving descendant, Athina, the daughter of Christina Onassis. Greeks had only had a fleeting glimpse on television some years before of a smiling, shy, 9 year old girl in a party dress getting into a speedboat with her father and family before it sped off across the straights from the island of Lefkada to Scorpios Island. During that visit cheering crowds and numerous policemen had lined the quay of the village of Nydri on Lefkada to catch a glimpse of the golden heiress and her family.

People abandoned their luggage to come and stare at the heiress and her family. Thierry for them was already a familiar figure.

"What do we do now?" Thierry asked somewhat self-consciously.

Gaby, caught up in the middle of the Israeli operation ordered from Greece, and uncertain about the truth of the kidnapping and murder scenario had read tens of negative articles in the Greek press directed against her husband and occasionally against herself. She looked at me with a sense of disbelief as I spoke of Greeks welcoming them. "I don't think so," she said in a very low voice, betraying, I felt, a hint of annoyance that I should have encouraged her husband's desire to bring the family to Greece at a time like this. I understood her reservations, but assured her now that many people had approached me to learn about the family and that reporters wanted stories and information about Athina and all of the Roussels. I addressed the children, but spoke primarily for the benefit of Athina.

"When we go outside those doors," I explained "we will be met by many people with cameras who will ask questions and make a lot of noise. This is because they all want to learn about you. In Greece people love you, especially in the schools where the pupils want to know all about you."

There were simple and effective ways of dealing with the media and a few basic rules to follow. I saw that imparting this knowledge to Athina and her siblings was an important part of my job as media adviser to the family. My other responsibility, a task of immense complexity owing to the damage that had been done to the family reputation by the Foundation Four was the preparation of the ground for the eventual return of the Onassis descendant to her dynastic hearth in Greece. From there Athina could then take the decision to claim her rightful position as head of the two Onassis Foundations and fulfill a public role that Aristotle Onassis had foreseen for his descendants and family when he donated half his fortune for this purpose.

On a yacht in Greece

The captain of the motorsailer sailed round to the bay of Lagonissi and anchored half a mile offshore owing to the shallow waters. When I saw its sleek lines and dark blue shiny finish I was impressed by the beauty of the yacht. It was large enough – 43 metres – to give a promise of stability and to overcome my initial misgivings. The captain assured me that its deep draft guaranteed a calm ride in the notoriously changeable windy conditions of Greece in the summer. It was the season of the *Meltemi*, the strong north-easterly Trade Winds that churn up the Aegean in July and August, but today was a day with what passes for moderate winds in our Greek summer – Force Five.

    The family and I gathered on the beach in front of Kalliroi's estate where the Roussel's were staying. The beach was a public one, as most are in Greece and the appearance of Nordic blonde heads and beefy bodyguards let everyone on the beach know that Athina was there with our party. It needed three trips in the tender to ferry us to the waiting yacht so in the meantime a few dozen holiday-makers left their towels and beach bags and made their way towards us, unselfconsciously creating a semicircle around our group while the yacht crew and bodyguards piled weekend bags and helped us into the rocking tender. Within fifteen minutes we were all on board the *Ariadne*. We shed our footwear into a basket on the rear deck and went into the chilly air-conditioned royal blue-carpeted lounge of the boat.

The Roussel children excitedly flitted from cabin to cabin, trying to decide which one was best. I took a cabin next to the stairs, which meant I could come and go without disturbing the others. Everyone settled in quickly, Thierry went for a nap in his cabin, Gaby settled down with a book and the children went out onto the deck to sunbathe and watch the changing scenery as we made our way towards Hydra island where none of the family had been before. The boat was, thankfully, stable, as the captain had assured me it would be.

I switched off my mobile phone and did not give the press our route details, only saying we would be in Hydra that evening. This was not enough for them so they scoured nearby islands to see where we would stop. The Roussel family wanted to swim and we anchored in a secluded bay opposite the island of Poros. Thierry, with a full stomach, and against the advice of all, dived in from the top of the roof of the boat and was followed by the children who went in, jumping off the ladder with a big splash as they hit the deep blue water. Soon we were all swimming. The bodyguards were strategically placed around us and our scuba diver was already three metres underwater to make sure that no one could sneak up on Athina. We spent an hour swimming in the sea and taking short breaks on board.

I was sitting on deck when I heard the chugging of a diesel engine approaching our bay. The guards immediately took up lookout positions and in a few moments a small overloaded fishing boat came round the corner about fifty yards away with three television camera crews precariously balanced on the narrow deck of the twelve foot vessel. It lurched as it came into the bay and I heard the scream of a female reporter as she and her cameraman very nearly tipped into the water with their camera and its tripod as their boat rocked when it turned to head for where we were.

"Yassou, Alexi," a voice called out. It was Eftichia from Star TV. Next to her were Alexia Koulouri from Skai TV and Alexia Tassouli from Mega. The three rivals had joined forces and they now had a scoop. Their cameras were rolling and had caught Athina on the ladder as she was getting ready to board one of the jet-skis. Sandrine was already on the other one with Emilios. Athina slowly backed up the ladder and went back inside. I told the reporters that she would not come out and just wanted to swim in private. They were not so easily put off and went to a vantage point about a hundred metres away where they laid in wait. I decided to see how Athina was taking this and descended into the main lounge where I saw she was in a fit of giggles with Erik as they looked through the smoked glass windows at the reporters knowing they could not see into the yacht. I had expected Athina to be upset by the arrival of the boat, because Thierry always insisted on how disturbed she was by the presence of any media. Athina though was thoroughly enjoying the game of hide-and-seek with the press.

Athina laughed and pointed to the press boat, telling Erik something in an aside which I couldn't hear. Seeing that Athina was okay I went back on deck, and descended to a tender which took me to the beach where Thierry, Gaby and the others had spread their towels.

After a while the overloaded grey press boat left. I knew the reporters had to get back to the Poros island phone company to transmit their news footage to their studios. It was before the days of Wi-Fi laptop and mobile file forwards.

We left the bay opposite Poros after a while and just as the sun was setting we approached the small amphitheatre-like harbour of Hydra through a luminous gold summer haze. The wind had died down completely and the metallic bronze sea was as flat as the top of a burnished table. The large stone-built mansions in the port and others built on the steep semi-circular hillside behind had been constructed by 18th century ship-owners, sea captains and pirates, and the mansions still looked as they did a hundred and fifty years ago. The small harbour at Hydra, accessible through a narrow opening on the left was full of weekend yachts and fishing boats. Our vessel was too big to enter the tiny harbour, so we tied up on the seaward side of the jetty which acted also as a breakwater, blocking off the harbour entrance. The Roussel children were fascinated by the three-storey mansions and the picture-postcard island. On the jetty now there were about 200 journalists, paparazzi, officials and onlookers. Among them I could make out the mayor of Hydra flanked by an escort of port police and island dignitaries. Athina seeing the crowd waiting for her did not want to come out of the boat and had gone back below deck. Thierry shrugged his shoulders while Sandrine,

Johanna and Erik waited excitedly, keen to disembark and explore the shops along the small waterfront.

Athina was sitting alone on one of the couches in the dark main lounge with her shoulders hunched. She was looking down at her feet, frightened and miserable. It was no longer the same hide and seek she had enjoyed earlier with the press from the safety of the boat. She knew that now the reporters were waiting for her outside the yacht and that they would not go away.

"Athina" I said, "I want to talk to you about something very important."

She looked at me, a distressed look on her face. She would have to understand now that we were managing the media for her own good, and not merely making appointments for journalists to upset her when all she wanted was to have a quiet holiday.

"You know now that in Greece everyone wants to know about you." I said. "That is because of their admiration for your grandfather and of their love for your mother, Christina. It is more than curiosity, it is real admiration."

She was looking at me now, listening intently. I continued "The Greek public demands that the media let them know about you."

Athina was following my words while fidgeting with a hairclip.

"The reporters want something to send back ever day to their papers and television stations. If they have that, then they will leave you alone for the rest of the day."

She was beginning to understand, though she was not happy.

"The next day the editors and station managers will ask for another picture and video footage, and the reporters will be obliged to get it."

I could see now that she understood the logic of what I was saying. The confusing situation outside was beginning to make some sense to her.

"If you spend just two minutes a day with the press, and let them take their pictures, then you will see that you will be left alone after that. You will even become friends with some of the reporters who are assigned to you. I in turn promise that I will talk to the media and tell them that they must not bother us after they have their first pictures."

I could now hear the clamour of the reporters outside as they grew impatient waiting to see the last Onassis. "Athina, Athina" they called out from the jetty by the stern of the *Ariadne*. Athina thought about what I had said for a few moments and then I saw her straighten her shoulders, stand up and heard her say "Alexis, let us go."

Athina had turned an important corner. She had realised what few stars of the cinema or public personas have understood about media relations. Give a little, and you get a lot – your peace. It was not to last as she withdrew into herself as she got older, resulting in the paranoid episodes like the one at the restaurant in Brazil where the waiters were told to line up holding sheets for the heiress to leave the eatery without being photographed.

It was only the beginning on a road that should have led her to a balanced relationship with the media and would have assured her of privacy on her own terms. But it did not as she became more and more obsessive about the presence of cameras as she grew older, and even about the use of photos that had already been taken of her. Her obsession by 2018 had reached the level almost of a Howard Hughes like phobia. She called it guarding her privacy but it was much more than that when she insisted through her lawyer in a curt note to me that an image of the two of us already published (with her consent) not be reprinted elsewhere and be withdrawn.

No one close to her mentioned to Athina that the family chauffeur was sent at night to the Paris Match offices in the French capital with a bulging envelope of photographs of Athina to be considered for publication.

Now waiting in the yacht at Hydra young Athina waited while I went out to negotiate with the reporters. I agreed with them that they could film her as she walked off the boat and along the waterfront by the shops for a distance of a hundred metres.

"Two hundred metres" called out Polydoras, a pleasant-mannered photographer. He was discreet but determined and was always the first to arrive on the scene along with Christos Bonis wherever Athina was expected.

"Okay," I agreed. I gave the signal and the mayor of the island came on board, surrounded by photographers whose cameras were now whirring and clicking. Athina and the other Roussels stood on the deck while the mayor welcomed them to the island. He gave them the flag of Hydra to fly on their yacht.

"This is the flag we gave to your grandfather," explained the mayor. "Aristotle Onassis' favourite island after Scorpios was Hydra. He came here often, the last time with Mrs. Kennedy-Onassis."

When the brief welcoming ceremony was over the port police opened a path for us and we disembarked. Athina, Thierry, the family and I walked along the waterfront, past cafés full of curious tourists and holiday-makers from Athens. Shopkeepers came out and stood in front of their store entrances each beckoning Thierry to come inside. We stopped at one shop with interesting handmade jewelry displayed in the window. The whole family went inside and Thierry asked me to translate for him.

"No need, Mr. Roussel." said the owner, "I speak seven languages."

The girls were interested in some rings with intricately carved classical Greek horse head motifs on them. Thierry bought rings for his daughters and ordered a gold necklace for Gaby while the excited crowd outside pressed their faces and cameras against the store window. Our bodyguards in the meantime were trying to keep the crowd at bay. When we reached the middle of the harbour front I turned to the press contingent.

"Okay, this is more than 200 metres, tomorrow again!"

There was some mumbling, but the paparazzi had their pictures and the television crews had plenty of footage to show on the news that night. Like a swarm of bees that suddenly changes direction and scatters, the press turned and made off through the narrow alleys to send their pictures to their offices. The television reporters went to the Flying Dolphin, the hydrofoil boat that runs from Athens to the Saronic Islands, to send off their video cartridges with Onassis granddaughter to their Athens studios in time for the evening news.

We entered the narrow side streets behind the row of historic stone mansions which fronted the toy town-like harbour. Hydra is an island where cars are not allowed and as a result all its streets and alleys are easy for pedestrians. The family stopped to look at artisan items, sweet shops and curio stalls. Half an hour later we found our way back through the labyrinthine alleys and backstreets to the harbour front again. Athina and especially Thierry were surprised to see that the reporters who had been in such hot pursuit of us in the fishing boat they had hired earlier on were now sitting in the waterfront cafes. The reporters had piled their equipment next to their tables and several of them were slouched in their chairs without lifting their eyes for more than a second or two as we walked past.

"That is what I meant, Athina," I said, nodding towards the camera crew from Mega TV who were relaxing, drinking iced coffee and puffing contentedly on Marlboros. Alexia Tassouli, the dark-haired reporter who worked for the station smiled as I walked by, and that was it. Tomorrow I knew that the chase would be on again.

That night the family was tired and Thierry was restless. His court case was coming up soon in Athens and the decision of the Swiss prosecutor regarding the kidnapping investigation was about to be announced any day now.

I sat on the covered deck of the *Ariadne* with him drinking a beer as we watched the activity unfolding in front of us in the port. I asked Thierry if he wanted anything else and he said no. Was I going to sleep early, he asked, as I got up to leave.

"No, Thierry" I teased him, "I unfortunately have to continue my duties even at this late hour, and have a meeting with the female press. They have demanded I have drinks with them at* Piratis Bar.*"

"And not just a drink!" said Thierry, a wry smile creeping across his face as he remembered his younger, wilder days.

I left him sitting in the dark on deck and made my way to *Piratis*, where most of the press had now congregated. Over drinks we caught up on the current gossip. We sat under the stars outside the bar relaxing in the close night air. There was not a breath of wind. All the crews and visitors on the sailing boats which filled the small harbour were on deck, talking in low voices. When they lit up a suntanned face would momentarily glow out of the dark before being lost again in the shadows. On the waterfront lovers walked with arms entwined. Affluent Athenian families, headed by fathers in baggy designer Bermuda shorts ambled by.

At around three in the morning I made my way back to the boat past closed waterfront cafes. It was almost totally dark in the tiny port. My path led me along the cobbles past the bright lights of a corner café where an American girl was sitting drinking with five newly-found male compatriots who had arrived aboard a 12 metre sailing yacht anchored opposite the

Ariadne. On the deck of our boat I saw David Weaver, the head bodyguard sitting in a bamboo chair, keeping watch. I said goodnight and climbed down the steep steps to the main lounge and from there down another level to my cabin. Within a few minutes I was blissfully settled into my bunk and drifted off into a deep and contented sleep. It had been a pleasant cruise that had gone well for everyone.

Alone at the Boislande mansion

Thierry and I were chatting on the covered rear deck of the *Ariadne*, as the dark blue motor sailer sliced its way through the transparent blue water as we travelled back from Hydra in July of 1998. Athina and the other children were sunbathing on the upper deck of the yacht.

"We are both proud of our own countries, Alexis," said Thierry, "and this is great" he continued, gesturing to the open expanse of cobalt blue sea as we made rapid progress under power, "but I want you to come to Spain, to understand what paradise is for me, to see how we live when we are alone and how peaceful our life is there. It is a place where no one outside our immediate family circle is allowed to come."

Being rather chauvinistic about the beauty of the Aegean Sea and the diversity of the Greek islands I admit I was sceptical about Thierry's Ibiza. Even so I was keen to take up the offer, my curiosity getting the better of me. The invitation came two days later from Athina when we were anchored in Hydra harbour. She had been tucking into a bowl of her favourite black Vodenon cherries; a rare variety found only in the north of Greece while next to her Erik was munching on a club sandwich. Athina asked me if I had been to Ibiza, and when I said no, both children, as if in a chorus, asked me to come back with them. Thierry who had been fiddling with a pair of binoculars sensed a good excuse to pile some more work on me and suggested a working holiday. Gaby, considerate as always leaned over towards me and said, "Come and have a good holiday, and NO work."

She looked reproachfully at Thierry, her expression chiding him for his suggestion that I should work as a condition for coming to their Spanish holiday home. I happily accepted their invitation.

Two weeks later the family had installed themselves in Ibiza and Thierry, true to his promise of a working holiday had booked a ticket for me to Ibiza with a two day stopover in Geneva first. I agreed to this arrangement because it would give me the opportunity at Boislande to select useful files from the comprehensive Onassis archive there. Boislande was the nerve center of the Roussel empire where secretaries, a financial controller and Pascale Luscher, Thierry's personal assistant, worked in the west wing of the house, while gardeners and a permanent staff of a cooks and a chauffeur operated out of a staff wing. Thierry had invited me to spend a week at La Jondal after I left Switzerland.

After arriving at the mansion I pored over files and documents, working primarily in Thierry's large first floor office which looks out over the rolling expanse of the front lawns, resembling those of a British public school. Fifty metres in front of the living room patio there is a 120m2 rectangular swimming pool and beyond that mature tree borders that surround the ten acre property. In the distance the grey waters of Lake Geneva stand out against a picture-postcard backdrop of smoke-blue mountains.

In Thierry's office, on the carved white marble mantelpiece, a bronze Rodin sculpture of an open hand stood next to a collection of photos and postcards. Impressionist paintings hang on the wall, slightly out of key with the glass, chrome and black leather decor of the spacious office.

After the secretaries had left that afternoon, isolating the archive wing by activating the burglar alarms, I decided to wind down in the gym by the indoor pool and then indulging myself by doing several slow laps in the outdoor pool to rid myself of the tension that had been so evident during Athina's visit, tension that had been aggravated by the security precautions and the hounding of Athina by the press in Greece. The signs of the battle between Thierry and the Greek co administrators of Athina's patrimony were apparent at the mansion. The Greek administrators, violating their duty, had excluded Thierry from their board meetings and had suspended payments of millions of dollars to him. Small but telling signs of the economic squeeze in the Roussel household could be seen in the state of the cars of the family and in details around the mansion. I noticed with some surprise that while the lawn was mowed it was full of weeds and wild flowers among the sowed grass. The wooden entrance gate to Boislande needed varnishing and Christina's Mercedes 500 SEL had problems with the driver's door sticking. Boislande was not the immaculate mansion I had seen on my first trips to the villa to meet Thierry for our legal and strategy conferences.

The drawing room had seen much drama when Christina was alive and had played a pivotal part in the battle for the Onassis fortune. It was here that Christina had signed her will. In this same room young Athina had played in front of her doting and tragic mother, unaware that she was to lose her so soon and be tossed into a bitter conflict with a group of men she did not know. It was a conflict that would ruin her teenage years and cause her to become a cover page item for dozens, if not hundreds of magazines and newspapers in the years that were to follow.

Framed photographs of the couple lined the bookcases and crowded the glass tops of the coffee tables. On the walls hung paintings of East African scenes, of lions and other fauna, mementos of the Black Marlin, the Roussel family beach home north of Mombasa at Mtwapa Creek in Kenya and at Thierry's father's sprawling game farm at Nanyuki below the snows of Mount Kenya.

I left Boislande the next day at noon, a hostage once again of Stanislaus, the mad Polish driver who was delighted at the opportunity of giving me another demonstration of his inimitable driving method. His technique was simple - drive flat out, honk the horn, throw French language insults peppered with heavily accented Polish vowels out of the window. *"Eembecile"'*, *"Ahh, Alorss, putten"*, *"Couchon!"*

Stanislaus made the drive even more hair-raising by opening the sunroof at 170 kilometers per hour and waving a pudgy hand out of the roof making rude circular gestures to a startled group of Czech workers in a battered green Zastava whom we overtook on the wrong side.

"A cette route. Eel ee a beaucoop dez acceedants. Monsierre" he announced cheerfully taking both hands

off the steering wheel to rummage for a cigarette lighter in his pockets. Miraculously, the car stayed on the road and we arrived at the airport in one piece.

Once we had parked Stanislaus nipped round to the back of the VW station wagon. He pulled out my suitcase with a large grunt before I could warn him that it was full of heavy files. Dumping my suitcase on the pavement with an expression of surprise he rubbed the small of his back with both hands.

"*Qu'est qu'eeel y a là dedanz. Monsièrre?*" (What is in there Monsieur) he asked, mystified by the unexpected weight of the case. "*Monsiere Roussel vous avait donnè de bricks d'or?*" (Has Mr. Roussel given you gold bricks to carry?)

I assured him Thierry had not given me gold to take to Spain and handed him a bottle of red wine for his trouble. He pretended he did not want to take it but happily gave in when he read the winery label, "*Ah Bon, Monsièrre, très bon!*"

An hour later I was on an Iberia plane ascending over the neat green fields behind Geneva as we left the blue strip of Lake Leman and the estate of Boislande behind us.

My long deserved holiday in Spain was about to start.

A fairytale Ibiza vacation with the family

The Iberia domestic airliner flying the hop from Madrid to Ibiza banked sharply to the left levelled its wings and began a rapid descent through the late summer evening haze, leaving the sun hanging on the horizon behind us. The toasted brown shape of Ibiza came suddenly into view as we dropped bumpily down for our final descent to the airport. Our plane quickly approached a strangely shaped rock formation jutting out to sea at the end of a wooded peninsula. I was a little nervous as we passed low over the sharp perpendicular rocks – a weird formation bearing an uncanny resemblance to what looked like the dorsal fin spikes of a huge half-submerged rock dinosaur. It seemed for a moment that the rock needles would scrape the belly of the plane but we passed safely over them and three minutes later we landed at Ibiza airport. As I stepped out of the cabin door onto the platform of the passenger staircase I felt a searing wind blowing from the direction of the rock needles inland past me to the dry coastal plain that lay beyond the airport.

    Ours was the only plane at the airport and the arrivals lounge was almost empty. My suitcase was nowhere to be seen and a search of the carousels and of the large arrivals lounge was unsuccessful. Before long the airport was totally deserted except for me and a rather forlorn Ivizenka, an attractive local girl who waited with me at the small Lost and Found cubicle for the man in charge to arrive. We pointed out various shapes to him on a poster in an effort to identify our errant luggage types. Another plane was due in two hours. My case would be on it I was assured by the helpful airport attendant who however spoke nothing except Spanish and Catalan. Looking around now I saw a rather confused man beyond the glass division in the distance holding up a piece of cardboard with my name on it. I nodded, motioning for him to wait until I finished the paperwork at the lost luggage desk.

It was dark by now, and when I went outside into the waiting area I was met by the smartly dressed man in crisp whites who had held up the sign. He identified himself as Didier, a Roussel employee who had been sent to collect me.

"Monsieur Thierry has gone to New York and Madame is out with the children and her brother's family. I have been instructed to take you to the house."

It was dark by now and we drove in silence for a while, passing small simple dwellings along a dry, dusty country road. The scene with its parched grass along the tarmac strip illuminated by our headlights reminded me of my native Crete in August. We passed over a small hill, and then descended via a steep dirt road to what I could barely make out to be a bay lying on our left.

"*Là! Monsieur,*" *said Didier.* "*C'est la maison de Monsieur Roussel.*"

Immediately opposite us was a steep hill with perhaps a hundred palm trees illuminated by concealed yellow floodlights. In addition to this a smattering of weak yellow lights like oil lanterns scattered on the hillside made the scene look like a Hollywood Arabian oasis movie set.

We followed the narrow road down and through a dry river bed, ascending on the other side for perhaps another hundred metres before stopping in front of a massive double fronted wooden gate bounded on both sides by a high white wall. Didier got out of the car and lifted my suitcase out of the boot.

"*C'est lourd Monsieur,*" (It is heavy, Sir) he said, with a slight hint of reproach, "*A ce n'est rien* (It's nothing)," I replied, wanting to make a joke. "*Je porte de bricks de l'or pour Monsieur Roussel,*" (I am carrying gold bricks for Mr. Roussel).

Didier looked at me in a quizzical way. My joke had fallen flat. Of course it would not have surprised the Roussel staff if someone had been carrying gold bars for the family. I decided it was too late to explain my joke to Didier so I helped him carry the suitcase inside the compound to a beautifully designed two-storied cream Spanish villa a few metres away.

The house, partially obscured by creeping flowering shrubs and a canopy of honeysuckle was lit by small amber lights sunk into the stairwells giving it a warm luminosity. Even with my help the suitcase still had to be carried upstairs in stages to give us time to catch our breath. I held on to my end of the case, careful not to step on my own toes and took a break on the tile landing of the porch by the front door of the villa. I was startled to hear the sound of gushing water and turned round. There, in front of me was an illuminated four metre high waterfall, about seven metres wide. It was a stunning sight and I now realized what Thierry had meant when he said he wanted me to come and see how the Roussel family lived away from the public eye. A large palm tree, floodlit from its wide gnarled base stood rooted in the sand to the right of the waterfall. Didier waited indulgently for me to get over my first reaction of admiration. It was clearly a scene he had witnessed with every new visitor and I noticed he had a glint of pride in his eye. «Magnifique" I said, picking up my end of the case once more to stagger with Didier up the last few tiled steps to the guest suite landing on the first floor. The guest apartment with its Spanish terracotta floors and hand-plastered walls was large, finished in turquoise and white with light blue and cream rugs and matching curtains. It was an atmosphere somewhat reminiscent of sybaritic Las Vegas hotel suites but in good taste. An elevated Jacuzzi tub and a picture window looked out onto some distant lights which I assumed to be villas on the other side of the dark bay. The high bed itself was large enough for three. I was happy to have all this space to roll around on but I was disappointed that Dimitra my wife had refused to come.

 Didier closed the curtains for me and pointing to a wall thermostat he asked «How many degrees would you like your room to be at, Monsieur?" Thierry and his family had provided well for me, and I was grateful now that after a tiring trip I would have the chance to relax my exhausted limbs in the cocoon of welcome luxury.

 "I will wait for you downstairs, Monsieur, to take you to dinner. At the main house," said Didier.

A few minutes later I was outside again, walking past the waterfall which I noticed was fed by a series of illuminated blue cascading shell-shaped swimming pools.

"How many pools Didier?"

"Eight monsieur!"

He was showing off again. Eight swimming pools were certainly beyond the reach of middle class living. It was probably excessive even by plutocratic standards so I had to excuse Didier's pride. I was in Thierry's wonderland now and I realised he had brought me here to knock a little bit of my Greek chauvinism off me. It was typical of the low-key foxy Frenchman not to have said anything before. He had had his own way and now he was probably sitting on the plane in mid-Atlantic, smiling wryly, knowing that he was impressing the pants off me with the summer mansion complex he had built for Athina.

"The main house is up", explained Didier, pointing to the top of the cliff which was barely visible through the mass of floodlit palm trees growing on the slope above us. "134 steps up. Sir, of course I will drive you to the villa."

I was not going to argue. The still humid night air was stifling hot. We went through the entry gate to the car parked outside and then drove round the boundary wall of the property, up a narrow winding tarred road leading to the top of a steep hill. We circled a small plateau, drove past a couple of other large estates before stopping in front of a massive pair of carved wooden doors. They had been brought here I later learned from a medieval monastery. Subdued lights lit the bushes and illuminated the long rough stone whitewashed perimeter walls of the property. Behind the doors was an octagonal tower. We entered the main house through a high-ceilinged hall passing through into a white dining and living area room with glass walls on three sides. In the room was a set of comfortable summer couches, one of which was occupied by a dozing white Labrador with a chewed slipper next to it. There were Mexican hand-carved coffee tables in the room and items of local folk art hung on the walls. Small wooden sculptures stood on a variety of glass shelves.

Didier showed me to my seat at the end of a long bare wooden table. Beyond the glass doors behind the dining area there was a terrace illuminated by a blue grotto-like glow of a rectangular swimming pool. Once again, as at Boislande, there was an almost total absence of sound. Only the gentle patter of servant's rubber-soled shoes and an occasional squeak when they swiveled to close a door quietly behind them interrupted the hush of the surroundings.

I was surprised to see that the members of the staff on-duty at this time were, apart from Didier, black. Three servants in matching white T-shirts and trousers came into the dining room to serve me. The setting brought back memories of my youth in Kenya on a sugar and sisal plantation we owned on the Nyanza plain near Lake Victoria.

After a long day I felt totally relaxed now. A wave of nostalgia engulfed me as I remembered evenings in our estate house in Kenya on a small hill looking out towards Lake Victoria on the horizon.

There was the same quiet night atmosphere, the same sound of rubber soles on tiles and on highly polished cement floors. It was as if I was back again on holiday from my colonial British boarding school in Nairobi. I looked up at the same gentle faces of the African servants in Thierry's house, the same faces with the familiar bone structure of other much loved retainers who had been with my family since the days my father was a young man exploring the savannahs and jungles of British and German East Africa. The words spoken in French by the servant brought me suddenly out of my time warp and back to the present – to Ibiza, to La Jondal - to Athina Onassis' holiday mansion.

After dinner Didier drove me back down the hill and dropped me off by the large gate outside the guest house. The ambient heat was stifling. Even though it was nearly midnight the temperature was 42 degrees Centigrade and extremely humid in the manner of the tropics, though the air here was filled with magnolia scent. I was startled when I approached the guest house to hear a voice call my name from the shadows, it was David Weaver, the head of the English bodyguard detail hired to watch over Athina day and night. I had been with David on several trips. Twice in Greece, and also in Switzerland at Lussy. I took my leave of him and went upstairs, relieved to enter the air-conditioned suite where I had a quick shower and slid into the crisp turquoise sheets of the king-size bed and within seconds fell into a deep sleep.

First morning in Ibiza- 8 pools and SAS bodyguards

I woke up early the next morning. When I opened the chintz curtains I saw an aquamarine-coloured bay about two hundred metres in front of the house. To the left a pine-covered hill tapered down to what I now recognized as the "dinosaur" rock ridge I had seen from the plane the day before. Several white sailing boats were anchored in the gulf.

I went downstairs and out of the house past a trestle covered by a tangle of jasmine, honeysuckle and wax-flower creepers and walked in the direction of the waterfall which was now strangely silent. A hidden timer had switched off the pump late at night.

I decided to be brave and go by foot up the steps to the main house. There was a landing a few metres up from where a semi-circular couch faced what was the lowest level of a series of shell-shaped swimming pools, set one below the other in the cliff-side. The water ran from one to another as each pool overflowed into the next one, and the next one down the cliff to where the last pool's ledge formed the top of the waterfall.

Further up the stairs I saw a large earthenware pot, turned on its side. This was the recycling source of the water for the cascading pools. The view from this elevation, over the roof of my villa, was spectacular. Several large white mansions had been constructed on the side of the cliff opposite. Out of breath by now, after climbing more steps I passed through an arch and then up a few more steps which led to a large open terrace. Here I saw the rectangular pool belonging to the main villa, which I recognised from the night before.

A Spanish servant was placing crockery on a table in front of a semicircular couch covered with large Bedouin-style cushions. The servant appeared surprised to see a holiday guest awake so early. He explained that breakfast could be taken at any time and that the family would wake up later. I settled onto the cushions. There was a wide selection of cereals, cheeses, croissants and muesli. A set of silver thermos-jugs containing fruit-juices, teas, coffee and milk were filled and ready for the family and their Greek guest. Soon after I heard a shuffle of feet coming up the steps from the lower north annex of the villa where the children were housed.

"Hello, Alexis!"

It was Athina followed closely by Erik and a sleepy looking stunningly beautiful Swedish au pair of around 24. "Are you going on the boat with us later?" Athina asked.

"It depends on your mother," I replied, "We haven't spoken yet."

Just then Gaby came into sight, greeted me with a kiss on the cheek and said "Of course he will."

Gaby was always the consummate hostess in spite of the enormous strain her personal life had been under with the attacks of Papadimitriou on Thierry, and the accusations that regularly surfaced in the press from the same quarter accusing Thierry of cavorting with other women. Evidence never produced, but sufficiently insidious to harm his reputation. I did wonder though why Gaby would allow such a beautiful blonde au pair to be living in the house around Thierry. As they say in Greece she was enough to tempt even a saint!

The family now gathered at the breakfast table. Gaby's brother Uv and his wife joined us. A close family friend, Bo Jacobssen, an architect working in Geneva and his family arrived with a breezy hello. Last to arrive was Johann, an intense young law student engaged to Gaby's niece Maria, who had brought him with her to Ibiza.

The family spoke Swedish to each other and English to me. I later asked Thierry if he spoke Swedish. He looked at me for a second with an expression of reproach before replying, "No, I am French".

Athina like the other children had an easy command of several languages. I watched the siblings with admiration as they switched from French to English to Swedish and back to English again. In a few years time her love affair with Doda de Miranda, the Brazilian horseman she would marry, encouraged her to learn Portuguese fluently.

Johanna, 6, after diving into the pool for a quick swim wrapped a large towel around her and joined us at the table.

After breakfast we arranged to meet at noon back at the villa from where we walked down a dirt path to the beach where Manuel, the captain of the *Pickwick* was waiting to take us out in the cruiser to a quiet spot to swim. When we got back Gaby asked if I wanted to go into town with one of the drivers to do some sightseeing. I needed to get a press release ready so I refused, but did ask Didier to drive me down to the guest house because 134 steep steps on a full stomach was more than I could handle.

 Didier proudly led me to the car pound where I saw that Thierry had more interesting toys than the nondescript and functional VW's parked in the front drive at Boislande. Here two Mercedes, a Bentley, a six-wheel Range Rover and several motorcycles stood out from the fleet of staff cars and station wagons in the plot. I made a mental note to ask permission to take a particularly powerful-looking black and chrome Honda motorcycle out for a spin later.

 At noon I met Gaby and the children by the main pool of the complex. We spoke about Greece and about the yacht cruise we had taken together to Hydra in July. Erik wanted to know if I had brought the video of him and his dad racing go-carts in Athens. This item had been broadcast on the eight o'clock news in Greece and Erik was dying now to prove to a disbelieving 13 year old Ibiza house guest that he had not been exaggerating when he claimed that he had appeared on Greek television driving a racing cart.

 "Erik, I have the video with me!" I replied. He nudged his friend with a smug "I told you so" expression. Erik, Thierry's only son resembled his father in many ways and when I met him some years later saw that he had inherited both the good looks of his father but also his interest in good looking girls. Erik had the manners of an older person and was one of the nicest boys I had ever met. Despite being only 13 he had proved on the last family visit to Greece that he was the consummate diplomat when a television reporter working for a television station with a connection to the Onassis Foundation thought she would get something out of him to embarrass Thierry. During an impromptu interview with Erik while we were having lunch in Tourkolimano the reporter had asked him a heavily charged question on air

"Do you prefer Greece or Spain?"

«I like *both* Greece and Spain. But Spain a little better because we have a house there. If later we build a house here in Greece I will maybe like it better here".

Thierry and I looked at each other and I winked. The reporter continued.

"Erik" she continued "do you want to learn Greek?"

A trick question. Papadimitriou had used Athina's lack of Greek as a propaganda weapon in the Greek media and in court to attack Thierry, whom he accused of isolating his daughter from her Greek roots. The matter of Athina not learning Greek had an emotional impact on the public in Greece, but also on the courts, who ignored the fact that three million Greek children in the US and Australia spoke not a word of their mother tongue, while young Athina, only half Greek, living with a French father and her Swedish stepmother in Switzerland was expected to know a language even her mother Christina did not learn until she was nearly 20 years old. The loaded question had now been put to Erik by the reporter. He looked at her with an expression of deceptive innocence, his blue eyes steadily holding her gaze.

"Greek is a very difficult language, more difficult than French, but I hope to be able to learn it in the future, and to speak it"

Erik had passed his first media test. When the reporter left I said to Thierry

"With Erik to talk to the media in Greece, I don't think you will need me much longer". Thierry laughed and proudly put his arm around his son.

***

"Swimming time!" Gaby announced.

We stood up as a series of crackles and beeps from bodyguards' walkie-talkies cut through the air silencing the cicadas in mid-chirp. I heard Manuel, the *Pickwick's* captain saying that the tender was being sent to the beach since the *Pickwick* was moored offshore. Christina had given the Dickensian protagonist's name to the yacht as a reference to "Mr Pickwick" and "Mrs Pickwick" that she and Thierry called each other when they were alone.

It was stiflingly hot and humid now. We walked down a steep, dusty path, the bodyguards flanking Athina who was walking a few yards in front of Gaby and I. Two more bodyguards brought up our rear. These silent former SAS commandos looked fit in spite of being over fifty. There was little doubt that they were still capable of the occasional physical stunt as one of them had demonstrated by jumping off the mast of our yacht in Greece through a lifesaver floating on the water. When he did this the Greek bodyguards guards came to complain to me that this was unprofessional. If something had gone wrong they said and the English guard had broken an arm or a leg, the whole holiday for the family would have been ruined.

The path ended at a rock and pebble beach where there was a small primitive restaurant and a shack selling pareos, goggles and other beach paraphernalia. Athina, with her teenager's curiosity, went off to the shack to look at some costume jewellery with Sandrine.

The tender was waiting to take us to the *Pickwick*, a cruiser of around forty feet. Manuel had manoeuvred the boat to about two hundred metres offshore. After climbing on board we settled on the open deck from where I could see a cook busily chopping salads in the galley as we chugged off into the open sea to seek a remote bay. After the nearly sterile seas of Greece, I was surprised to see how many fish were in the water around our yacht. The water was a clear turquoise colour, with occasional cobalt patches succeeding one another as we went over deeper stretches of water.

We anchored in about four fathoms of water and spent the next few hours diving over the side of the boat, gossiping and generally messing about, while the children put on goggles and swam underwater occasionally breaking the surface to excitedly comment to us adults on some feature of the sea bottom that looked interesting to them. Athina, tall and willow-like was an accomplished swimmer, like her father, and looked born to the sea as had been her grandfather Ari Onassis.

Standing on the rear deck of the *Pickwick* I was looking out to sea towards the island of

Formenteira when I suddenly noticed a tattooed frogman carrying a harpoon gun swimming towards us. He had come in from a distance and was silently approaching us on the blind side of the yacht. I called for Athina and the other children to come back onto the boat which they did without asking why. Gaby saw what was happening and sent a bodyguard to tell the frogman to get away from the vicinity of the yacht. He did not hesitate when he saw a row of beefy bodyguards leaning over the rail of the deck motioning for him to move away. The incident ended there.

Thierry came back to Ibiza on the second day I was there. He drove me into town and to a dock where he was looking at some inflatable boats he had constructed in a new facility in Morocco. Thierry explained that he intended to sell inflatable boats to coast guards and port police around the world. On the way back he made a call to a restaurant and booked a table for three for nine o'clock. I presumed it was for him, Gaby and me. When we arrived back at the villa it was about five in the evening and Thierry went to his private penthouse floor with his own swimming pool at the top of the villa. Gaby was lodged in the children's wing which was one level down the hill from the ground floor of the mansion on Pogorroi bay.

"Would you like to come and play *boules* with us?" asked Athina.

"I don't know how," I replied,

"It's easy" said Erik," I'll show you how! You can be my partner"

I accompanied the children and Gaby to the shaded area at the side of the main house where there was a rolled sand pitch. Erik handed me a patterned steel ball which was surprisingly heavy for its size. I proceeded to spin a coin with the girls to see which couple would go first. There were three teams, Athina and Sandrine, Gaby and little Johanna, and Erik and I. Johanna was given a three metre handicap and rolled the first ball. The game from there proceeded in a happy atmosphere of friendly competition. Erik showed me how to play but was a clearly a little disappointed that I was not a fast learner, my first ball falling way short of the desired mark. After a few rounds little Johanna and Gaby had beaten me and Erik. Athina and Sandrine won and we all congratulated them, but it was time to go back now and get ready since the Jakobsson family was coming for dinner. Their three girls were almost the same age as Athina's siblings and were her best friends. Today one of the Jakobsson girls had a birthday and Athina was putting on a dinner party for her. As the Roussel house guest I too was invited. We all left to get some rest, have showers and to dress. I had forgotten completely about Thierry's restaurant date.

I went to my room, attended to some messages that had been sent to me. I relaxed, showered and changed and waited until it was time to meet the others for dinner. Thierry was nowhere to be seen as was so often the case but no one seemed to miss him when we all sat down at a long table that had been set out on the north terrace next to the illuminated main swimming pool. As we sat down at the long table Gaby and the rest of us heard peals of laughter and girlish giggles coming from the staircase leading up to the main pool level where we were. Athina, two of the girls and Erik came through the arch, barefoot, holding their shoes in their hands. When the giggles stopped they breathlessly told us that they had gone to dance in the "secret discotheque" located behind the waterfall in front of the guest house and that their shoes had got stuck to the dance floor. What they did not know when they had gone there to dance to a new cassette one of the Jakobsson girls had brought for Athina was that two members of the villa maintenance staff had painted the floor with thick black paint that afternoon and the paint had not dried when Athina and her friends unsuspectingly went onto the wet dance floor of the discotheque.

Uv and Marie's fiancé had left that day for Sweden, so Erik and I were the only males among a swarm of women and girls. Present were Gaby, Athina, Sandrine, Johanna, the three blonde Jakobsson sisters, their mother, UV's fiancée Marie and the Swedish babysitter. It was a very hot summer night, completely airless and humid with the heavy scent of jasmine in the atmosphere. Above us, despite the humidity, there was a clear sky filled with stars while the candles on the table and the wavelike blue reflection of the illuminated pool danced on the villa walls near us. It was a happy evening, Athina was sitting directly opposite me at the long table and I could see she was in a cheerful mood. Presents were brought and it was a moment of delight to see the childish curiosity of Athina who turned and looked to see what each present contained as her friend sitting next to her excitedly opened the small packages. It was a moment of pure innocence and I relished it, seeing Athina, around whom bitter public battles were taking place, excited like any child at the opening of each new present given to her good friend. I wondered how long this innocence would last knowing that it was only a matter of time before she would be forced to look people in the eye to see what they wanted of her. That day would come soon, and not always with the clarity of perspective that would allow the motives, good and bad, of others to be distinguished by the heiress. What I had not foreseen was the true, still hidden, character of the heiress that would be revealed to me several years later when I had given her the notorious red file with documents collected by Doda's longtime call girl mistress, Nicky. It was in a cancer ward in Athens (described in a chapter later in this book) that the final seal was broken to reveal a dark facet of the soul of the last Onassis

Five French chefs worked for the Roussels and they were all here at La Jondal today. Thierry soon after, in order to economize, fired them all; something that made Gaby put her foot down. She would NOT become a kitchen slave for Thierry, she said, and so Thierry kept one of the chefs at Lussy for her. A cake with candles and lit sparklers was presented and the Jakobsson birthday girl extinguished the candles amid much puffing and laughter as we all sang *"Happy Birthday to you!"*

Dinner was served by the African staff Thierry had brought from his Kilifi seaside estate on the Kenya coast. When the waiter came round for second helpings I said to him quietly in Swahili "*Nataka viazei tu*" – meaning "I only want potatoes". For a moment the servant did not react but when he realised that someone at the table had spoken his native language he looked around startled at all the white faces, unable to fit the Swahili phrase to a guest. I repeated my request, telling him I had grown up in Kenya, after which he was exceptionally attentive to me for the rest of the evening.

Looking round I noticed that Athina and I were the only two brown-haired and olive skinned people amid what seemed like a sea of blonde-haired, Nordic pale-skinned dinner guests.

"Athina," I said, leaning forward so that the others would not hear me, 'We are the only two Greeks here!" She broke out into a wide grin with a sparkle in her fawn-like light brown eyes, clearly agreeing with me. And so it was. The only surviving member of the fabled Greek Onassis dynasty and her Greek press representative and friend were in Spain, at a dinner table surrounded by foreign family, friends, and dozens of staff, at a celebration in that magical softly illuminated hillside mansion complex. We had a bond between us that she did not share with anyone else there. I thought back to the times that I had sat near her grandfather Aristotle in the Grande Bretagne Hotel bar and in nightclubs when he was at the next table and wondered how he would have reacted if he knew that the twenty-five year old near him would one day become deeply involved with his granddaughter's family while a huge battle for control of her fortune and her upbringing ebbed and surged.

At around 11pm Thierry cheerfully showed up wearing a slim-fit black shirt, a black belt with a silver buckle and silver studs all round and black narrow trousers. The image of the tall slim blond man in black would have taken many a young woman's breath away and Thierry knew he was making a grand entrance now. Despite being 45, married twice with a brood of children, and immersed to his ears in international corporate financial issues he was dressed and looked the playboy that he was.

He had eaten, he said, and asked Gaby and me to sit with him on a wide semicircular couch under a thatch umbrella. We put our legs up on the canvas cushions of the couch and ordered alcoholic drinks, relaxing finally after what had been for Athina, Thierry, Gaby and me one of the most stressful years of our lives as the battle with Papadimitriou and the Onassis Foundation had gone into high gear with important court cases coming up in Greece and in Switzerland. As we wound down under the moonless starry Ibiza sky, with Pogorroi Bay with its pinpricks of lights coming from mast lights of sailing yachts anchored in the bay, Thierry said "Now you know what I meant when I said come and see how we live away from the media, Alexis."

It was indeed a magical moment. Watching Athina and her teenage friends absorbed in a cheerful conversation, gathered in a circle as they sat on the Spanish handmade terracotta tiles by a large geranium-filled urn next to the illuminated pool I had to agree that life for Athina and her family here in this mansion hideaway with its eight cascading swimming pools, secret discotheque, waterfall and palm forest was as close to a private paradise as I had ever seen. I had yet to visit Scorpios but that would come later, in November, when Athina, Thierry and I would go to the island for the memorial service for the tenth anniversary of Christina Onassis's death.

Goings on at Scorpios

Scorpios was a playground for the Onassis family and their friends. In Ari's time it was a jet-set stop for Rudolph Nureyev, the Russian ballet dancer, the Kennedy family, Greta Garbo, Maria Callas, well-known politicians and heads of state. When Christina took over, the excesses of her partying were second only to her legendary hospitality when she sent her Lear jet to bring her friends and acquaintances to wherever she was. She ordered her pilots to pick up delicacies unavailable in Greece to bring back to Scorpios. The one thing she would not tolerate was to walk in and find a maid in her bedroom or in one of the cabanas on East Beach, or one making eye contact. The servant would be promptly fired.

The island became a party haven shared by her husbands, lovers and hangers-on when the heiress was there. Every whim was catered for by forty staff members and her managers.

Once hearing the phrase "If Pigs could fly" from one of her guests she immediately called her pilot and demanded that he arrange for a pig to be fitted with a parachute and released from the family helicopter over Scorpios. The pilot used to Christina's notoriously erratic behaviour, acquiesced. A pig was taken from the Scorpios farm enclosure, fitted with a parachute at the heliport on the top of the island behind the Forest House and hoisted on board with much squealing. Christina, beaming, watched as the helicopter lifted off and hovered above until a signal was given from the ground to let the pig "fly".

An assortment of her friends and some bemused local Greek Scorpios staff not familiar with British nursery rhymes watched as a large pink bundle was pushed out of the plane. The parachute failed to open properly and the unfortunate animal sped towards the ground where it landed with a resounding *splat*. The Onassis heiress question as to whether pigs could fly had been answered.

The Orthodox Church reaches out to Onassis' granddaughter

It was a swelteringly hot day in July of 1998. Thierry, Athina, I and Athina's aunt Marilena had dodged into a café in an arcade to avoid several TV crews which had blocked off the pavement of Ermou St, the main shopping thoroughfare of Athens, just off Constitution Square.

While we sat at a small table we kept our eyes on a wall clock, counting the minutes as they dragged by. We had an important appointment coming up. Athina, dressed in a white silk dress and a grey jacket, was sitting next to me with Thierry on her other side, while Marilena sat opposite us.

The customers in the café started turning their heads, recognizing our party from prime time news broadcasts of the previous two days. The bodyguards were busy in the café now, firmly intercepting well-wishers and the curious who wanted to come to our table.

The atmosphere was tense as the minute hand of the wall clock inched towards the twelve o'clock mark. Thierry was telling Athina to relax, but to no avail. She was understandably awed and I could see that she was nervous. It was difficult for her at that moment to understand the welcome she would receive from the head of the Orthodox Church of Greece and was understandably apprehensive since this was the first time she had ever met a person like Archbishop Christodoulos. I saw her momentarily fight back tears welling up in her large, deer-like brown eyes, but she became calm again when her father stroked her shoulder to reassure her.

At exactly two minutes to twelve I nodded to Thierry and we got up. We made our way back into the bright sunshine of Ermou Street. Our guards and the policemen on duty outside cleared a path for us to walk along Ayias Filotheis alley to the neoclassical building next to the Athens Cathedral where His Beatitude Archbishop Christodoulos (translation - Servant of the Lord) of Athens and All of Greece, had his offices.

When Athina was born Thierry and Christina had decided that Athina should be christened into the Orthodox faith of her mother. The christening took place on Scorpios, and was presided over by Father Apostolis, the local priest whom Onassis had always invited to carry out family ceremonies. George Livanos, Christina's uncle was the godfather at a ceremony attended by the whole family. After Christina's sudden death Athina moved to Thierry's house to be with her half-brother Erik, her half-sister Sandrine, and Gaby. The religious situation in the Roussel household was one of tolerance and piety, with the family praying every night. When the children were at an age where they could understand scripture tales, they attended church lessons in Lausanne. The Roussel family was an interesting mix of faiths. Gaby, Erik, Sandrine and Johanna were Episcopalian Protestant, Thierry was a laid-back Catholic, and Athina was Greek Orthodox. Despite this the family had no difficulty in matters of faith. Thierry had made a promise to respect Christina's wish regarding Athina's religion and so the time came in 1988 when Athina was fourteen he told me of his plans for her. He said that she was growing up now and day-by-day was enquiring about her Onassis family history. She had questions about the Greek faith also, and Thierry asked me my opinion as to whom she should see in Greece to talk to her about these matters. There was one person whom I considered ideally suited for this. The newly elected Archbishop Christodoulos of Athens and the Whole of Greece and it was the right time. Three months earlier Archbishop Seraphim, the former head of the mainland Greek Church had died, well into his eighties. He had been a man of little culture, speaking in a strong peasant vernacular, had rough manners and to many Greeks was a living relic of a divisive and troubled past. He had been accused of consorting with the colonels of the Greek junta when only a few yards away young Greek men and women were suffering physical torture and moral debasement in the dank cells of the military police. Seraphim, though controversial, had staunch supporters and was a master politician, managing to survive in his position until he died in 1998. He was replaced by a rising star of the Church, Christodoulos, who was highly educated, spoke several languages and had a shrewd understanding that in the new millennium the master of the game would be he who understood and used the media.

  Archbishop Christodoulos, a little over fifty at the time when we were to meet him had an expression that made one think he was bearing all the worries of the world on his shoulders. His eyes bore an uncanny resemblance to those of the late, great actor Dirk Bogarde, with that sad, knowing quality that said, "I have seen it all before". Christodoulos could light up in mirth in a second, transforming himself into a ho-ho-ho Santa Claus-like figure. He was adored by children and the younger generation in Greece who found him "cool" and direct in his manner. He spoke also with Bogarde's polished actor's delivery when making speeches of importance.

The majority of the Greek public, with the notable exception of some leftist Greek politicians, immediately fell in love with him and churches very soon could have put up "Full House" signs wherever the Archbishop went. The young, traditionally indifferent to matters of religion, soon took to the priest with his straight talk and wise advice, sending him numerous invitations to come to their schools or even to share a drink with them at their school parties. Christodoulos did not disappoint them. Within three months of being elected he topped all the opinion polls in Greece as the country's most popular figure. He was a man who understood teenagers and so I sent him a letter asking if he would see Athina and her father. I requested that he bless her, since she belonged to a family with a long history of tragedy and pain.

Two days later I received a phone call from the Archbishop's office granting my request. We set the date for the meeting for July 7th. We further agreed that since cameras followed the Archbishop everywhere, as they did Athina, there should not be a leak to the press. We decided to allow only one TV crew and a photographer to attend the first moments of their meeting. Word inevitably leaked out and I was deluged by reporters. I denied any meeting had been arranged. A Greek newspaper "Typos tou Mitsi" wrote a strong article attacking the Archbishop, telling him not to fall in with Roussel's plans to "squander Athina's fortune".

I wondered whether the Archbishop would go ahead with the meeting now that he was being threatened with being dragged into a very highly charged controversy. Christodoulos ignored the paper and was at that moment waiting for us upstairs at the Church of Greece headquarters.

As we progressed down the alley towards the Metropolis cathedral I was relieved to see only a handful of journalists. I was surprised at the relative quiet as we wound our way through the noon shoppers. At the Archbishop's headquarters we were met by a priest in the Orthodox traditional black cassock and stove-pipe hat. He motioned for us to follow him up the steep marble steps into the Church headquarters building. Athina nervously hung onto her father's sleeve as we entered the gloom of a large high-ceilinged hall. Suddenly there was a blinding barrage of flashlights and a noisy rush of more than thirty paparazzi towards us. In a second or two we were engulfed. They were next to us, pushing, pulling, shouting "Athina", "Athina", as they tugged at our sleeves. I was locked into a scrum and carried forward up the steep stairs leading to the upper level where the Archbishop was waiting for us.

I was squeezed against the wall by a wedge of reporters and cut off from Thierry and a bewildered Athina who kept looking round to see where I was.

Reaching the landing a large door opened and our disheveled party went inside.

Before entering the building Thierry had asked me what the correct protocol was for greeting the Archbishop. I explained that Athina should follow Orthodox tradition and kiss his hand, while Thierry as a Catholic was not expected to do so. Thierry had not seen the Archbishop so he was not aware what he looked like. In the confusion of our entry to the upper floor, Thierry took the hand of a young priest by the door and bent to kiss it. The priest, surprised and flattered, did not react.

A bald paparazzo wearing a black and white candy stripe suit forced himself ahead of me, holding me back as two young priests by the doors pushed them shut, leaving me outside in the seething mass of excited cameramen and journalists. A furious banging on the door by me caused the priests inside to open it a chink, and when they saw who it was, they allowed me through, pushing back the reporters who tried to enter with me. It was absolute pandemonium.

A smiling Archbishop Christodoulos was waiting to receive us by the door. Athina bent to kiss his hand but he withdrew it and kissed her on both cheeks in a warm welcome. Thierry likewise bent forward, but again the Archbishop withdrew his hand, not allowing Thierry to be in a position of homage that the hand-kissing symbolized. Instead he greeted Thierry warmly with a traditional kiss on both cheeks. As the massive wooden door shut behind me I looked up to see a flushed Thierry and Athina looking at me. The bodyguards were straightening their jackets and ties while along the opposite wall of the large red-carpeted reception room stood a row of black-cassocked bearded Orthodox priests. Athina was somewhat bewildered by the medieval atmosphere of the moment. One of the priests, a kindly man with jolly eyes, understanding her fears stepped forward slowly, so as not to startle her and said "Athina, don't let our appearance worry you. We are good people!"

He turned to me and said in Greek "Dressed like this we must look somber and frightening to the little lady". It was in part true. The priests proved to be civilized and discreet and tried to put Onassis' granddaughter at ease, asking her and her father questions in English and in French. It was obvious that they were impressed by the young teenager who carried the Onassis legend on her slim shoulders.

Thierry had asked that the meeting with the Archbishop be in private - just the Archbishop, he and Athina were to be present as there were family matters to be discussed. Marilena Patronikola, Athina's aunt and I therefore waited in the Archbishop's antechamber while Christodoulos spoke with the Roussels.

The meeting was expected to last for no more than fifteen minutes. Twenty minutes passed, then a further fifteen minutes, and another fifteen minutes. Marilena and I wondered what was being said by the Archbishop to father and daughter. Meanwhile, outside, delegations from all over Greece and one from Australia had arrived and were waiting for their own audience with the Archbishop.

The silence in the room where we were sitting under the gaze of the fifteen or so standing priests was broken every few minutes with the ringing of a mobile phone, followed by a rustling of robes as the priest in question dug into his cassock pockets to locate the ringing phone. I tried to stifle a laugh when one phone started chiming to the tune of "Auld Lang Syne".

At a quarter past one the door to the Archbishop's office opened and Marilena and I were invited to go in. The Archbishop asked us to sit opposite him at his desk next to Thierry and Athina. We talked for a few minutes, and by this time it was obvious that Athina had been surprised that the Archbishop was so friendly and that he spoke good French as Thierry later confirmed. Christodoulos told us that when he was a schoolboy he had attended the Leontios School, an exclusive educational establishment run by French Catholic priests. We sat for a few more minutes and then the personal photographer of the Archbishop, Christos Bonis, was called in to take our photos.

All this time we could hear the muffled shuffling of chairs and a lot of whispering from the ante room. The priests at the door had allowed the paparazzi to enter the room in preparation for a photo shoot of Athina with the Archbishop. Christodoulos' assistants had now wisely put up a dividing rope to keep the photographers at a secure distance in the room. A photo session lasted for five minutes with the Archbishop standing next to Thierry and Athina. For Thierry's enemies it was a clear message that the Orthodox Church had its doors open for Athina, but for Thierry too. From the Onassis Foundation there was, as expected, public criticism about the meeting. The meeting had touched on several matters related to Athina. Archbishop Christodoulos discussed Christina and Aristotle with her, and told her that whenever Athina wanted she could contact him. If she wanted to see an Orthodox priest in Lausanne he would arrange it for her, but there was no pressure of any sort and she should know this.

  I did not have a chance to talk to Thierry until that afternoon when I joined him on the motor sailer, the *Ariadne*, anchored about half a mile offshore at Lagonissi opposite Aunt Kalliroi's villa which the Roussels were using as a base for their Greek holiday.

  Thierry had already made himself at home sitting on the curved settee on the covered rear deck of the yacht. He was relaxing, smoking a cigarette, but I could see he was waiting to tell me of his impressions of the meeting with the Archbishop. We did not have much time for this because I had found the opportunity to arrange two important interviews in the next half an hour.

  Thierry was not in the mood to talk to journalists but I had felt very strongly that this was an important opportunity to let his side of the dispute be known, so he accepted with a shrug and a sigh of feigned suffering. Roussel trusted my judgment after seeing the change in public opinion and in the media since I had started to work for him.

  "The *pope* gave me his mobile phone number!" said Thierry, astonished that a high ranking cleric would have this electronic toy among his paraphernalia.

"I told you he was modern, Thierry. What about Athina?" I asked.

"She was very worried when we went there before she saw him. But he spoke well to her and besides he speaks good French. We talked about the family and other things. Athina though cried on the way back – the strain and anticipation of the meeting was too much for her. But we made a friend, I think, and that is important."

The two of us sat in silence for a while. It was obvious that the meeting had in certain ways which were not yet obvious changed Thierry and Athina. I knew it was for the best, but as so often happens, the importance of pivotal events often dawns last on those who are closest and most affected by them.

A woman's shout from the side of the boat and the purring of an outboard motor indicated that the first journalist had arrived at the yacht. In the yacht tender, hanging onto her soundman was Angeliki Kourouni, the reporter from Tribune De Geneve and young Stefanos Dianellos, a well-mannered columnist from "Ta NEA", an Athens paper.

Oblivious to the people around her Angeliki Kourouni was screaming as the tender pitched in the water. It took a good five minutes and much protesting by her to get her up the ladder and onto the yacht.

"I hate boats!" she announced loudly and demanded to go downstairs into the main lounge where the sea would not be visible to her. Thierry, I, and her soundman, a silent and gaunt looking Swiss national sat down at a table where the sounds of the sea were muffled by the plate glass windows and the thick blue wall-to-wall carpeting.

Ms. Kourouni had not been a particularly supportive journalist but she represented an important group of radio and television stations in Europe as well as the main Geneva paper. It was for this reason that I invited her to interview Thierry. It was a calculated risk but I hoped the benefits of the meeting would outweigh the risks.

Kourouni made it plain immediately that she was not there to write pleasant things about Roussel – she wanted a story, and she was not going to show any appreciation for the foreign press exclusive interview we had granted her. In fact the whole scene was difficult. After the urbane and usually well-groomed girls who covered the Onassis family saga, the appearance of this journalist was a shock to us. She had short, brightly-coloured magenta hair in a wild perm, a faded outsize sweater with what appeared to be a tear in one sleeve and the rest of her outfit consisted of baggy cotton clothes of a different print. The interview was not helped by the fact that her silent and gaunt assistant kept twiddling his thumbs while she unsuccessfully played with knobs on her tape recorder, lifting her eyebrows to indicate to him that it wasn't working, while all the time firing off questions one after another at Thierry. When I asked what was wrong she told me that she had come back from Kosovo three days before, where an Albanian Liberation Army UCK bullet aimed at her had struck the tape recorder. She had survived, but the recorder now needed assistance since the "play" and "record" buttons would not stay down when pressed. She hissed at her silent sound man to put his thumbs on the two buttons concurrently.

For the next hour and a half he kept them there as Thierry unwound with his side of the dispute and spoke of Athina, Christina and Papadimitriou. Not once did Ms Kourouni smile. It was obvious that from the front lines of a civil war in Yugoslavia to go straight onboard a 43 metre sailing schooner and report on the problems of the rich would have been a provocation to any war correspondent's sense of social justice. Kourouni though seemed supremely professional and I told Thierry that we would have to wait and see what she would write in the Tribune de Geneve. Above all we did not want the visit to the Archbishop to be dragged into the overall dispute.

Two days later the Tribune de Geneve had a front page story on Athina Onassis-Roussel and how she had appeared in front of the head of the Orthodox Church in a provocatively short white miniskirt. Later when the pictures for the visit were published, they showed Athina, clad in a modest white dress that came way down past her calves, and a long jacket. Once again Athina had been victimized.

Contrarily in Greece the press fawned now on Athina. Full page photographs of Onassis' granddaughter appeared in many papers and there were pages of glowing reports in most magazines. That evening the main item on all the Greek TV news stations was the meeting of the Onassis descendant with the head of the Orthodox Church of Greece. There was not one press word in discord. The Tribune de Geneve stood alone in its criticism of a 14 year-old girl who had gone to see her religious mentor.

Two weeks later, when I finally managed to trace Ms Kourouni on her crackling mobile, I understood that she was at the grisly scene of a new Balkan outrage. She explained that she had sent the article by fax to Switzerland and that it had been edited by a new reporter who added the miniskirt jibe without her knowledge. It may have been so.

My last thought was for Ms Kourouni's sullen, hollow-checked soundman who no doubt at that moment was a few feet away from her, with thumbs still glued to the "play" and "record" buttons of the tape recorder while sniper rounds from angry UCK militia combatants sorting out centuries of hatred kicked up spurts of dust around him. It is a sad fact of life, and one that shames us all, that the readers of the Tribune de Geneve, to whom the soundman was valiantly offering his technical services, would first choose to read what young Athina Onassis was wearing on the motor sailer *Ariadne* and only afterwards read how many people had died that day in Pristina's outskirts.

A determined stalker and other admirers

I first saw him carrying a large battered suitcase outside the Evelpidon law courts in Athens during Thierry's case with the Onassis Foundation board members. It was a bitterly cold but sunny day in March of 1998. We were waiting for Thierry's defamation case to be heard. The man who was in his mid-sixties was wearing a heavily creased beige suit. He approached me at the entrance to the court, put down his suitcase with a grunt and said -

"I want to talk to Mr. Roussel. I have something important to tell him."

"What is your name?" I asked.

"Petros."

The name meant nothing to me.

"It is very important," he said." I have the solution to the court disputes here in my suitcase. All the documents are here."

I realised in a flash that the man standing in front of me was the obsessive former Onassis employee who had written countless letters to Athina and Thierry. Over the years he had also pestered them with hundreds of phone calls.

I told him to wait and went over to where Stefanos our head of security was standing outside the room where Thierry and the lawyers were in conference. I explained to Stefanos who the man was.

"If you do have evidence which will be useful for this case you should take it to someone on the other side, they are the ones who took the initiative of bringing this case to court," I told Petros.

He looked confused for a second then he stooped to pick up his case. Nodding to me he walked off to look for Papadimitriou closely accompanied by Stefanos who from that moment made sure the man had no more contact with us that day. When I returned to the waiting room I told Thierry and Gaby about my encounter.

"Do you know that we once found him in our garden in Switzerland?" said Gaby. "He came to the house three times. He is obsessed with Athina."

"What is in his suitcase?" I asked.

"Hundreds of press clippings and letters regarding our family," Thierry answered. "He has sent us more than 700 letters!"

After that morning I forgot about him. Ten days later I received a call on my mobile phone. A polite voice was on the other end "May I speak to Mr. Mantheakis'"

"Who is it?" I responded.

"Petros - with the suitcase."

Someone had given him my mobile number. He continued, "I must explain to you that I have the whole solution to the problem of Mr. Roussel and his quarrel with the Foundation."

I decided to humour him in the hope that I could deflect his interest.

"I am the incarnation of Onassis. In fact I am Onassis the Second. An improved and more moral version of the original, because Onassis Number One was a real bastard!"

Our conversation was somewhere beyond the outer limits of logic now. I realized my choices of dealing with the man were limited: I could either hang up, in which case he would call again, or I could try and fend him off.

"What is it that you really want?" I asked, thinking of the options open to me to get rid of him.

"Mr. Roussel has four children, that is too many. I want to marry Athina and Sandrine. He can keep Erik and Johanna."

Athina was thirteen and Sandrine eleven.

"And how old are you?" I asked.

"Sixty two."

"You should be ashamed of yourself! They are just children!" I replied, feigning anger.

"I will be a father to them and later I will give them many children. I already have a house ready for them. And don't worry about my performance; I can satisfy five 20 year old women."

I hung up.

Petros of course dogged me from that day on. He had read in the papers that I was the only person in Greece in close contact with the Roussel family and this convinced him that I was the solution to his problem.

"Only you, Mr. Mantheakis..." was the phrase that I heard again and again. This usually followed a telephone call that he had previously made to Katia Ioannides, the younger former Olympic Airlines employee who had married Pavlos Ioannides of the Onassis Foundation. Katia of course was not in contact with the Roussels and was unable to help Petros, so inevitably the next call was to me.

I tried to come to an accommodation with him so that he would not call me every day. We made a deal for our contact by phone to be limited to once a week, but then he would get excited by some news item he saw regarding Athina and he would call me. My postman became accustomed to delivering heavy large brown envelopes from the provincial Greek town of Agrinion. These envelopes were marked *Strictly Private and Personal*. The envelopes contained Petros' cosmic theory as well as letters to Thierry and Athina. They came in regularly, and there were telephone calls at all times of day, on my mobile and to my office number to ask whether I had received the latest letters. One day I opened an envelope to see the results of an examination at a fertility clinic. It was an analysis of a sperm count of Petros who included a note telling me that here was the proof that he would be a productive husband for Athina and Sandrine!

I became exasperated when I started getting five and six calls a day. I noticed after a while that I was starting to act irrationally toward him, while Petros himself was calm and polite. Sometimes I would hang in there, and the conversation would often be about his days as a first engineer on the Onassis tankers. In the middle of the conversation he would stop and say, "Of course you remember that I am Onassis reincarnated? Onassis the Second!"

One Sunday morning Petros called to ask me if I believed in the transmigration of souls and in reincarnation. Caught unawares I made the fatal mistake of saying that our Ancient Greek philosophers believed in the theory as did perhaps a quarter of the population of the world. The Buddhists too were convinced it was true. From that day on Petros hung on to me like a limpet. He had found what he was sure was a fellow believer.

"Ah, Mister Mantheakis," he would say, "You are my saviour, everyone thinks I am mad, but you yourself admitted that reincarnation is possible and from now on I will only talk to you because we are kindred souls in a hostile and unbelieving world."

I talked to people who knew him from his Onassis days to try and understand where his problem lay. They told me that he had been sent home with a pension after he behaved strangely on several occasions on board. Petros himself recounted how he had married a Russian girl who now lived with his son in Moscow.

"I wanted to see them, but the Russians would not let me so I wrote a hundred letters to Brezhnev and later to Gorbachev. I went to Moscow and sat outside the Kremlin shouting for them to give my son back."

I was horrified at the thought. "What happened Petros?" I asked, wondering how the Russian communist regime had reacted to Onassis the Second waving his arms and shouting insults at them in the Kremlin from Red Square.

"They threw me in jail. Communists are completely materialistic in their theory. They could not understand that I was reincarnated."

He told me how he was deported from Moscow and had not been able to see his son, who was now seventeen. It was a tragic story.

"I will settle everything when I marry Athina," he said with finality and hung up.

One day I was on the yacht of a Greek shipowner for whom Petros had worked after being fired from the Onassis group. The captain of the yacht who knew Petros from his tanker days told me that Petros had brought his Russian wife, a child bride of 16, onto the tankers which were breaking the oil blockade in the Gulf during the Iran-Iraq war. Petros' child-bride found herself in a totally foreign and bewildering environment. She was on the tanker when it was strafed by aircraft, rocketed by shore batteries and hit by an Exocet missile. Terrified, disoriented and insecure she had found security in the bunks of Petros' fellow officers. This for her husband's fragile mind had been the final straw. Petros started hallucinating regularly and was soon sent home to Greece. He looked for an outlet for his frustration and before long locked onto a new target. He became obsessed by the granddaughter of Onassis and her half-sister Sandrine.

I found out later that Petros had been seriously affected by a traumatic episode in his family when he was 5 years old. He recounted to me that he had seen his father murder his mother in front of his eyes. Petros was then passed on to relatives who brought him up. On occasion when I discussed these things with him, hoping to ease the isolation he felt, he would open up but would soon get back onto his favourite subject, Athina. He was not a man to lose sight of his quarry for long. He confided to me that he was furious with the Roussel secretary working at the Roussel apartment at 88 Avenue Foch, near the Arc De Triomphe in Paris.

"Just imagine! I travelled all the way to Paris to ask Thierry for Athina's and Sandrine's hand in marriage. When I arrived at the apartment I rang the bell and a secretary opened the door. She let me in, but when I told her my name she locked me in the guest toilet. She then brought a concierge who threw me out. No sense of hospitality to travellers, Mr. Mantheakis, these French, I tell you, absolutely shocking!"

I could imagine the panic of the secretary when, standing alone with the "family friend' inside the Roussel apartment she realised that she had opened the door to the obsessive stalker-suitor Petros.

One afternoon at Lussy just before Athina was to return home from school Thierry was in his study when one of the bodyguards noticed a furtive figure in a far corner of the garden near where Athina kept her two sheep. The British guard gave out the alarm. Other guards rushed to apprehend the intruder who immediately lifted his hands in a motion of surrender. He was quickly taken to the kitchen where he was interrogated by the bodyguards. Thierry looked in to see what all the fuss was about and saw Petros in the middle of all the excitement. Thierry ordered the guards to release him after they told him not to come back again, explaining to him that he could have been shot. Petros had not only disturbed the Roussels at home that day but had another victim nearby. He had seriously annoyed a resident of the local youth hostel where he had slept the night before. Petros told me the story himself. He had run out of money by using all his resources to finance his expedition to Switzerland. On the previous evening in the youth hostel he had felt hungry. He had a plan he told me. He waited for the others in the dormitory to leave and at that propitious moment he started searching in the satchels of the absent students who were lodged in the same room. Petros was looking for food. In one bag he found two sandwiches, meticulously prepared and wrapped in cling film and aluminium foil. Petros ate the sandwiches quickly and wolfed down a bar of Nestle chocolate he found in the same bag. Pleased with himself, his hunger pangs now satisfied, he settled down on his bunk and drifted off into a contented sleep. Half an hour later he was rudely awoken by a commotion in the dormitory. Some of the students had returned.

Petros recounted what happened next. "One of the youths, a Japanese boy, was waving his arms about and protesting loudly that his sandwiches had been stolen. He looked at me accusingly. 'You were the only person here.' He said."

Petros told the complaining youth that he had indeed eaten his sandwiches, but that two thousand years ago St Paul had preached that "for the sick and for travellers there is no sin".

The protesting and hungry Japanese youth, deprived of his sandwiches, was understandably unwilling to accept this tenet of western religious philosophy and continued complaining for some time until Petros was thrown out of the dorm and found shelter in a nearby park.

This failed expedition to Switzerland made Petros even more determined. He was a man with a mission.

"I am packing my bags to go back," he said to me some months later, "but I am short of money, so I will have to wait and save up my pension payments. I will call you after I marry Athina." With that he hung up.

Every Christmas a large parcel of olives of the best quality and a fine cheese was sent to me by Petros. A similar package was delivered to Athina and Sandrine in Switzerland. It was difficult for me to be angry with him even though he exasperated me at times. He only stopped calling me when Athina married Doda.

Athina's admirers were of all ages and dispositions. Some were cultured, more like opera fans, some adoring, while others were abusive and demanding. One day during Thierry's court case in Athens in 1998 a rough looking man of around 35 with a flushed red face and disheveled clothes came up to me demanding to talk to Thierry. I told him that Mr. Roussel was busy with his court case and was not available. The man became insistent. At that moment there was a recess in the courtroom and Thierry came outside to talk to me.

"What does he want?" Thierry asked, seeing that the man had fixed him with a determined scowl.

"Tell him that I have come five hundred kilometres from my village. I want to marry Athina!"

"That is not possible," I answered," She is too young for such things and must finish her school first," giving him my standard answer whenever I was in this situation.

I translated what had been said to Thierry, thinking the situation rather funny. I saw that Thierry had a look of concern in his eyes. I turned round and saw that the suitor was now red in the face and was sputtering with fury.

"I came all the way here and will not leave without Athina. Tell Mr. Roussel to send for her right now!" he barked. I realised the man was dangerous and was likely to attack at any time.

"It's okay," said a reassuring voice just behind me. It was Costas our bodyguard and driver who made a quick move, grabbed the man in a vice-like grip by the elbow and handed him over to two policemen on guard duty at the door of the court building. The bell rang to indicate that our court was back in session and we quickly forgot the incident.

There is a permanent population of cranks who spend all day attending various trials in Athens, playing out their own fantasies and finding refuge, and possibly reassurance, in the drama of others. I had noticed in November 1998 that for a whole week there was a skinny blondish youth of around twenty sitting in the back of Thierry's courtroom, always in the same seat. He wore a beige raincoat and motorcycle boots. One day in recess he approached me and asked, without introducing himself "When is *my* issue going to be taken care of?"

"What issue?" I asked, mystified.

"My appointment as President of the Onassis Public Benefit Foundation."

Here we go again, I thought.

From that day the youth pestered me regularly and eventually one evening he followed me to the hotel where Athina was staying after we returned from the Drakos wedding with the Roussel family. One of our guards called me on my mobile.

"Sorry to call so late but we have caught a chap here who says he wants to see Athina. He looks a little vague."

"Does he have a blue motorbike?" I asked.

"That's him".

"Hold him at all costs, and don't let him through. He has been stalking Athina and Thierry for months.

Stefanos had been on guard at the gate of the Astir Palace Hotel in Vouliagmeni, the large luxury resort hotel of several hundred acres where we were staying. It was past midnight. There were three of the Greek state VIP special branch police with Stefanos. They took the man's identification card, noted his name and told him to hop it otherwise he would find himself in jail.

That was the end of him. Or so I thought. One day the entry phone at my house rang. I saw the face of the man on the screen of the videophone.

"I have brought some presents for Athina."

I asked him for identification. He had an Arabic name. He explained that he was half-Syrian and lived in Greece. I did not let him into the house but I did send the presents to Athina, and thanked him on his inevitable reappearance a couple of months later. The last time I saw him he was in a Greek airman's uniform. Lowering his voice he confided that he had taken a leave of absence from the Syrian secret service for which he had been a specially trained agent.

He regularly popped up whenever Thierry was in Athens. My last encounter with him was when I saw him standing outside my gate. I asked what he wanted.

"Just to say hello" he beamed. I knew he was hiding something.

"What is it, Abdullah?" I asked.

"I have just come back from Switzerland. I spent a month on holiday there and visited Athina's house several times, though the guards would not let me in."

He was radiant with happiness at having got so close to the object of his admiration.

As Athina grew older she became an attractive young woman with a certain air of mystery about her. She was wrapped in the myth of being the last survivor of the legendary Greek Onassis dynasty - a person beyond the reach of ordinary people. She entered the Greek national psyche as an idol. For a teenager it was a difficult and demanding position to be in, but she adapted well, keeping a tantalizing distance from the media. In a symbolic way she reminded me during her teens of the stories recounted by early European explorers in the Congo who described the existence of a graceful long-necked deer the natives called the Okapi. It was a slim animal which would appear for a few seconds in some small clearing in the vast Ituri forest before infuriatingly disappearing into the shadows, not allowing itself to be captured or photographed. For many years the elusive African deer was a legend. The African Okapi with its huge fawn eyes was real though, and so, of course, was Athina, but to the Greek public she remained a mysterious embodiment of the Onassis myth. As such she would always have her admirers, whether it was the obsessed Petros with his hundreds of letters or others with meticulously kept diaries of Athina sightings, while yet others sent presents for the heiress at Christmas and birthdays.

Petrol station attendants when they recognised me would say "Tell Athina to come to Greece", or warn "Tell her to be careful". The same thing happened regularly at income tax offices, in ministries, in tavernas and when I went to church. Everyone, from judges and government ministers to cleaning women wanted to know "What is she like?"

Return with Athina to Scorpios, November 1998

I held on tightly to the handrail of the heavily loaded Bertram cruiser as it crashed and slewed over each successive wave of the black sea. Ahead of us loomed Scorpios Island, a dark tree-covered mass barely distinguishable from the dark sea and the low grey rain clouds of that November evening.

Athina and Thierry were standing just in front of me, looking silently ahead, while the bodyguards who had found seats among the piles of luggage made their best to avoid the lashing streams of sea spray. As we approached the island where the Onassis family were buried the tension in the boat was palpable. Athina had just a few hours ago left her school in Switzerland and her cheerful place among the Roussel family, of which she was an integral part, to find herself suddenly an Onassis.

Athina who had not been to Scorpios for several years was understandably apprehensive as we approached the place where her mother was buried. I saw her move closer to the reassuring figure of her father as we rapidly approached the dark place where her Greek mother Christina was interred in a small private chapel with three other members of the Onassis dynasty. A few minutes later we pulled alongside a large jetty. There old Onassis-family retainers had come to welcome back the heiress and owner of the island. For me it was a relief to be at the end of our journey since the trip had not been an easy one.

Earlier we had been flying in an 18 seat chartered Olympic Airways Dornier from Athens.

"There is a storm ahead," the captain had announced thirty minutes after take-off. Accompanying Thierry, Athina and me were eight worried-looking journalists whose colour became ashen as we started losing height.
"Why are we descending?" asked Thierry, leaning into the aisle.
 "The clouds are getting lower," the pilot explained "We need to get under them to retain visual flight rules".

    Just then there was a nasty jolt. The plane bucked, then banked and dipped suddenly to the right. In front of us all I could see through the cockpit windscreen were clouds, less than half a mile away. We descended hurriedly to perhaps a thousand metres above sea level before the captain eased the plane out of the dive and levelled its wings. Below us the crinkled surface of the grey sea appeared immobile like in a photograph. We crept along now with reduced power, hanging just under a brooding ceiling of dark clouds that seemed almost to touch the roof of our plane.

    The pilot saw a break in the cloud bank and sharply veered the plane's nose up and to the left, aiming it at the chasm of clear sky between what looked like two perpendicular cliffs, steep cloud formations bearing in on either side of us. The captain gave power to the props and started a full throttle ascent. The noise and vibration inside the small cabin of the Dornier were deafening. Through the open slice of sky between the two cloud banks a looming mountainous mass - the Peloponnese peninsula - was approaching us at an alarming rate.

I held my breath until we cleared the mountain tops and then asked the co-pilot why we did not go over the clouds.

"We have no oxygen or pressurization system" he mimed over the din in the cabin.

The plane was bouncing now, once again buffeted by clouds into which we had wandered. It felt like an age but must have been only minutes before we broke clear again skimming over white cloud tips into a dazzlingly blue sky with the sunshine reflected off tiny almost horizontal glistening trails of water on the outside of the cabin windows.

The girl reporters in the plane were unusually silent. I turned in my seat to see a row of anxious faces. Alexia from Skai TV, a pale, freckled girl with a white skin, more Scottish than Greek in appearance, had a deathly pallor. Noticing she was gripping the armrests I teased her, in an attempt to cheer her up, but with little success. Eftichia, from Star, a slim dark Cretan girl in her late twenties, was calmer. I could see that their personal video cams had been put away and the reporters were silently watching Athina who was in the single seat immediately behind me. The SAS bodyguards, all muscles, balding heads and wide shoulders were reassuringly relaxed.

Athina had dozed off to sleep. A photo of her grandfather Aristotle Onassis, the founder of Olympic Airways, was staring up at his granddaughter from the open page in the complementary flight magazine in her lap. Athina looked totally relaxed. She was calm in adversity.

A few minutes later when we entered the clouds again, Thierry stood up, agitated. The plane was completely enveloped in cloud now and the interior of the cabin became dark. Outside I saw that visibility was no more than ten or fifteen metres.

"They are not allowed to fly in cloud," Thierry said to me, more anxious for Athina than for himself. "I am going to talk to the captain."

He peeked through the door to the cockpit and then turned back, his tall frame bent almost in two because of the low cabin ceiling. He nodded to me as he sat down. "They are on IFR now." We were both relieved to see that the plane had the necessary instruments for flight in cloud conditions.

After a while the plane suddenly lost altitude once again. The pilots explained that the cloud ceiling was lifting and they could fly now by sight, which meant going under the cloud cover. Flying below the low cloud ceiling for half an hour more we started to descend. Below us there was a fertile coastal area with flat emerald green fields. Then we saw the airport runways. In minutes we touched down and after coming to a halt we were met by the airport director. A row of taxis and Mercedes cars were waiting for us in front of the small country airport building.

Thierry and Athina rode in the car ahead of me, following a patrol car which had turned on its rotating blue beacon. Behind us a convoy of taxis carrying press and security personnel jockeyed for position. My mobile was ringing constantly, reporters wanting to know where we would stop. Associated Press called to ask if the rumor that Athina was going to Scorpios was true. I could see Athina and Thierry in the car in front. At that moment she turned and smiled at me. I confirmed that Athina Roussel was indeed on her way to Scorpios. In a few minutes Associated Press had put the item on world-wide release.

A few minutes later CNN rang, then three paparazzi in quick succession, and then Thierry rang anxiously asking where I was, as he could not see my car. I told his driver on the mobile to slow down because two press vans had wedged themselves between us and I had lost sight of him. To add to this confusion three hired cars came alongside with cameramen hanging out of the windows, their heavy professional cameras pointing at us. The reporters were travelling parallel to us, in the wrong lane of the narrow winding country road. Over the car radio I could hear a Greek station giving a live broadcast of the pending arrival of the Onassis heiress at Scorpios. A mile from Nydri, the island resort opposite Scorpios I had a call from an unofficial representative of the paparazzi asking whether we would bypass Nydri and get into a boat to avoid them and go straight on to Scorpios Island.

"No, we are arriving now," I reassured him as we entered Nydri. The village was strangely deserted. I wondered where everyone was. The answer came when we turned off the main street into a narrow passage between some shops and turned out again along the quay in front of a row of tavernas and folk art shops. Just ahead there was a crowd of perhaps five hundred people - villagers and journalists - waiting for us. The whole village was there.

Athina stepped out of the car and took her father by the arm after the bodyguards had taken up their positions, Thierry motioned for me to approach and then we were engulfed by the welcoming villagers. A gap opened and directly in front of us there stood a line of local officials. The mayor of Nydri, Mr. Gazis was there, while next to him was Father Apostolis, the sprightly octogenarian priest who had baptized Athina and had presided over the funerals of three members of the Onassis family. In a moving reversal of roles he bowed his tiny frame and kissed Athina's hand.

Eftichia, a streetwise reporter not normally one to be sentimental whispered to me. "I am in shock, I am in shock!"

Her eyes had misted over as she looked at Athina standing just in front of us. At that moment the teenage heiress was standing in for Aristotle Onassis, her uncle Alexander and for her mother Christina. The occasion was no longer a private visit. It had assumed all the formality of a minor state occasion.

I was now directly behind Athina, less than a foot away. The image of the last Onassis, this tall dark young beauty in her immaculately cut charcoal two-piece trouser suit, being respectfully received by the village was moving. I felt goose bumps on my arms and an involuntary shiver went down my spine. There are no words to properly describe that moment. It was local history in the making, the return of the Onassis dynasty from the dead. All of those present, including me and the camera crews felt the symbolism of the moment while a strange hush fell over the crowd.

One would have expected this slim, dignified 13 year-old girl to be bewildered by the reception.

More so since the officials and the villagers addressed her one by one in Greek, a language she did not understand. I stepped forward and stood next to her in case she wanted a translator, but I saw in her eyes that she knew exactly what the mayor was saying and understood what was happening.

The Onassis family had risen from its ashes.

There was an immediate, almost fairytale feudal rapport between Athina and the villagers. The legendary family was here again, in the flesh.

"Life in this village stopped ten years ago when your mother, Christina Onassis died," said the mayor to Athina. "Today life has returned to Scorpios and to us. Welcome home, Athina."

Three awed schoolgirls stepped forward and shyly gave Athina a large bouquet of daffodils, irises and red roses.

Athina had been an awkward and homely little girl when she last visited the island four years previously. Today the chrysalis of death which had trapped her family had opened and a beautiful butterfly had emerged. The spell was suddenly broken when one of the Scorpios employees stepped forward into the barrage of flashbulbs and tugged at Thierry's sleeve.

"The boat for Scorpios is ready," he said.

The Bertram cruiser carrying us with the bodyguards and a mountain of luggage was bumping noisily over the waves as the sea became choppier. Scorpios, heavily wooded, loomed in front of us when we turned round a headland and before long we tied up at the large jetty Onassis had built to hold his 340 foot superyacht the *Christina*.

Captain Anastassiades, the former yacht captain, was waiting with a row of cars for us. He motioned for us to enter the first vehicle, but Thierry had other ideas. He was not a guest here. He took the keys of the two white Mini Mokes, famously featured in photos of Onassis wedding to Jackie. He tossed me the keys of the second Moke.

"Alexis, drive that one," he said authoritatively, making it plain to all there that the owners were back on their island.

We were met at the Pink House by Mme. Olga who had been the housekeeper from the time Christina and Thierry had lived on the island. She was crying as she spoke to Thierry saying how happy she was to see the family back at last, but I noticed that Thierry and Athina were being no more than polite in listening to her. The reason for their reserve I later learned was that Olga and most of the staff had allied themselves with the Foundation and some of the staff had given critical press interviews about the family. The fact that they were being paid their salaries by Athina and owed her their loyalty escaped them. For the Onassis descendant this did not go unnoticed.

What surprised me when we entered the villa was how perfectly at home Athina was. She walked straight in, looked briefly round the room and collapsed on a sofa, stretching her legs out. It was the same sofa that her grandfather Aristotle had specifically had made for the Pink House so that he could stretch out and catnap in front of the fireplace.

Thierry sat next to Athina and lit a cigarette, loosening his tie. I left them to chat and went with the housekeeper to a villa a hundred yards further up the road. This was the Hill House, the simply furnished villa where Onassis himself lived when he was on the island and not sleeping on his yacht. Below the villa, down some twenty steps in the garden were the kitchens and staff quarters where our two English bodyguards had installed themselves in one room while Emilios and Petros, the Greek guards, took the adjacent one.

After unpacking I went back to the Pink House and asked Emilios who was outside now, where Thierry was.

"He went down towards the chapel on foot" he replied. I decided to follow Thierry, in order not to leave him alone. I walked for about half kilometer along the paved road past olive groves and a densely planted pine and cedar wood. Along the roadside there were rows of white and red oleander trees leading to the chapel near the bottom of the road on a bend where it approached the large dock.

I saw no sign of Thierry in the main room of the chapel. I then looked in a room to the left that contained the tombs of Aristotle and Artemis, Onassis' older sister. There was nobody there. Passing through a small arch into a chamber to the right I saw Thierry standing in front of Christina's white marble tomb with his back to me. His head was bent and his hand was resting lightly, gently stroking the polished marble surface of the raised tomb. He had not heard me approach and was deeply absorbed in his thoughts as he looked down at where the remains of Christina lay. For a while he stayed like that, and I made no noise or movement to disturb him.

It was strange for me to see to see this much-maligned man, accused of not caring for his first wife, of being a man with few feelings, here in this chapel, praying in private and obviously communicating in his own way with his dead wife and mother of his child. They were intensely private moments and I felt like an intruder. For anyone who could have witnessed the scene in the chapel there could be no doubt that he still harboured feelings for Christina. Suddenly, as if awaking from a trance he turned and saw me. There were tears running down his cheeks and his eyes were bloodshot. I stepped back to light a candle for each of the four of the Onassis family members who were buried in the chapel and followed Thierry outside.

We walked back without exchanging a word. Thierry only spoke when we reached the Pink House, asking me to come in. I told him I wanted to take a shower and change at the Hill House and would see him later on.

As soon as I entered my room the phone rang. It was the chef who wanted to know what I would like for dinner. This service was one of the pleasures of Scorpios. A guest could order anything to eat from the chefs who were on duty day and night. The five villas on Scorpios Island offer their guests the support facilities of a luxury hotel. There are professional standard laundry rooms, large kitchens and stores, a twenty-four hour telephone operator when guests are on the island and a large machine room and desalination plant on the south west corner of Scorpios. Additionally there are stables for horses and a farm which formerly housed cows to produce milk and cheese, while 36 staff kept the island running smoothly. When we arrived we saw no trace though of the Scorpios-bred pheasants, apparently they had flown off or been shot by members of the staff. On a later trip I was happy to see the pheasants were back in large numbers. The cost of maintenance of the island and its services ran to in excess of a million Euros a year.

 Thierry and Athina went across by boat to Nydri for a dinner I had booked for them at a fish taverna. Though I was a friend of the family I decided that while we were on Scorpios it would be better for me to stay out of sight of the television cameras and the paparazzi because the occasion of our visit was Christina's memorial. It was, and had to remain, a strictly family affair.

 When I had showered and changed I went down to the Pink House, the villa that Jackie had spent many months and a very large amount of Onassis' money to refurbish. It was her home for weeks at a time when she was on the island.

 Dinner was grilled sea bass, a salad of Scorpios-grown vegetables and an exquisite fruit flan. The quality of the cooking was expectedly on a par with that of a Michelin three-star restaurant since the chef was the same one who had cooked for Onassis, Jackie, Maria Callas and all the famous and demanding guests who had been on the "Christina".

 After dinner I settled on a couch and switched on the television. Our arrival at Scorpios was on every station. Three channels had live coverage of Athina and Thierry dining at the restaurant in Nydri. There was even an interview with the owner, who explained that Athina's mother used to eat at his taverna whenever she came to Scorpios. It wasn't exactly true, but it sounded good and no doubt brought him a lot of extra business the following summer.

At eleven fifteen Athina and Thierry returned, exhausted from their long day. Athina with a sigh of relief plopped onto one of the couches in an adjacent lounge. Thierry went to the bar asking me to join him for a drink. I noticed a row of bamboo chairs stacked against the wall behind the bar and remembered hearing that this was all that remained of Jackie's refurbishing of the villa. Jackie, soon after marrying Aristotle Onassis had remodeled and redecorating several of the Onassis properties, just as she had done at the White House after she married Jack Kennedy. Christina had thrown out everything that reminded her of the former first lady of the US whom she despised, saying that Jackie was only interested in her father's money and had brought bad luck everywhere she went.

Thierry and I sat and spoke for a long time. He told me about Christina and what their life had been like. He recounted stories of their stays on Scorpios and how different things were now.

"The island's facilities were quite basic, even primitive in some aspects, when Onassis had it, but he liked it that way," explained Thierry, "Christina had different ideas. I remember, Alexis, how surprised I was when I first came here and saw that the main bathroom had a half-tub, the ones you sit up in. Christina later upgraded the island houses and added "Main House" where we lived. The pool came later."

I had heard that Onassis never wanted a pool because he considered it excessive to have such fine beaches and the turquoise Ionian waters at one's feet and swim instead in recycled chlorinated water.

"Christina built most of the roads and put in the luxury touches," Thierry said. "We were happy here, but it did not last. There was too much pressure on us from people who had interests in the management of the fortune. None of Christina's marriages survived these attacks from the outside."

I asked him about Athina. Did she know much about Christina?

"Now that she is older I have started to tell her more about her mother. Tonight I will show her a letter her mother wrote before she died. She had asked me to give it to Athina when she grew up. There are things in it......" His voice trailed off and I saw him thinking about the woman he had once loved. It had been a doomed love. Christina, deeply troubled from her teenage days followed a lonely road after her divorce from Thierry, often begging him to go back and sometimes hurting him with her behaviour. It was a road that finally led her to Buenos Aires in 1988, to die alone kneeling next to a bathtub.

I finished my drink and left Thierry with his memories, making my way up the winding path towards the Hill house. Outside the door I saw the reassuring and vigilant figure of Emilios standing in the dark, keeping watch over the house where Athina was with her father. As I passed the kitchens and staff quarters further up the hill I heard the voice of men laughing and glimpsed the British bodyguards relaxing with the chef and his daughter. In front of them on the kitchen table a neat row of empty beer and whiskey bottles signalled the signs of an end to their career as Onassis bodyguards. I shook my head and went up to my room.

I was woken by the sound of the shutters banging. It was dawn and a strong breeze had picked up across the sea, forcing its way over the island, bending the oleander bushes almost flat along the edge of the lawn while low rain clouds hung in the sky. I decided to take a Mini Moke and went on a drive round the wooded island, stopping at various places along the way to admire the scenery and some of the 250 types of exotic trees Onassis had imported from around the world. The lawns surrounding the villas were from seed brought from Cape Town. On a later trip I was surprised to see the sheep and goats on the island had not chewed up the lawn and asked the gardener about this.

"Ah, Mr. Alexis," he replied, "Mr. Onassis chose this lawn because the grass is bitter and animals will not eat it". The genius of Onassis I thought, and how these details showed a man set apart in his thinking from other men.

I stopped briefly at the large jetty below the chapel to meet Stefanos Dianellos, the young journalist from "Ta NEA" newspaper and a female photographer he had brought with him to take photos of the memorial service. Thierry had been adamant about not having press on the island. He did not want Athina exposed to the media at anytime on

Scorpios and especially not while praying at her mother's tomb. He had promised this to Athina. On the other hand I explained to him that for historical importance, and for Athina herself, the return to Scorpios and the attendance by Thierry and Athina at Christina's memorial was too important an occasion, both for the Onassis family, and for Greece, not to be on record. He reluctantly agreed with my logic and spoke to Athina. We both made a promise to her that there would be no interview and no photographer in the chapel.

When I returned Emilios told me that Mr. Roussel was waiting for me for breakfast at the Pink House. I entered and I saw Thierry dressed somberly in a dark suit and tie, while Athina was wearing a charcoal grey suit and a white blouse. I was shocked at the change in their appearance from the night before. Thierry's eyes were red and his face drawn. Athina's eyelids were swollen and her eyes too were bloodshot. There was no doubt that the hours they had spent alone had been a time of great emotional strain as Thierry told Athina much more about her tragic mother. Thierry took me aside and said "I spoke to Athina about Christina last night. I read her the letter her mother wrote to her...» He had spoken at great depth to her about the woman who had died a few years previously and was buried in the chapel down the road.

Athina had obviously been crying for much of the time when Christina Onassis and her tragic life story was unfolded for her, sentence by sentence, by the man who had known her mother better than anyone else. Thierry carried a message across time and from beyond the grave to his daughter. I could see this morning that Athina was a changed girl and that she was ready and prepared to participate in the memorial service at the tomb of her mother.

There was understandably little conversation at breakfast; Thierry drank coffee while Athina pecked at a croissant. When it was time Athina went to fix her hair and Thierry took me out onto the rear terrace of the Pink House on the side that faces Lefkada Island and the village of Nydri three miles away.

"I didn't sleep at all last night," said Thierry, "Athina was upset about her mother. There was so much to talk about."

Athina came outside asking her father in French if it was time to go. Thierry nodded to her and they left by the stone steps, descending towards the drive that leads to the chapel. They were followed by Emilio and Petros. I had asked the guards to keep a discreet distance from the Roussels because of the media. I did not want bodyguards to appear in any shots of the memorial service for Christina. Leaving to go up to my room I saw the two ex-SAS guards standing outside, taking photographs of each other with the Pink House as background. I informed them that the Roussel's had already left and they had better get a move on if they were to catch up. Thierry later confided to me that he was going to replace the security team with a younger group when they returned to Switzerland because he was not happy with their recent performance.

Looking down the wooded slope I could now see a row of fishing and day boats anchored about fifty metres offshore. Their decks were tightly packed with paparazzi and television camera crews. Telephoto lenses pointed at Thierry and Athina as they walked towards the chapel. These distant shots were all the media would get because the entrance was on the other side of the chapel, facing away from the sea and from the journalist's hired boats.

I went back inside and waited for Athina and Thierry to return from the memorial service presided over by tiny Father Apostolis. I sat down once again and fielded a series of telephone calls from the press for the next hour until I heard the crackling of walkie-talkies and the sound of shuffling feet on the steps outside the house.

"It was a very good ceremony" said Thierry, "but we had a problem with the photographer. Athina was very upset."

"What happened?" I asked, surprised.

"She came very close and photographed Athina during the ceremony. Athina was distracted by the sound of the shutter clicking all the time and became very distressed."

I had specifically given instructions to the photographer not to approach to a distance of less than thirty metres in order to avoid just such an occurrence. For the young female photographer the temptation of having a world exclusive of the Onassis descendant bowing in prayer over her mother's grave was too much. The photographer had gone right up to the open chapel door to record the service inside.

"Come, let's go for lunch," said Thierry, suddenly cheering up.

Father Apostolis walked by my side, wanting to tell me all about the ceremony. He spoke no English and asked me to translate his words for Athina and Thierry who were walking next to us.

We entered the cavernous reception room of the Hill House where the staff of Scorpios had in the meantime laid out a series of dishes on a long buffet table. The main item was a whole sea bass boiled in herbs and served with home-made mayonnaise, steamed new potatoes and young carrots. Fish is the traditional dish served at Greek Orthodox memorial services and is associated with early Christian times when a fish symbol was the secret sign of recognition among Christians. Today boiled fish is still eaten in Greece after memorial services in honour of the souls of the departed.

We served ourselves and sat at one of the round tables next to the open doors leading to the terrace. The sun was out again but it was too bright to sit outside, something not unusual in Greece even in November. Father Apostolis dressed in his black cassock and sprightly for his eighty-odd years was fascinated by young Athina, seeing how much she had grown since he last saw her. She had been an infant then and he had baptized her here in this same room.

"I can see her mother in her" he said to me, and then addressing Athina in Greek "I remember your baptism here, when the whole family were present. It was a happy occasion".

He turned to me "Don't tell them this, it is not the right time, but Athina's godfather, George Livanos – Christina's uncle - did not give Athina and

Thierry the support which his duty to them demanded."

Later Father Apostolis bravely made this same statement on camera for the eight o'clock news, knowing that the four administrators in the Onassis Foundation and Athina's uncle would be displeased by anyone coming out in public to support Thierry or his daughter.

After lunch the four of us went out onto the terrace to admire the view.

"This is the beauty of Scorpios" said Thierry "It is how I remember the island. It is so green and the sea on a calm winter day like today is just like blue glass. Christina and I used to sit here in the evenings and watch the moon come up from behind the hills over there." He pointed to a row of granite mountains wrapped in a mantle of silver-blue haze on the other side of a wide stretch of the sparkling Ionian Sea in front of us.

Athina wandered back inside the house to choose some out-of-season cherries from the buffet table leaving Thierry and me alone with the priest. Thierry took out a bulging white envelope from his jacket pocket and gave it to Father Apostolis.

"Ask him to give it to a needy family in Nydri," instructed Thierry. How unlike his daughter's later attitude of indifference to the suffering of others this act of generosity by Thierry was. I translated the request.

The priest was visibly moved. "Thank them both dearly from me," he said and added "The gift will do good. I assure them of that."

A bodyguard came out onto the terrace and discreetly pointed to his watch, letting me know it was time for us to leave for the airport.

We returned to Athens on the midday commercial flight from nearby Aktion airport. There was a minor panic because of a delay in take-off which put Athina in danger of missing her Athens connection to Geneva. This was taken care of when the captain radioed ahead to the control tower at Athens airport. A patrol car was waiting on the airport runway to lead our minibus across the tarmac to the runways at the Olympic terminal at the East International Airport where the Swissair plane was waiting for its last scheduled passenger. Athina kissed her father goodbye and hurriedly went up the steps of the plane with her bodyguards, relieved to have caught her flight because she had an important exam at school the next morning.

I dropped Thierry off at the Athenaeum Intercontinental Hotel. He too had an important, though less pleasant, appointment the next day. He had to be in courtroom number 9 for the resumption of his defamation case.

A Romantic Onassis wedding by the sea

The beginning of 1999 was a period of the intense legal confrontation between Thierry and the 4 Greeks. The mosaic of court actions and counter actions was so complicated, and the jurisdictions so widespread with overlapping decisions that it took me months to understand the overall picture. In the forefront were two civil court cases which had been heard in Greece. Other cases were under deliberation in the Cantonal courts of Switzerland. The Swiss Juvenile Authority - the Tutelle - an independent court authority responsible for overseeing the financial affairs of minors, had recently handed down a historic decision ejecting Papadimitriou and the entire board of the patrimony. This decision was superseded three days later by another Swiss court ruling. The new decision now suspended the Tutelle decision which had in turn given management of the fortune to KPMG, the international auditing firm. The management was now given back to the Greeks. Almost at the same time the Federal High Court of Switzerland passed down a ruling allowing the Tutelle to install another international auditing firm, Ernst and Young, to check on certain transactions carried out by the board over the previous three years. Thierry himself had an appeal coming up in Greece, against the defamation sentence passed on him in December 1998, while yet another criminal court was considering charging Papadimitriou for defamatory statements in the press against Thierry. It was a matter of note that many of the court cases initiated by the Four Greeks were defined as being "*gegen*

Athina Roussel" – against Athina Roussel. The legal expenses for these cases were charged to her by her four administrators.

Fourteen legal firms located in Greece, France and Switzerland were working for the Roussel family, while a number of expensive legal firms had been employed by Papadimitriou and the Foundation in an effort to get Thierry out of their hair, allowing them to retain management of Athina's money. Against this incredibly complicated background of international suit and counter suit were the psychologically disturbing scenarios that had previously terrified Athina. 1999 was a very difficult time for the children and for Thierry as well.

Suddenly there was a welcome change of climate - an Onassis wedding in Greece. After three funerals in the family it was a most welcome change. Thierry called me to say that George Drakos, Athina's second cousin and grandson of Aunt Kalliroi, was getting married to Vicki Ioannides, the daughter of an Olympic airline pilot (no relation to Paul Ioannides of the Foundation). The wedding, Thierry explained, was to take place at the private chapel of Aunt Kalliroi's seaside estate at Lagonissi on July 3rd. Over five hundred guests were expected. The arrival of Athina at the centre of such a large family gathering would firmly place the Roussel family back in the centre of Athenian society and put the family into the proper perspective regarding their position as Onassis' rightful heirs. Papadimitriou and his associates were not invited to the wedding. It was the first public snub by the Greek members of the Onassis family against the former family employee-executives who had acted so badly against Aristotle's granddaughter and her father.

When Gaby announced to the children that they would be coming to Greece, young Johanna asked "Mum, is that the country where everybody pushes everyone else?" The rush of the paparazzi and the pressing TV crews during their previous visits had made Athina's little sister think that this is how everybody behaved in Greece!

The short walk from the VIP lounge of the East Air Terminal to our waiting cars was accomplished by our bodyguards and Greek police escort driving a wedge through the crowd of paparazzi, television reporters and well-wishers. When we settled into our cars I was pleased to see that Athina new bodyguards, two of whom were black former SAS commandos with intimidating looks and shaven heads, had an incredibly alert manner and were continuously in communication with the other members of our security team. The Greek Minister of Public Order and the head of the VIP section of the police headquarters had given us an additional escort of highly trained police officers, the same ones who looked after President Clinton and Prince Charles on their visits in the same year. Additionally I had Stefanos, our private head of security, Emilios, and a motorcycle outrider to ride next to the rear wheel of Athina's minivan as well as some other men to coordinate the team.

Our convoy made quick progress to the Astir Palace Hotel at Vouliagmeni, the exclusive seaside suburb resort of Athens. The hotel is accessed along a wide palm lined avenue that turns onto a large pine-forested peninsula. There among large villas and exclusive resort apartments lies the hotel complex in a hundred acres of lush semi-tropical grounds. Gaby had requested me to book rooms there after seeing the hotel with its three private beaches on a previous trip when we had sought refuge from the press while waiting for a delayed flight to Switzerland to be announced. The hotel staff were waiting for us and the entry bar had already been lifted at the gates as we arrived, chased by press cars and motorcycles. Getting out of our cars we swept into a large lounge overlooking the sea: heads everywhere turned to look at our party as conversation in the large hotel lobby stopped. Athina was by now used to the fuss made over her in Greece and just wanted to get up to her room to eat something as it was nearly four o'clock. The rest of us were in a hurry to change out of our jackets and ties as the temperature was over 40 degrees centigrade.

Our bookings at the hotel had been cancelled by accident from Boislande and the hotel management had at the last moment miraculously found a row of rooms for us on the top floor, no mean feat at this time of the year when the hotel was full of Greek ship-owners, minor Arab princes and international businessmen and politicians. Connie Perez, the hotel's Columbian PR head undertook to escort Athina and her family and to make things smooth for their stay.

The children disappeared into their rooms in a state of excitement while Thierry, Gaby and I settled down to have a snack and a drink and to briefly catch up on what had been happening. I was surprised at the change in Thierry since I last had seen him. He looked unusually haggard, his hair was long and shaggy over his collar and the whites of his eyes were a malarial yellow. He looked quite ill. I was worried to see that he had also lost an alarming amount of weight, a fact that could not be hidden by the padded shoulders of his blue suit. The jacket drooped on his shoulders. It was unlike Thierry to be like this and it showed me that he must have been under considerable stress for quite a while.

"What news of Papadimitriou?" he asked. It was his standard question.

"I am always optimistic about our cases, Thierry," I answered. "The Four are not the people they were two years ago."

Thierry was not to be cheered up.

"We are finished - they have the management of Athina's patrimony now, and I am very afraid they will not give Athina her inheritance easily. Athina will not be able to fight Papadimitriou alone. It is over. "

Thierry had never in the past shown this defeatism.

"Why do you say that?" I asked.

"The Swiss court gave them back the management 3 days after the Tutelle ruled it must go to KPMG."

I admit that this ruling had been a shock at the time. Later when I discussed it with lawyers in Greece they explained that it would be quite normal for a stay to be granted until the Four Greeks appeal had been heard, otherwise it would mean that the fortune would go back and forth like a ping-pong ball. All the secrets of Athina's accounts and holdings would then have to be revealed to an outside company (KPMG) before the courts had ruled definitively on who should have the management of the patrimony.

I explained this to Thierry, but he was too dejected to be persuaded by my argument.

"There is of course no guarantee that the courts will not overturn the original decision and leave the management to Papadimitriou, Thierry," I added, "but there is a logic to the way the Swiss are handling the matter."

"I don't think so," concluded Thierry. I, though, was still optimistic and told him so. He was very tired and so I left him to take a nap. He would need this break because we had to leave for the wedding in less than two hours.

At six o'clock our convoy left the Astir Palace hotel. There were once more a group of photographers inside the grounds, a situation which unfortunately was allowed by the management who otherwise were very accommodating of their famous young client.

Emilios was riding a motorcycle in front of us, shrilly blowing a whistle to warn pedestrians and other cars of our approach, while the accompanying police cars followed us, their rotating beacons warning other cars to give way. Our convoy drove rapidly along the tight curves of the coastal road, past the barren brown scenery which lies between Vouliagmeni and Lagonissi where the wedding was to take place. On the way the busy road passes in front of several typically South Mediterranean resort settlements, with their mix of apartment houses, villas, tourist shops and cafes. The presence of two parked patrol cars at the 37.5 km marker of the Athens–Cape Sounion road signalled that we had arrived at Aunt Kalliroi's lush beachfront estate. There were cameras crews and paparazzi there waiting for us. Uniformed police held them back so we could go through the gates into the property where Athina's aunt Marilena Patronikola, the mother of the groom, was waiting for us in the forecourt of the villa, next to the chapel. Marilena was with her companion, the motorcycle-riding surgeon Mihalis Gyras, a man known for his intelligent humour and his three beautiful daughters from his previous marriages. Marilena was Christina Onassis's first cousin and had been very close to her. I had met with her several times before and had been surprised the first time I saw her how like Christina she was.

Marilena, of medium height was attractive and intelligent and common Athenian folklore said that in addition to her former husbands (among whom was a well known industrialist, and the head of the largest state bank in Greece) there had been famous admirers who had kneeled at her feet – one a charismatic serving prime minister and another a famous singer whose silken voice and matinee idol good looks melted the hearts of most of the Greek female population between the ages of sixteen and eighty.

In the van behind me the Roussels were now stumbling over the folded seats of the vehicle and stepping down onto the gravel forecourt, brushing their jackets and straightening their clothes. All activity in the forecourt stopped as waiters and guests alike turned to stare at the Roussel family. Athina was wearing a long white dress, slit to above the knee, and a red jacket. Her hair had been cut short, a fact that was to be widely reported in the domestic and international media hungry for anything that had to do with the Onassis heiress.

No journalists were allowed into the wedding area because Thierry was aware that all attention would centre on Athina, something that could potentially spoil the wedding for the bride and groom. This after all was their day. The media making do of a difficult situation for them lined up outside the villa hedge. We could hear them calling out in the hope that Athina would turn round to be photographed. At the front entrance where we had parked ushers in dinner jackets were guiding the guests through the interior of the house to the lawns which bordered the beach in the front of the villa. We had arrived early and so were able to stretch our legs before the ceremony began.

Thierry was talking to my wife Dimitra, who had come independently, and I found an opportunity to sit on a swinging garden settee from where I could observe the guests arriving. Athina and Gaby went inside the house to talk to Aunt Kalliroi, while Johanna, Sandrine and Erik wandered off to the pool, wishing they could change into swimsuits and dive in from the high board as they had done the summer before.

Smart starched linen and heavy silverware had been laid out on round tables, allowing for a total of eight hundred guests to be seated in the garden. Several attractive-looking young women in evening wear moved from table to table to make sure that everything was in place. One girl who wore a tight semi-transparent white dress caught the attention of the males who were wandering around. The girl was responsible for making sure that bowls of professionally arranged flowers were placed on every table. The image of her bending forward and tantalizingly revealing the outline of string panties through the white dress with its low cut back was broadcast by all the news channels reporting on the Onassis family wedding that day. Unknowingly, the anonymous blonde girl entered the news archives in Greece for ever; her image now part of the Onassis family heritage whenever the wedding footage is shown on television.

Looking out to the beach I saw a series of caravans parked on the sand with camera crews and their tripods precariously balanced on the vehicle roofs just beyond the perimeter fence of the Patronikola villa. Already tiny red lights indicated which cameras were rolling. Tall telescopic antennae and satellite dishes sent out the images to the television studios.

The wedding started an hour later at 8 p.m. outside the chapel near the entrance to the villa. As I stood on the lawn, among the hundreds of other guests outside the chapel, I had the opportunity to observe how at home Athina seemed here among her Greek relatives. The presence of the other guests, whose attention was on her most of the time, did not in the least bit perturb her. Athina knew who she was, and though she was just fourteen I could see that her family upbringing had given her the poise to deal with her situation.

The ceremony and reception made for an evening of unsurpassed glamour. Diamonds, emeralds and rubies from Harry Winston in New York and Cartier in Paris were in evidence throughout, together with heavy hand-beaten gold necklaces and earrings from Lalaounis and Zolotas in Athens, Geneva and Paris. Creations were displayed like the treasures of a maharani's dowry. As the bearded priest in his gold-thread embroidered robes went through the colourful Greek Orthodox ceremony, my wandering eye could not help observing the enormous expense many guests had gone to in order to make their appearance at the Onassis family estate that evening. Details stuck in my mind, especially the virgin beige soles of women's footwear indicating that much of the extraordinarily expensive apparel had been bought or budgeted for specifically for the wedding where the granddaughter of the "richest man on earth" would be in attendance.

When the chapel ceremony was over the Roussel family, I and Dimitra went and sat at table Number 2. With us was the second sister of Ari Onassis, Merope Konialides from Monte Carlo, and her Swedish daughter-in-law. Athina sat on my left, Dimitra on my right, next to Thierry, who was next to Aunt Merope. Gaby was next and the younger Roussel children were next to Gaby.

The sun had gone down now, and the whole setting was softly lit by candles and garden lights, while four long buffet tables under white awnings were receiving the attention of high-hatted chefs and meat carvers.

The guests present represented every section of Greek high society. Ship-owners from Monte Carlo and London, Athenian industrialists, some with glamorous younger wives, politicians working the crowd. Internationally known film directors and some actors were also present. Onassis relatives were there and so were their relatives. A young glamorous twenty-something crowd of scions of famous families sat down next to well-exercised girlfriends with perfect tans and shiny hair. Women in thirty thousand dollar designer gowns walked by, wearing the mortgage price of an oil tanker in emeralds, rubies or diamonds on their necks and wrists, while less expensively dressed ladies hung onto the arms of expatriate banking and marine insurance executives.

When the guests were all seated the klieg lights on the roof of the TV vans were turned on, and the live band played for the entry of the bride and groom. How different indeed was the rough and contemptuous treatment of the media in Brazil when Athina and Doda wed six years later. Viki Ioannides, the bride, was ravishing in her long white embroidered gown as she swept in, accompanied by the full sound of the band, holding her wide wedding dress so as not to have it trail on the paths leading through the lawn. Viki and George went to sit at the elevated long table which was reserved for the immediate family.

From almost the moment we sat down the Swedish relative next to Athina took out a camera from her handbag and started taking pictures of the heiress, the flashbulb blinding us every few seconds. This went on all through dinner. For a moment we breathed in relief, thinking she had run out of film, but then she brought out another camera and continued shooting. I knew how Athina hated photographs and cameras because of the hounding the paparazzi had subjected her to since she was a baby, but she was concealing her feelings very well at the table. Thierry and Gaby showed no visible response to the photo intrusion by Athina's distant Swedish aunt, but I knew that they too must be annoyed, as we all were.

I had wondered when the first suitors would make their appearance at our table. I overheard the Swedish woman telling her teenage son and daughter to make sure they sat near Athina when a chair was available. This plan was put into action sooner than I expected. When I returned from the buffet I found the woman's son firmly ensconced in my chair next to Athina. He saw me standing with my plate in my hand, and ignored me.

"Young man," I said menacingly, "That is my chair."

He looked at me with an expression of annoyance. It was clear he was not happy to have to vacate his newly occupied territory so close to a famous quarry. The same thing happened when I got up to greet a friend who came over from one of the other tables. When I turned round, the daughter of the Swedish lady had enthroned herself on my chair and was not budging. I told her once to please get up and was ignored. With the second reminder, she looked up, as did her brother, staring daggers. Their mother seeing all the time what was going on took it all quite in her stride. I was standing up with nowhere to sit, while my food was getting cold, but still the woman made no move to tell her kids to vacate my seat. It was time for action. I stepped forward, grabbed the back of my chair and tipped it forward, necessitating a quick evacuation of the chiffon-laced teenage butterball who was in dire danger of rolling on the lawn at Athina's feet. But I was not the only victim of these little predators. Thierry and I got up at some point to fetch ice-cream and fruit. This time Dimitra, to protect my rights, put her hand firmly on my chair seat, but Thierry's chair, now vacant, was plucked from the table and placed next to Athina. Thierry, when he returned and seeing he had nowhere to sit, gave up and went over to another table whose guests had left earlier. Athina, accustomed to hangers on and persistent pests suffered this attention but was obviously relieved when Sandrine and Johanna suggested they all go over to the dance floor now that the music had begun.

In spite of the festive atmosphere around us Thierry was pre-occupied and Gaby sensed this, keeping by his side for most of the time to cheer him up. Later she went to dance with little Johanna who was having the time of her life, oblivious to the television cameras forty yards away which were filming every move the family made.

When Athina returned I noticed a small distinguished-looking man with a goatee circling round our table, his attention on us. I guessed that he was waiting for a chance to introduce himself and was not wrong. He came and spoke to Thierry. It was Nicolas Gage, the best selling Greek-American author of the book "Eleni" that had been made into a successful film. He later wrote a long article for American Vanity Fair about the heiress, and as a result is often quoted in the media. He describes this brief meeting with the heiress in his article and he was able to speak to her twice by phone later while preparing his story. In fact he was one of the very few journalists ever to speak to the heiress, though Thierry refused to answer his questions directly and I had to act as go-between in order to give the journalist the answers he wanted from Roussel.

For Athina the wedding at her aunt's house was to be her emergence from the Roussel family chrysalis into the heart of Athenian society. The evening was pleasant. I always had fun in those days with Athina, who was intelligent and had a mature sense of humour. Often, on other occasions, I used to make little jokes when media pressure became intense to distract her, but this evening there was to be more fun of an unspoken kind regarding the state of siege enacted by the society hopefuls circling our table, prompted on by their own ambition or those of ambitious parents who saw in the Onassis heiress the answer to so many of their prayers. An additional spur to their interest was that Athina was now a young woman with exceptionally good looks. She sensed this power, and though we did not discuss it directly, a casual glance between us and the twinkle of mirth in her eyes indicated that even at fourteen she knew the attraction that both her name but also her good looks were having on the young men who wandered deliberately close to our table.

I found Athina interesting because beneath her poise and air of nonchalance in public their was a very normal and curious teenager who would often show great surprise at some story I would have to tell, or laugh at some titbit of innocent gossip.

Having brought up a teenage daughter to whom I had always been close I had a feeling for what little girls and teenagers found interesting and what annoyed them in adults. I enjoyed seeing the amusement of Athina at some little thing I said, or her curiosity for an unknown fact. Journalists always asked me the standard question "What impresses a girl with a billion dollars and the whole world at her feet?"

"Little things," I said, "and a sense of humour."

Athina, tall and poised – 1.78m - moved among the crowd that evening with the confidence of someone who knows that all eyes are on her. The next day two television directors confronted me, accusing me of coaching Athina how to act that evening in front of the cameras.

"Why do you say that?" I asked.

"Every time she got up to get something from the buffet, she would walk for a few steps looking at the various dishes on the table, as if reviewing a guard of honour, than she would stop, pause, and turn 3/4 profile to the cameras. After this she continued walking without once showing she was aware of our six cameras filming her. Her pacing and her pauses were too professional a performance to have been accidental."

"I am innocent!" I replied laughing, though I knew they were not convinced. But it was the truth. Athina was the perfect media girl that evening. She had both the Roussel poise and the Onassis flair in handling the press. Sadly this was to change when things went terribly wrong three years later in the Roussel household.

We left the wedding reception at 2 a.m. Athina had stolen the show all evening. Normally blasé multi-millionaires and granddames of legendary shipping dynasties had been reduced to eating out of her hand. It was clear that on July 3rd 1999 the granddaughter of Onassis had stepped into her famous grandfather's shoes for all to see, and I could see how proud Thierry and Gaby were of the way she had carried herself that evening in front of eight hundred critical pairs of eyes present and the adoring eyes of millions of television viewers watching the live television broadcast of the heiress with the Mona Lisa smile.

The next morning I picked up my newspapers from Mrs. Meli, who owned the newsagents shop near my apartment in Melissia.

"Athina was a princess. Onassis would have been proud and so would her mother if she were alive," she said, handing me a pile of morning papers with full page articles on Athina. There were large photos of her with admiring headlines

Beautiful Athina returns, An Onassis wedding – glamour again, Athina stuns with her new look".

Of all the headlines the truest one was -

A Star is Born

The television footage of the wedding that evening showed Athina walking on the lawns by the sea among the hundreds of glamorous guests. Tens of black-tied waiters, the illuminated pool, the live orchestra playing Latin, Greek and pop music and the flickering candlelight under the star-filled sky brought back memories of a distant past to another member of the Onassis family. Most of those at our table were on the dance floor moving to the rhythms of classics like "Day by Day" and "Vamos A La Playa". I was sitting now next to Merope Konialides, Aristotle's sister. She told me what life was like in Argentina when she and Aristotle had lived there.

"It was like this every night," she explained, "until Peron's regime took over and ruined the country."

Despite the romanticized Argentina we had all seen in "Evita" I knew the reality was very different and that a way of life that had been the envy of the world and the inspiration for movies such as *Gilda* had been destroyed by the violent social changes which the populist dictatorial regime Peron had brought in.

"This reminds me so much of Buenos Aires in the Thirties and Forties," Merope repeated, her eyes misting as memories of her youth flooded back. Then she looked up and seeing that Athina had returned and was sitting next to me, on my left once again, chatting with some friends, said quietly, "If only Aristotle had been alive tonight to see Athina." Her hopes, as were those of nearly everyone, were very high for the heiress who seemed to have everything and the world stage was waiting for her to enter from the wings to centre stage after her coming of age.

There was a strange closeness, like a presence at the table at that moment. I think we all felt it. Perhaps Onassis *was* there, sitting with us and watching his granddaughter. Or perhaps it was just the scented moist sea air which hugged each of us as the atmosphere cooled with the approach of dawn of a new summer day.

Christina's demons

"Thierry" I said, "I never understood your refusal to father another child with Christina."

"Alexis, there was a reason," he replied, "and it had to do with when I first married Christina."

We were now standing on the small covered wooden balcony facing out over the rolling Boislande lawns. The shining silver strip of water which was Lake Leman lay in the distance. As Thierry spoke I could not but help see why Christina should have had such a desire to have another child by this stunningly good-looking aristocrat with his intense deep-blue eyes, and thick blond-accented hair.

"The problem existed even when I married Christina. She was taking drugs all the time. Amphetamines to wake her up, other pills to boost her in the day, barbiturates to make her sleep. It was awful. I told her that she would have to stop the drugs. Especially if we were to have a child. Finally I gave Christina an ultimatum and to her credit she broke her habit."

I myself had heard of Christina's reliance on drugs and her binges in the past. There have been numerous passages in the international press about this. The drug problem was never denied by those who were close to her.

"The worst thing was that Christina would go through sudden changes in mood," explained Thierry, "I did not want the future mother of my children to take drugs. Anyway, Christina who was a very strong person understood this and stayed clean for months.

She eventually became pregnant with Athina. We were in Eleuthera in the Bahamas when we found out and it was one of the happiest times of our life together."

Thierry looked down for a moment, his face clouding.

"One day I came back and saw that Christina was completely confused. It was obvious she had taken a large dose of pills again. The sight of her swollen belly made me angry and I worried that she could have done such a thing. I wondered where she had got the drugs from, and we had a big fight with Christina. Eleni, who had just come from New York, was a witness to the scene."

As he told the story I could see Thierry was in a state of distress at the painful memory of those days.

"One day I walked into the house and Christina was not there. Eleni had not seen her either, so I went into the garden to look for her. Christina was lying on her back on the lawn, unconscious. I rushed her to the clinic and the doctor confirmed that she had again taken a large dose of drugs. She regained consciousness later and we returned home. I was worried sick as to whether our baby would be affected by what Christina was doing and so we flew to Paris where I sent Christina to our obstetrician for a check, and also to prepare for when she would have the baby. The obstetrician, when we went to see him, called me outside the room, looking very concerned.

"Mr. Roussel," he said to me, "with the amount of drugs your wife is taking I am worried for the baby unless something is done quickly""

Thierry's mobile phone rang at that moment; it was the driver saying that he was waiting downstairs to take him back to Lussy. Thierry rang off and returned to our conversation.

"The doctor said that in order to save the child Christina would have to have a Caesarean operation. The baby would be premature but if we waited then there was no guarantee as to what could happen".

"You were the best, Ari, and you were the worst!"

Ari Onassis drank. He enjoyed alcohol just as he enjoyed chasing women and making money. I remember Onassis on several occasions as he sat at one of the adjacent tables in the gloomy Grande Bretagne Hotel bar, drinking with his business colleague and friend Professor Georgakis. Late at night when Ari had things on his mind he would go to Tourkolimano, the well- known C- shaped picturesque yacht harbour in Piraeus. There, in one of the hole-in-the-wall eateries with rough stucco whitewashed walls decorated haphazardly with bits of fishing nets, fading posters of Fix beer, bits of mirror and dog-eared calendars Onassis would sit on one of the Spartan wood and raffia *kafeneio* chairs knocking back one glass after another of Tsantali ouzo or Johnny Walker whisky. He did this, eating *mezedes* as he took the pulse of street life, chatting with a hodge-podge of out-of-work sailors, labourers, lottery ticket sellers and prostitutes who came in to have a bite to eat and something to drink. Bars and alcohol were a way of life for Onassis. It was a chance meeting in a bar in Buenos Aires when he was in his twenties that was to change his life and connect him to shipping.

Costas Gratsos was the son of an established Greek ship-owner. It was customary in those days before the invention of training simulators for the scions of shipping families to travel on the family vessels to get firsthand knowledge of how the ships were run, how the crew functioned, where to get supplies and to meet their agents and Greek Consuls in far away harbours where the family-owned fleet plied its trade. Costas Gratsos was an urbane young man and accepted this apprenticeship as a necessary part of his training as a rite-of-passage to becoming a full-fledged ship-owner. This was not to say that he did not miss the night life and the girls when he sat with the captain on the bridge of a boat looking out across dark seas on a stormy night. But each trip ended with a harbour and Gratsos looked forward to the next landfall and its welcoming fleshpots.

The boat he was travelling on during one particular trip docked in Buenos Aires. That evening after showering and changing into his smart hand-tailored land clothes Costas Gratsos made his way to a bar in the city. As he sat in the gloomy interior he noticed a short young man of Mediterranean complexion sitting a couple of stools away. Gratsos cosmopolitan eye observed the expensive cut of the young man's clothes and discerned an unusual confidence for a man who was barely into his twenties. The two of them soon struck up a conversation and Gratsos was happy to find that his new found drinking companion in this exotic setting was a fellow Greek. The man told Gratsos that his name was Ari Onassis. He was a refugee from Asia Minor and was now in the cigarette trade in Argentina. Gratsos was immediately impressed by the young and brash Onassis. There was something compelling in his confidence and in the way he spoke. Onassis it was obvious was fiercely determined to make money, something Gratsos already had. As the two Greeks sat drinking their talk turned to women, something for which they both shared a passion. From that day on their friendship was sealed. Gratsos was constantly with Onassis, acting as a mentor. Onassis in the meantime, with Gratsos at his side, made money and more money. He also admired Gratsos cosmopolitan ways. Gratsos was a bachelor who spent a fortune on expensive hotels, glamorous women and a high profile lifestyle. Onassis soon followed suit, mimicking and soon surpassing his friend's penchant for the good things in life.

When the two met Onassis was having a problem with his cigarette business. Rents were high in Buenos Aires and Onassis did not know where to store his stock of cigarettes. Gratsos suggested that Ari should look at one or two of the small ships which were tied up in port. There was a recession at the time and there were many boats off-charter going for a song. Onassis went down to the harbour with Gratsos the next day and bought a small vessel to use as a floating storage warehouse. The first step had been taken, Onassis had become a ship-owner and it was Costas Gratsos who had set him on his way to becoming the world's best known shipping tycoon

Gratsos stayed with Onassis for the rest of his life. There was a bond between them which was stronger than that among many brothers. After Onassis died in 1975 Christina slowly pushed Gratsos out of her life. It was said that she was influenced in this by Papadimitriou. What is known is that a member of the Onassis Foundation, Vlassopoulos, a shipowner's son himself and a childhood friend who went to work for Onassis wrote in his book "Memories of a Life" that he had an argument with Papadimitriou because the latter kept speaking badly about Gratsos to other members of the Onassis Foundation after Gratsos' death.

In October of 2001 during a television interview I casually mentioned Gratsos and his lifelong friendship with Onassis. I explained that Papadimitriou had been an employee of Onassis and one of his in-house lawyers but that he was never a bosom friend as he had been presented in some Greek newspapers. I supported this with the fact that few knew Papadimitriou before the conflict with Thierry Roussel. Those who did know him knew him primarily as one of Onassis legal staff. It had always been Onassis and Gratsos as long as I could remember. Gratsos was the only lifetime friend of Onassis.

The next morning I received a call from the Gratsos shipping offices in central Athens. It was Constantine Gratsos, the nephew of Costas on the phone, telling me he had seen the programme the previous evening and was pleased that I had finally put the record right regarding his uncle. We chatted for a while and agreed to meet. A few weeks later I went to the glass and marble Gratsos Shipping Building on Panepistimiou St where Constantine and his brother have their Standard Bulk Shipping fleet offices on the 6th and 7th floors.

On entering the reception area I saw the usual metal ship scale models in glass display cases but here the woodwork of the offices, the expensive blue and grey carpets, bleached wood paneling and white marble radiated opulent good taste. The Gratsos offices smelled of "Old Money", something that Onassis had respected.

I met Constantine Gratsos upstairs in his large office and we chatted about Onassis and about Costas Gratsos who had been the *bon viveur* of the family. Constantine Gratsos the younger had many tales to tell me about Ari Onassis. He recounted how one night before the war Ari and uncle Costas Gratsos were at Claridge's Hotel in London. As usual the two men were drinking in the bar. One drink followed another, and then another, and then another. Onassis mentioned to Gratsos that he had booked a flight to Oslo the next morning to meet some Norwegian ship-owners about a deal he was setting up. As the evening progressed the two friends became more and more intoxicated. When the night wore on even further Gratsos finally decided it was time for him to return to his suite. Onassis stayed behind to finish his drink.

In the morning when Gratsos came down for breakfast he noticed that there was some agitated discussion in the reception area. He asked what was happening and was informed that there had been an aviation disaster that morning. The flight from London to Oslo had crashed, killing all aboard. Gratsos was stunned. It was Onassis' flight. Not knowing what to do he headed directly for the bar to mourn his friend.

After the second or third drink he heard a rasping sound by his feet. Looking down he saw Onassis happily snoring on the floor. He had passed out at the bar and spent all night hugging the foot rail. Onassis had missed his flight and saved his life. As I sat listening to these stories the door to Constantine Gratsos office opened and a man came in who introduced himself as the other Gratsos brother. He sat down and joined in the conversation with his own reminiscences. The Gratsos nephews have many memories of Ari, something attested to by several photos in the office showing their father with Onassis at their villa and on the "Christina".

Whenever one hears of Onassis and Gratsos one will inevitably hear in the same breath some anecdote concerning ships, a drinking episode, or glamorous women. One of these episodes had to do with the time when the two young friends were walking in Manhattan on their way to P.J.Clarke's, the famous New York bar and watering hole of the rich and famous. Onassis and Gratsos were regular clients at P.J.'s, whose proprietor had a soft spot for his sybaritic Greek clients. Onassis however had a problem with P.J.'s. He did not like the food there so he made an arrangement which allowed him to bring his own sausages to be grilled and served to him at the bar.

On this particular occasion Ari and Gratsos were on the way to the bar when they were stopped in the street by a man called Moore, the then President of Citibank. It was a time when everyone in New York knew everyone. Moore was curious to know what was in the limp package Onassis was carrying under his arm. Ari obliged him by taking out a string of sausages and explaining to the startled banker that this was the fare that he had arranged for the owner of P.J.'s to cook for him and Gratsos. The banker looked in wonder as the two young Greek millionaires disappeared inside the bar carrying their sausages with them.

It was at this time that anyone who was anyone would dine at the El Morocco. In the famous club there were three zones with strict social delineation. First there was a seating area for celebrity clients, and then there was the dance floor. Directly beyond this was a third section, a seating area known as Siberia because only the tourists and unknowns would be seated there.

Onassis and Gratsos arrived at El Morocco one evening without a reservation. The celebrity seating area was full and there was no question of the proprietor seating them in Siberia, so he put a table for the two Greeks on the raised dance floor. This was the Holy of Holies for diners. Only one other table was allowed on the dance floor that night. When Onassis looked over he nodded almost imperceptibly to its sole occupant, so as not to be noticed. The table was occupied by a much feared Sicilian mafia boss who controlled the New York waterfront. Onassis of course knew him. Without the don's blessing and cooperation no ship could load and unload if the owner wanted to avoid problems and Onassis was not a man to have his ships delayed by striking dockworkers.

Years later the services of Gratsos were called for by the Onassis family in a particularly delicate matter. Christina, against the wishes of her family, had married Serge Kausov, a Russian shipping manager who was reputed to be a KGB agent. Gratsos, acting for the family undertook to go to Moscow where Christina was living in a two room flat. Larger dwellings were just not available nor were they of course for sale under the Soviet Communist regime.

Instead of returning with Christina Gratsos ended up staying months in Moscow after succumbing to Christina's pleading for him to help her get a better apartment. Gratsos called upon the services of an old student-days friend to do the impossible. The Russian friend in question had been with Gratsos in Paris and in Zurich in the Twenties. The Russian was an exiled prince who had escaped the Bolsheviks with his life and little else. With Gratsos they had shared in high jinks as students. One notorious incident involved the hoisting of a Communist flag in conservative Zurich shortly after the Russian revolution. The effect on the conservative burghers of Zurich on seeing the Red flag waving in the central square can only be imagined. The prince being a man of supreme practicality and exhibiting acute judgment for new opportunities later decided to go home to Russia where he buried his royal past and became an active member of the Revolutionary Communist party. His rise to the top of the Union of Soviet Socialist People's Republics' power structure was rapid. By the seventies when Christina was in Moscow without a decent home, Gratsos found that his old friend was now a member of the Supreme Soviet Politburo, the governing body of the Soviet Union.

After some marathon drinking bouts and tearfully nostalgic reminiscences with his princely friend, interspersed no doubt with eyeing and discussing the potential for bedding several blonde *Krassny Narodny* Volunteers Gratsos' friend pulled the right strings and like magic a seven-room apartment materialised for Christina. After this Gratsos took his leave of the Kaousov's and returned to the Free World to resume his capitalist preoccupation with making money and living the good life.

What wounded Gratsos soon after this episode was that people close to Christina managed to turn her against this most loyal of her father's friends. When Costas Gratsos died Christina sent a large wreath of flowers to the funeral but she herself did not to attend the burial ceremony because she had checked herself into a hospital that morning. It was a betrayal of the sort that the Onassis have sprung on close friends with each new generation.

After Costas Gratsos, perhaps the best known of Onassis' associates was Professor Georgakis, a brilliant man described by his enemies as being a man with many weaknesses. In the years immediately before Onassis death Georgakis was constantly by his side though few knew that this friendship also had a Gratsos connection.

During the Second World War the brother of Costas Gratsos had been active in the Greek resistance as part of the underground network which hid Allied pilots and helped them escape Nazi-occupied Greece. The penalty for harbouring Allied airmen was death, and Greeks hosts were being sent daily to the firing squads. Gratsos brother's underground cell was betrayed ironically by a Cypriot whom Gratsos' brother's group had helped. The Germans arrested Gratsos' brother and threw him into Averoff prison on Alexandras Avenue. Soon after his arrest he was brought before a German occupation military court. His wife desperately sought help to save his life and found this in two Greek lawyers who were prepared to defend him. The first lawyer (who later became the head of a Greek ministry) demanded payment of a substantial amount which he insisted be in British gold sovereigns. The money was paid in advance. The second lawyer, a young man in his twenties, did not mention his fee.

It was an open and shut case. There was a prosecution witness, the Cypriot, and the expected penalty would be a death sentence. When the prisoner was asked by the German military judge if he had anything to say, Gratsos' brother answered in his own defence in German. He spoke fluent German, having received a PhD in Zurich prior to the outbreak of the war. The German judge was impressed and said in his verdict "The prisoner is found not guilty since it is inconceivable that anyone who has been exposed to German culture will do anything to harm the interests of the Third Reich."

Gratsos brother was free. When he left the prison he asked the younger lawyer what his fee was.

"I do not charge money to patriots," came the answer.

The young lawyer's name was Yannis Georgakis and Gratsos brother did not forget him. When Onassis asked Gratsos some years later if he had any suggestions for a good lawyer, Gratsos mentioned Georgakis who by now was a well known law professor. Onassis asked to meet Georgakis, took a liking to him and immediately hired him. They became good friends and would often be seen in the late hours staggering out of a bar. I saw them on several occasions in the Plaka, the old part of Athens whose narrow streets with whitewashed houses, tourist tavernas and noisy discotheques had become a Mecca for wealthy Athenian youth and foreign hippies in the Seventies.

In Plaka there was a youth dive called *The Trip* where I saw Onassis and Georgakis on more than one occasion wander in after two in the morning to sit at the bar. Onassis was just at home rubbing shoulders with 18 year-old girls and boys there as he was at a society gala in Monte Carlo. This ability to mix with everybody was one of the reasons that the Greeks adored him.

Gratsos always liked to tease Ari about the time he had interceded for Onassis to go to visit one of the world's biggest ship-owners. Ari desperately wanted to do a deal with the Norwegians and had begged Gratsos to help make the contact for him. After a couple of weeks Gratsos called the Norwegian shipping tycoon to find out how Onassis was getting on.

"I really don't know what to say about your friend," said the puzzled Norwegian to Gratsos. "Onassis is the laziest person I have ever met: he is also the most brilliant."

The Norwegian had been amazed by the acuteness of young Onassis and his original ideas, but had been thoroughly shocked by Ari's penchant for waking up at two and three in the afternoon after revelling all night in Oslo's red-light district.

When Onassis died Gratsos stood over the coffin and pronounced the last judgment on his gifted and flawed friend.

"You were the best, Ari, and you were the worst".

A Doll made of Steel

Athina's inheritance was in the hands of the Onassis Foundation administrators led by Stelios Papadimitriou. In fact there was doubt as to whether Papadimitriou would actually hand over the fortune to the heiress on her 18th birthday as Christina Onassis had ordered in her will. He had stated that he himself "would decide" if he would hand over the inheritance to Athina or not on her 18th birthday.

I had been close to Thierry and Athina from 1998 when their fortune and Thierry's freedom hung from a thread. Attitudes changed slowly after we got the campaign going. After a while people would stop me in the street, in offices and in courtrooms asking about Athina and Thierry.

I had been Athina and Thierry's material witness in numerous court cases in Greece. For three years I had the doubtful honour of being dragged through the courts by Papadimitriou and the Onassis Foundation after helping Thierry win a 15 million dollar court case that had been brought against him. The tide of public, press, judicial and political hostility had been turned, bit by bit, until Athina was voted in a magazine poll as "the person who will be most influential individual in Greece in the next ten years". We had come a long way.

Oprah, Dan Rather and Larry King asked me to arrange interviews with Athina while one man who recognised Thierry in an elevator at the Athens Hilton burst out "Mr. Roussel I want to congratulate you for what you have done for Athina." Whereupon he grabbed a startled Thierry by the shoulders and planted a noisy kiss on both his cheeks. Thierry flushed red as a beetroot, but the incident was indicative of the sea change that had taken place in the public's perception of Athina and her father.

Thierry had moved like the fox he was, managing to take over control of Athina's fortune after she inherited it on her 18th birthday. It was cleverly done. Some years previously, before meeting the Roussels, I had written an article suggesting that the solution to the dispute with the Onassis Foundation would be for a trust to be set up to be managed by prestigious private asset administrators. I had suggested Julius Baer, the oldest private bank in Switzerland, Bank Leu, and some other financial institutions in Switzerland, saying that they should be in charge of her patrimony until Athina "got to know the ropes", After this, I had written, the heiress would be able to take over her fortune and that of the Onassis Foundation. The article had been the reason Thierry invited me to meet him in Switzerland. What I did not know was that Thierry had squirrelled away my formula and set up a trust with friendly professional trustees and him on the Board of Trustees so that Athina would not be managing her money upon inheriting it. It was a major coup for Thierry. Unknown to me he pulled the plan out of his memory chest and during the turbulent first weeks when the conflict over her new boyfriend and future husband Doda had begun he told Athina that her money must be safeguarded. Athina in order not to aggravate their relationship further agreed to have her money put into a trust, as Thierry had suggested to her. It made sense at the time for both sides. Athina could prove thus that Doda was not interested in the fortune because she had his approval for the trust, and Thierry would be happy to be in the driver's seat once again after having been thrown out illegally from the Onassis patrimony board by his Greek co-administrators, and later legally, in 1999, by the Authorite de Tutelle of Upper Engaddin in Switzerland which appointed KPMG to manage the patrimony until the heiress's coming of age.

My information regarding the trust was that Yves Repiquet had prepared a power of attorney for Athina to sign allowing Thierry to establish a trust to be managed by four private banks and by him. Thierry had also got Athina to agree to settle amounts of money on her Roussel siblings from her Onassis inheritance. The presence of the banks on the board was a guarantee to Athina that Thierry would not be in sole charge of her money and the involvement of these respected bankers was a further guarantee for the safe and conservative management of her fortune. Doda, who was a new fixture in Athina's life knew of the objections of Athina's father to their relationship and was understandably keen to keep himself out of any inter-Roussel family dispute about the management of the Onassis fortune. He had enough public image problems of his own not to be called a fortune hunter by the father of his new-found love so he wisely kept his distance waiting for a more convenient time to assert his position.

On the 29th of January, 2003 amid massive press speculation Thierry got Athina to sign the powers of attorney allowing him to set up a trust with Julius Baer Bank of Zurich, Rothschild, Citicorp and HSBC. Thierry was the fifth trustee. He was now in excellent and reputable financial company and was working with the most trusted names in private banking in the world. Not bad for a former playboy and "useless clown" as Papadimitriou had called him in the infamous press conference that took place at the Onassis Foundation headquarters in 1997 in Athens! Thierry could always be counted on to pull a rabbit out of a hat to confound his friends and enemies. His worst enemy though was often his own impatience, a symptom of an over-privileged upbringing, and his impetuousness, as noted in a dry comment in a letter sent to him and me by his Zurich lawyer, Marc Bonnant, a former president of the Swiss Bar Association, who had referred to Thierry's "charactere eruptif".

When Athina came of age she inherited Christina Onassis' vast personal fortune that include the apartment at 88, Avenue Foch, the islands of Scorpios and Sparti in Greece, the Pogorroi Bay mansion complex "La Jondal" in Ibiza, 140 offshore companies, a prime seaside Onassis plot in Glyfada, scattered properties in Switzerland, Greece, Spain and France as well as a substantial portfolio of shares, bonds, cash, precious metals, Impressionist paintings, the 20 million Euro Onassis chalet 'Villa Crystal' in St Moritz", a stunning collection of jewellery that had belonged to Christina and to Athina's grandmother, Tina Livanos-Blandford-Onassis-Niarchos, and numerous other valuable items. With the passing of this fortune into her hands Athina voluntarily gave up control by agreeing to put her assets into the trust.

Thierry had pulled off a major coup. He had taken the entire Onassis fortune inherited by Athina out of her hands and was once more a trustee, managing the fortune as he had been after the opening of Christina's will. This time there was a basic difference, Thierry Roussel did not have rivals as colleagues - as the Greek dominated Papadimitriou board had been - instead he had willing, and no doubt appreciative, partners pleased to have been invited by him onto the Athina Onassis trust board. These institutions and their directors were valuable to Thierry who were a bottomless mine of information regarding the management of important private fortunes.

Thierry now dropped from the media radar in keeping with his father's advice that to live well one must live "cache" – hidden. His business affairs, as Papadimitriou kept reminding everyone, were somewhat sketchy. Few knew what he was up to and I was perhaps one of those, but I never knew what his purpose and eventual goals were. There was a small boatbuilding facility in Morocco and a house in Casablanca. He had also set up a sheep farming operation with 5,000 animals in partnership with a Moroccan princess. Both of these ventures reminded me of what a relative of his had once said. "With Thierry you never quite know what he is doing professionally - he is a bit here and a bit there." To be fair to him when he was getting 2.4 million dollars a year from Christina's will (inflation indexed from 1988) he did not need to earn a living or to prove himself to anyone. The Italian saying "dolce fa niente" would have been perfectly acceptable for a person of his social standing given the income he had for life from Christina's estate.

The Moroccan ventures were not businesses that would make him millions but Thierry all the same seemed to enjoy having a Moroccan base and perhaps these businesses occupied his spare time and offered him more than just the prospect of increasing his income. Morocco was a secluded playground for the very rich and famous from early in the twentieth century and it was a place where they could enjoy themselves in the privacy of an exotic, film-set atmosphere, primarily in Casablanca, with an unlimited supply of cheap servants, sybaritic pleasures on hand and a chance to be away from the rules and strictures of bourgeois Europe. Many celebrities and high net worth individuals had played out their fantasies there. Their stories are legion and during Thierry's time in Morocco there were rumours circulating regarding a European neighbour of Roussel's nicknamed "The White Pasha of Casablanca". Local legend has it that this eccentric playboy in his late fifties liked to sit on a carved throne dressed in an embroidered black caftan while twenty attractive young hand-picked Moroccan girls danced in a circle in transparent oriental veils in front of him in his exquisitely decorated Moroccan palace-style throne room. As each girl passed in front of him the White Pasha liked to lift the silk veils and stroke the bodies of whichever dancers took his fancy on that day. The story goes that the attractive young women were recruited by a salaried "mother hen" and were permanently on call whenever the Pasha was in residence in Casablanca. There were other colourful characters too. The servants of a glamorous European couple were amused to hear the couple's children referring to their parents in the kitchen as "Bonny and Clyde". "Clyde's" car would be seen on occasion cruising the Bois de Boulogne at night where the chauffeur had been instructed to pick up one or two prostitutes to take back to the Ritz whenever his employer was passing through Paris. Whether apocryphal or not these stories are of less importance than the fact that Casablanca can still spawn gossip to tickle the imagination of those who do not live there.

Athina appeared, accompanying her stepmother Gaby, was now a stunning, mature young woman with perfectly coiffed blonde-streaked hair, immaculately tailored clothes and the poise of a princess when she came out of the hotel's front entrance to go to dinner with Aunt Kalliroi, Onassis' half sister. It was the first time I saw signs of a change in Athina.

Coming out of the hotel Athina was greeted by several of the young women TV journalists who had spoken to her at my daughter's birthday dinner in Vouliagmeni, had slept in café chairs all night to cover our yacht visit to Hydra island in 1999, had spent hours in flimsy boats off Scorpios in choppy waters when we went to the island for the memorial service for Christina and had become familiar faces and names to Athina. As I watched the scene on TV I could hear the press corps girls welcoming calls "Hello Athina!" "Welcome to Greece" "How was your trip?" "Did you have a good flight?" "Yassou Athina!" but Athina was preoccupied with something else, looking at her mobile phone and did not respond.

I had in the past, when asked to describe the sensitive and shy Onassis heiress said that she had another side to her that would become apparent, in my view, after she became 18 and was free to do as she liked. I was quoted in a Swiss weekly "L'Illustre" saying that young Athina was a "Poupee d'Acier" - a doll made of steel. I believed that under the shy exterior she could be as tough as any Onassis and my prediction of how hard she was going to turn out came true when she finally had had enough of Doda and those around him by 2016 when she instigated divorce proceedings against him. She put up the houses for sale, disposed of her Florida stables, sold the cars he was driven about in and the horses he rode including his beloved Cornetto that he had ridden in the 2016 Olympics in Brazil. It was without doubt part Onassis hereditary behavior, and partly self-protection on behalf of a sensitive and hurt young woman.

It was to be the last time that Athina would see her favourite aunt. Kalliroi called Athina aside and asked her if she was sure of Doda's sentiments.

"You must be careful Athina," she said, "because many men will approach you for your money."

Thierry and Athina. A very expensive dispute

When Athina came of age on January 29th of 2003 and inherited her Onassis fortune Thierry seemed unready to accept that the daughter he had acted for and brought up was now an adult. Athina had been receiving a small amount of pocket money over the years, amounts in keeping with that of a middle class family, not those of the richest teenager in the world. Through the trust Thierry set up with Athina her allowance was increased to several thousand dollars a month and any extras that were needed were met by the trustees on a case-by-case basis. Boislande, where Thierry had his financial services and property company, SGFC, took care of the details and Thierry's staff was available to Athina.

Thierry told me that when Athina wanted to buy Doda a horse that cost 50,000 USD the money was immediately released. It was a reasonable amount for a horse but when a demand came in for a multiple of this sum for another show jumping equine Thierry was not happy and communicated this to Athina. Again the money was given since it was, after all, Athina's own money.

Soon afterwards Athina needed some funds when her monthly allowance had run out. She called Boislande and asked for the money to be wired to her account. The secretary in charge of payments to Athina told her dryly "You have drawn all your allowance for this month."

This was the last straw for the heiress. Athina, furious, told Doda what had happened. According to reports from a source close to the heiress she contacted several of the banks where her money, estimated at hundreds of millions was in accounts in her name. Account after account was said now to have been found empty. It transpired that Thierry had transferred the money from the banks to the trust set up by him with the agreement of Athina. His motive for setting up the trust was to protect her inheritance until she was older, Thierry explained to me over lunch at the Noga Hilton in Geneva in 2004.

The offhand remark of the secretary from Thierry's office precipitated a chain of events that was to cause a deep rift in the family and cost tens of millions of dollars. Those close to Athina supported her, saying that she was the Onassis heiress and nobody could talk to her like that. Athina was trapped. Her money was in the trust where her father, as a co-trustee had a say, while she had none. When she checked to see if she could break the trust and get her money back she was informed that Switzerland's trust laws were among the most watertight in the world and unless gross mismanagement or violation of a will could be proved there was very little room to do anything.

The fracas proved that Thierry had grossly miscalculated his current influence over his daughter, thinking that Athina would carry on now that she was an adult as she had when she was the frightened and shy little girl hanging on his arm. He thought too that she would be content, as before, to live within her allowance as she had done when she was a minor. Her frustration now, and the realisation that as the Onassis heiress she had acquiesced to blocking access to her own money caused her to blow up. Advised that she could not break the trust she turned to Baker and Mackenzie, a top UK law firm and put the matter into their hands, apparently at the suggestion of Doda. Thierry told me that they investigated him and his management of her patrimony for months. But, he added, he had increased the value of Athina's trust portfolio 12.5% in two years and he had the letters from his co-trustees, the bankers, to prove it. Of course, he explained, there was a clock ticking at the side of the team of lawyers Athina had hired. I estimated the fees to have been around 600 pounds sterling per hour for each lawyer from the UK law firm. A similar amount was charged by Allen and Overy, the law firm Thierry hired to protect himself and prove that he had carried out his fiduciary duties diligently. Thierry told me that the total cost of Athina's anger and determination to expose him was 30 million dollars. 20 Million was paid to Athina's lawyers and Thierry paid 10 million to his own legal team. It was one of the most expensive father/daughter spats in history. While we were having coffee at the Perle du Lac restaurant at the lakeside in Geneva Thierry explained the aspects of the dispute and its result. He was in a good mood, having just finished lunch with five international bankers where, as I learned later, they agreed to support Thierry in his plans to register a hedge Fund of Funds in Luxembourg, to be run from his Swiss offices, now at Nyon.

He told me now that the only expense that he had paid over the years as an administrator of Athina's patrimony that was not accepted was a bill for 250 Euros for some phone calls he had made.

After the investigation Athina had no grounds to sue her father as she had threatened to do when the dispute began. Though both father and daughter backed off for the moment it was clear that the rift was too deep for Thierry to be acceptable as a trustee by Athina. Athina, probably with the agreement of Doda who was not on good terms with his future father-in-law, who perhaps saw too much of himself in the Brazilian rider, looked for another way to dislodge her father from the management of her fortune

    I asked Thierry if Athina was aware of the pain and humiliation that he had been through for six years in his battle with the Papadimitriou group. Was she aware of what he had done for her and her fortune as a father, I asked him? Thierry thought about it and asked me to intercede with Athina. Could I write a letter from the heart to be presented to Athina, describing all the humiliations I had seen Thierry suffer in Greece, the months he had spent in Athens criminal courts, the attacks by the Onassis Foundation presidency on him personally, the destruction of his reputation and his health that this had resulted in. It had been a father's battle, as I would explain, for his daughter's rights to control her fortune and to establish her inalienable right to become president of the Alexander Onassis Foundations upon becoming 21.

    I voiced my objections, for what they were worth, to Thierry and to Nuot Saratz, his Swiss lawyer. Thierry of course took no notice and took off to Nyon on Lake Leman to establish his hedge fund called GMT Multi Strategy Fund of Funds at 6a

Chemin de Joran, with the prestigious support of Banque Privee de Edmond Rothschild as the custodian and agent for GMT. Of course the fund did well, at least for the three years that its performance was posted for non-subscribers on the web. Thierry Roussel had finally achieved what he had craved all his life, to be a respected businessman and financier. He was at the top of the tree now and had finally shaken off the stigma of the failed strawberry farms and the Guyana timber project. His small inflatable boat venture and the sheep rearing farm in Morocco were peanuts now. Thierry was among the financial big boys: and ones with great prestige at that. He could now finally live as he wanted, and he did. Hidden from public view.

A year or so previously I had been in contact with a leading lawyer in Vaduz to whom I had set out the question of Athina's right to the Onassis Foundation presidency. He had seen the deed of charter signed by the board, which had included Papadimitriou, several Onassis relatives and Christina Onassis who was the first - and by general admission - very successful Onassis Foundation president. The founding deed of the stiftung, or Foundation, stated clearly that an Onassis descendant would always be president, without the need of election upon becoming 21. It further stated that the deed's articles relating to the presidency could never be modified. There was a clear cut case for Athina to become president of her family-financed Foundation with its fleet of super tankers, Manhattan skyscraper, Nash Terrace real estate, and numerous multi-million dollar assets around the world. Papadimitriou and the Greek board members of the Foundation had come out regularly against Athina's automatic right to the presidency as described in the Deed of Charter. They did not want Athina as president - that was clear. The Lichtenstein lawyer who saw the documents was amused to see that on the board of the Foundation was a man called Peter Marxer who, a lawyer himself, was the brother of a former prime minister of the tiny principality.

"A very shrewd move by the Greeks," the lawyer said, "to put a close relative of a prime minister onto their board!"

Thierry had always spoken about how his battle with the Onassis Foundation and the Greek co-administrators of Athina's patrimony was to assure her of her rights and to protect the Foundation. It was, he had always maintained, a battle for her right to become head of the Onassis Foundation. When in 1999 the hold of the Papadimitriou Four on Athina's patrimony was broken by a series of legal decisions in Switzerland and the patrimony was assured of passing into her hands on her coming of age, the second issue of the Foundation presidency loomed large and needed to be addressed. Sometime later I started looking into the issue and finally had what I needed when I had finished preparing the thick Onassis Foundation file with hundreds of documents, depositions, legal decisions, wills, interpretation of laws and it was up to Athina now to take what was hers according to the deed of the Onassis Foundation.

I arranged a meeting with Thierry and Yves Repiquet at Yves' Avenue Mozart offices in Paris, not declaring over the phone, for reasons of confidentiality, what the subject of our meeting would be. I booked my plane tickets and hotel and flew to Paris with a file I had prepared for Thierry and a briefcase full of documents. He was a man who loved papers and wanted everything laid out clearly for him with a covering note or letter to explain what was being presented each time. He had demanded and received a fax from me almost every day including the weekends for the years I had acting as his spokesman, media advisor and coordinator of his legal offices.

Yves and Thierry were waiting for me in the elegant conference room at Yves' legal partnership's offices. The large room was similar to other law offices I had seen in Paris, with its *decappe* bleached oak wall paneling and bookcase lined walls. The muffled buzz of early evening Paris traffic filtered through large double-glazed windows. Thierry was in a jocular mood, heavier than the last time we had met, again wearing his favourite dark blue suit, white monogrammed shirt and Tod's driving loafers. He had come to the meeting from the heavily gilded ornate Onassis apartment at 88 Avenue Foch which was his Paris base, just a step away from the Arc de Triomphe. Thierry smiled at me and said, somewhat impatiently "Yes, Alexis. What is it?" It was a stance I had seen on other occasions when Thierry had made arrangements to go somewhere else immediately after a meeting, usually after business hours.

I handed a copy of the thick Liechtenstein file to Thierry and to Yves and began my introduction, starting to explain that everything was ready for

Athina to instigate a legal process in Vaduz for the presidency of the Alexander Onassis Business and Public Benefit Foundations. This had been our object for years and we had fought together in courts of law and in the world's media for Athina to get what was her Onassis birthright and to be able to play a public role that had been provided for her by her grandfather Aristotle and her mother Christina. Sixteen legal offices had represented the heiress and her father and I had been a go-between for most of them because someone was needed who understood the briefs in their different languages and jurisdictions and could organise what documents would be presented to which lawyers and in what courts.

Thierry closed the file, pushing it away from him.

"Alexis, Athina has her money now. She has enough not to care about the Foundation. We are not interested."

With that he stood up, checked his heavy gold sports watch, glanced at his reflection in a pane of glass, fixing a wayward lock of chemically highlighted blond hair and came round the table to shake my hand.

"Thanks Alexis, for coming from Athens."

I picked up my files, put them back in my briefcase and took a photo of Thierry and Yves as was my habit as proof that the meeting had taken place. I left in the elevator, as the office door closed behind me, leaving the two old childhood friends to get ready for their evening outing. They had been together from their teenage years, sharing tents when camping, girlfriends when older, and experiences during the difficult years. They had now put behind them, for the moment at least the matter of the Onassis Presidency for Athina.

What was equally strange was something Thierry said to me in 2004 when we were having lunch on the first floor of the Noga Hilton in Geneva. Erik, Athina's half brother, was now a mature and handsome young man with a soft-spoken manner about him. He told me he was working for a bank as an intern. I congratulated him on hearing this and said "Erik, after we help Athina get the presidency of her grandfather's Foundation it will be nice for her to have her brother with her now that you are getting banking experience. You will be able to do great things for the Foundation and for Greece too."

Erik clearly had not thought of being with his sister on the Onassis Foundation board and he looked interested at what I had suggested, but Thierry immediately interrupted, waving a hand, saying, "No! No! It is not for Erik."

His categorical statement made me wonder. Why would Thierry not want his son to be on the board of a prestigious international foundation and one that had been established by Athina's mother and grandfather with the Onassis family in mind? Did the same apply for his daughter? Thierry called for the waiter to bring the bill, making it obvious that he did not want the conversation with Erik to continue.

After the meeting at Yves Repiquet's Paris office I wondered if the whole conflict had boiled down to a matter of "enough money'. Was this the only thing that now interested Athina? What of the

Onassis dynasty and its obligations? Was she afraid of starting a new conflict? I recalled what Thierry had declared, when he was choking back tears of anger and frustration as we walked through a crowd of paparazzi and a bank of TV cameras in the Athens courtroom just after the sentence of five years imprisonment had been handed down to him for perjury, defamation of the Onassis Foundation and false accusation. Standing there defiantly before the massed media he had declared to the Swiss correspondent of the Tribune de Geneve and to a French radio station that was broadcasting live from the courtroom *"It is Athina's great responsibility to her grandfather to serve the Onassis Foundation whose money built the Foundation. If I have to I will go to every court in the world to defend her right to the Foundation".*

In the now empty office building's old fashioned elevator memories flooded back of what Thierry had said in the court late that night when the sentence had been handed down. We had spent 42 days in court, Thierry in the dock and me one row behind him for support and to deal with the ever present media. Images flashed by and I remembered all the visits to and by the Roussel family, of anxieties shared in close family circumstances across Europe with Thierry, Gaby and Athina. Images of stressful days with Thierry and Gaby in hostile law courts, of late night half-hour calls from Thierry, of nights alone poring over court and police depositions in French, German, English and Greek, of Thierry calling from Switzerland to say that Athina was in hysterics because Papadimitriou had had a confiscation notice for their properties served at

Boislande, of me going to talk to people in all walks of public life to explain why we were campaigning so hard on behalf of Athina and Thierry, of three years I had sat in court, falsely accused by the Foundation, before I won the case with a unanimous decision by the three judges.

I stepped out into the street to take a taxi back to my hotel near the Louvre. The coloured lights of Paris flashed by the cab window as the young driver zipped in an out at speed from lane to lane along by the banks of the Seine and I felt empty.

I wondered about a board meeting of the Onassis Foundation where they had altered the statutes of the Foundation regarding the rights of Onassis descendants to the presidency. The statutes had been changed, taking away Athina's birthright to the presidency despite the Deed of Charter saying that none of the clauses referring to the presidential rights of Onassis descendants could be altered. I wondered too why the Onassis Foundation governing committee had met in Lausanne, just a kilometer or two from where Thierry and Athina lived, a place so far from Greece where the Foundation members lived, but just round the corner from the Roussel residence at Lussy sur Morges. Had there been a meeting between the two sides? It remains one of the few unsolved mysteries of the Onassis story for me even today.

Thierry in a late night call to me said in desperation that Athina had changed in character, was being isolated by the Brazilians and that Gaby too had commented on her altered behaviour after accompanying Athina to Athens to see Aunt Kalliroi.

Cybele's suicide and the Onassis Curse

A series of premature deaths, suicides and fatal accidents in the Onassis family and those near them has for years fed the myth of curse that has followed the family from early days in Asia Minor to Europe and to South America. The "Onassis Curse" was never mentioned as such in the Roussel household and I debunked it whenever any journalist referred to it. When Athina grew up it seemed that the chapter with the string of deaths that had been a part of the Onassis dynasty's tragedy-ridden history had closed for good.

By 2005 Athina was independent, married, albeit not to have children by Doda and master of her vast inherited fortune. But since her coming of age fatal accidents started to happen again. Two young women were killed riding a Roussel family-owned jet ski in front of Athina's seafront Ibiza mansion estate. More were to follow.

Cybele Dorsa, Doda's former companion and mother of their daughter Vivienne committed suicide after sending a damning letter to the editor of the leading Brazilian lifestyle magazine CARAS (FACES) naming Athina and Doda. The letter was rife with accusation. As the last communication of someone about to die it did not help to dispel the existence of an Onassis curse.

Some time before she died Cybele had granted a telephone interview to a Greek journalist making it clear she was distraught at having to give up her daughter into Doda and Athina's custody. The reporter asked if Athina was going to adopt Vivienne and how Cybele viewed Athina and Doda bringing up her daughter.

"I wish (them) happiness, you know," answered Cybele, "I just want my daughter back. That is my business; the other things are not my business. If Athina is good for my daughter I like (it). I want my daughter here; I believe she belongs in Brazil."

To another Greek journalist, Athanasia Anezaki from ALTER TV she said "Doda is always without money. His father sends him money."

The story of 17 year-old Athina meeting and falling in love with Doda at the Pessoa Riding School is well known now. The young impressionable teenage Onassis heiress fell head over heels for the handsome Brazilian twice-Olympic medallist at the riding school, and against her father's wishes she moved in to live with the older man. Doda had been living with Cybele Dorsa, a glamorous Cindy Crawford look-alike Brazilian model, actress and presenter at Radio Transamerica. When Doda left Cybele for Athina she went to the media and expressed her bitterness at having lost her companion of eight years saying he had left her for Athina's money. Dorsa said much more, that Doda used to laugh at Athina, remarking to Cybele that the then-chubby Greek heiress was "like an elephant". Cybele told the media that Doda was so short of money that he did not even have a car. A search of the Belgian tax records would be enough to see if she was telling the truth about the state of Doda's finances when he met Athina or if she was being spiteful.

Doda took little notice of what Cybele was telling the press now that he was with the Onassis heiress and he did not look back. Soon afterwards he took Vivienne to live with him and Athina in Belgium. How they managed this and why a judge in Brazil gave custody to Doda is a mystery. There was talk that it was not something sinister but that Cybele was on drugs and this affected the decision of the court to give her daughter into Doda and Athina's care.

Cybele understandably deeply resented the loss of her daughter but started her life over again, this time in a luxury 7th floor flat in an apartment building called *The Flowers*. She worked for a while as an actress appearing in several plays, and found a new love, an older man with whom she appeared to have a measure of happiness and stability, despite the constant pain of the loss of Vivienne who now appeared in photos in the media with her arms around Athina's neck or sitting next to her.

Worse for Cybele were press reports that Vivienne was looking up to Athina as her mother. Cybele's link to the Onassis family via Doda had brought her nothing but anguish and despair. She had lost her beloved long-time companion to the young heiress, her family had been broken up by the arrival of Doda's new love and Cybele had been forced by circumstances that she alluded to in her suicide letter to give up her young daughter because of a plan involving money.

Cybele seemed happy with her older companion and was slowly putting her life together when pre-dawn car accident after a party killed her companion and seriously injured Cybele, causing her to be hospitalised for three months. Cybele was a fighter and even this new loss did not break her spirit. Left with a son, Fe – Fernando - from a previous partner Cybele put together the pieces of her broken body and of her life and started over again. She also managed to write a book called "Men in Your Pocket".

She subsequently met and fell in love with a young television presenter, Gilberto Scarpa, a dashing-looking well-known TV personality. With him she seemed to be genuinely happy. He too was in love with her, something that showed in the photos and videos they posted of themselves on the internet after they made plans to wed. But it was not to be, and those who believe in an Onassis curse were not surprised to hear of another death when the news from Brazil came that 27 year old Gilberto had taken his life by jumping to his death from Cybele's seventh floor apartment in south Sao Paolo. Cybele had run down to the street to see Gilberto lying on his back with his eyes open, and started speaking to him, convinced he could hear her. But Gilberto Scarpa was dead, his life snuffed out by the shame of a drug habit he could not beat. Pride had been greater than what he saw as the alternative - to live as an addict. For Cybele this was the latest tragedy in a life turned on its head from the day that an Onassis had walked into it taking away her companion and her daughter.

A friend in Sao Paolo, the journalist and musician Harold Emert, had spoken at length with Cybele before Gilberto's death and she had poured out her heart to him.

"She is a decent woman. Alexis," Harold said to me the next day, "and she seems to be making a go of it, but she does have problems."

But it had all been too much for Cybele. With Doda, Vivienne, her older lover and Gilberto gone her life was a desert landscape. She was overtaken by loneliness and two months after Gilberto jumped from her apartment Cybele wrote a heart rending letter with her final thoughts and penned accusations about Doda. She then opened the balcony window and let herself fall to her death.

It was a tragic end to the tragic life of a 36 year-old woman who had fought and had lost, beaten by circumstance, habits, and bad luck. Like an injured butterfly she had spun down through the air, down seven floors to leave her broken mortal shell on the pavement as her soul broke free. Cybele left behind one of the most moving and damning suicide letters ever; a letter that contained a heartfelt apology to her children, harsh accusations against Doda, and a prediction for Athina.

Doda's reaction to the suicide of his former partner and mother of their daughter was to deny any responsibility and to immediately have a Brazilian court issue an injunction against his name being mentioned in Cybele's emailed letter which was published in CARAS magazine. The editor and staff at the magazine were furious with Doda for issuing the court order banning the printing of his name. The issue was already off the presses when the staff at the magazine had to go back and delete his name with a black marker wherever Cybele had included it in her note. The ban also applied to CARAS' website. The magazine's editor told the press that it was the first time that censorship had been exercised on any article printed in his magazine and added that even in a dictatorship this would not happen.

Eight days after the ban the editor of CARAS won a court victory. His appeal filed before the Court of San Paolo was granted, ensuring the publication in full of the letter sent by the Cybele to the magazine before she committed suicide on the night of March 26.

CARAS wrote –

"Now, thanks to the court's decision, CARAS can again fulfil Cybele's last wish before dying. Read below the complete letter sent by Cybele Dorsa before she died."

(Excerpts from Cybele's death note) –

"Of all the men who passed through (my life) the one who harmed me most was undoubtedly Doda, father of the daughter with whom I will have no more contact. The man who did me the most good, when he was alive, was Gilberto.

Living without my two children and without the love of my life tears me completely apart, as if I had woken up during heart surgery, I feel my heart being cut by an electric knife that never stops. I cannot stand crying… It does not stop, ever! I cannot stand to live or rather to survive. My food does not go down, I feel a lump in my throat, I'm getting thinner every day, I feel my skin peeling off my body. The question is, if I end my life, am I committing suicide?

... the death scene of my love (Gilberto) comes back to me constantly, I remember the body of Gilberto in the middle of the street, but his eyes were open and I thought he could hear me so I talked to him a lot ... I do not consider myself suicidal, I am suffering more pain now than when I had the car accident. Now there is no morphine, nothing to soothe the pain, nothing to stop this feeling of drilling in my chest. Moreover, Doda never seems to tire of humiliating me, he would not even meet (me). He was the worst man I ever met in my life, a wolf in sheep's clothing.

Fernando and Vivienne -
Forgive me, your mother, but loneliness is a terrible prison, it feels like I'm locked inside myself, I'm tired, I'm sorry by the lack of (having) you, I confess with Gilberto here it was easier to bear, I love him so much, I do not know how I can continue ... here at home it was cold... I'll find my love. You guys do not even need me. One day ask Carla your aunt or my uncle and know the whole truth. I love you guys and I'll be looking at you guys from up there...

Vivi, we will meet each other in other lives. I never abandoned you. Your father made a millionaire's plan to take you away from me and I had no other option. Fe(rnando) ditto ... I'll be rooting for you at football, in realizing their dreams...

Doda-,

...One day God will forgive you for what you did and do to me, with Athina and with children, try to be someone better, I'm sorry... Athina will never know a real man, one love. I am suffering now, however, I was totally happy with Gilberto, a man of truth, who showed his face that did not lie, hid nothing and so it was until the end. He jumped off the building out of shame at having been defeated by drugs... for shame.

Mother, Carla, Uncle, Father, Bruna, Maciel and Dantino-

Forgive me... it did not work, I tried for almost two months but the pain is hell. I'm going alone... do not worry, I'm sure God understands someone who dies for love. Obsessed I'm not, I am very aware of what I'm doing, my life became a lie, and you guys know, I opted for the truth.

Cybele Dorsa
P.S. I want to be buried in the same grave as Gilberto. Please... I want my coffin on top of his.

For those who are not superstitious and believe only in statistics the 14 untimely deaths, suicides and incidents connected to the Onassis family will only be seen as coincidence, while the rest believe that there is a century-old curse connected to the House of Onassis that has descended on Athina and will accompany her until the end...

Cancer Ward

The tiny embedded blue led lights in the horizontal white panel above the partially raised hospital bed bathed the two-bed hospital room on the fourth floor of the Athens urban public hospital in a ghostly dim light. The sound of bubbling oxygen being fed by a transparent plastic tube into the lungs of the female patient by whose bed I was sitting, keeping watch over her in the surgical cancer wing, was all I could hear in the pervading silence engulfing the hospital now, hours after the last visitors had left. Three night nurses were in attendance and a doctor in green overalls who came by every three hours to check on the patients in their rooms.

The occasional groan of a male patient vomiting from an empty stomach came as a rasping interruption from time to time from another room along the silent neon-lit corridor as the patient's body reacted to the toxic chemotherapy administered earlier that day to him.

The deathly silence in the room I was in was offset by the continuous gentle hypnotic buzz of late night traffic on one of the capital's main streets close to the Athens hospital. The sound of an occasional noisy moped ridden by a delivery boy was all that came in above the murmur of traffic through the slightly ajar hospital window, left open to refresh the air in the room for the patient breathing heavily next to me.

Tubes and catheters were in vital parts of her body; one in her nose going deep down to drain her stomach, another in her lower abdomen to drain trauma overflow juices from the five hour operation that had taken place two days previously. More tubes, thinner ones this time, were attached with butterfly valves to bruised veins in her hands. These valves kept blocking every few hours as the body's immune system valiantly tried to defend itself from the invading needles by forming clots around the point of their entry.

The nurses came to check the patient and pump more serum into her veins, hurting her, to clear the blockage or to look for a new vein when that one was rendered useless. Another catheter, from the patient's bladder, came out from under the starched top sheet to slowly empty yellow body waste into a deflated plastic bag on the floor. In all seven tubes were connected to the woman's injured body.

I had spent two days and nights since the operation in a hard uncomfortable armchair, but noticed little discomfort as my attention was concentrated on the pale woman with her blonde hair next to me fighting for her life with nurses in smartly starched white uniforms coming in every half hour to replace the morphine, antibiotics and other drugs hanging overhead from the hook of the mobile stand next to the bed, to help her recover.

We desperately needed a private night nurse since I was unable to lift or handle the patient on my own, and the ward nurses were not available for this as they were occupied in changing serum bottles, aerolin lung expanding containers attached to catheters, emptying bags of blood and body liquids and administering medicines.

I felt a dark presence in the room, hanging over us. Was it the wandering spirit of a lonely person far away slowly breaking out from her cocoon of burnished steel to reveal herself to me in response to a final sms I was about to send her for help? I really did not know, it was just a feeling I had in that unreal box of a room I was in with the cancer patient next to me.

The atmosphere in the dimly lit, immaculately clean cancer ward accommodating the woman I was watching over was surreal, like one from a movie; a setting divorced from the morning reality of bright sunshine, dogs barking on balconies, bus doors opening with a hiss at an adjacent bus stop, schoolchildren spilling out of the front gates of their downtown Athens schools with squeals of delight following the ringing of the last bell, ignoring the honking of horns of drivers forced to brake suddenly to avoid them.

The blue dim light and colourless grey tones of the room that night reminded me of looking out of a hotel window with this same woman on a late December afternoon in Rovanyemi, below the Arctic Circle in Finland, after the winter sun had set at 2pm. The diffusion of cold blue and white lights outside the Finnish hotel had been strange to us coming from the South where the Mediterranean sun left its fiery traces in the sky for a while even after it sank over the Saronic Sea and the distant ancient mountain range of the Peloponnese on the darkest of summer nights. The weak Arctic winter light reflected from the blue grey street lamps by the ice of the desolate street in Rovanyemi had been so like that in the Athens hospital room with its sedated surgical patient.

The crisp sheet covering the patient's suffering and damaged body held together by synthetic thread, staples and sterile bandages was motionless except for her chest section that raised itself gently, rhythmically, for a few centimetres and lowered itself again, continuing its mechanical motion as her soul wandered in reverie to places unknown in a deep morphine-induced sleep.

'Sharper than a serpent's tooth is a thankless child' (King Lear, William Shakespeare)

When we first arrived at Nydri village opposite Scorpios in 1998 with Athina I commented that she was like a beautiful butterfly that had just emerged from a chrysalis. Such was her recent transformation, but there was to be another one, another cocoon into which the Onassis butterfly would enter with her gilded wings and slender body to metamorphose once again, not physically this time, but psychologically.

The change in her had been coming for a long time, away from the public eye, apparent after she emerged from her shell to reveal in 2017 the real Athina Onassis, the mature woman who had rid herself of her husband, had taken charge of her life and was now alone in the world, estranged from family, with few friends, and with only her horses, her trainer, bankers and lawyers to keep her company, along with her stable hands.

During the formative years, after she received her inheritance she had started to show signs of a hard and uncaring character.

Christina Onassis until her death had adored young Athina, she had doted on her. Athina was the light of her life and Christina left everything to her daughter in her will - houses, hundreds of millions in cash, property, and jewellery, shares, currencies, gold bars, Scorpios Island and her personal effects. Athina after 1998 when we went to Scorpios on my suggestion to Thierry for Christina's ten year memorial service, never went back to the island to light a single candle at the graves of her dead mother or her grandfather who had made her equestrian life, the LAOHS, the jet planes, the mansions, the servants, the bodyguards and billionaire lifestyle possible. Not one candle. Nor was a single day set aside out of the whole year to visit the white marble tomb of the devoted and loving woman who had stayed up nights by her bed and watched over her every step as Athina grew to be an adored three year old, when Christina had suddenly had her life snuffed out.

Not once did Athina, the beneficiary of so much generosity, take the time to show her appreciation to the mother and grandfather who had given her everything, without which she would have been who knows what; a shop assistant, a hotel clerk, a teacher, a stable manager, an airline flight attendant?

The young soul of the pretty brunette heiress inside that cocoon was slowly morphing into something different from the timid girl everyone saw in the occasional television newscast, but how harsh few could have imagined.

There had been signs of this quiet transformation previously when her fragile Aunt Olga Onassis, 84, had come to me in Athens in tears saying that Athina's accountants had cut off the small monthly income that she had been receiving from the time of Aristotle Onassis, through Christina, and then from the patrimony when the Four Greeks were managing Athina's inheritance. Olga Onassis was eating out of garbage cans in the streets of Athens the press wrote, and other media reported she was standing in a church soup line for a daily plate of food in order to survive. I informed the office at *Boislande* and Thierry gave me an envelope with several thousand dollars of his own money to give the old lady for Christmas, which delighted her and her family. But it was Thierry's money and not his obligation.

Athina, like an unemotional doll of steel was unmoved and did not respond to the call to continue what her mother Christina and Grandfather Aristotle had always done for the old lady. Soon after Olga Onassis went to the Grande Bretagne Hotel in Athens when she heard Athina and Gaby were staying there, and sat until 2 am waiting in the reception area to give a letter to her billionaire niece, but Athina's bodyguards did not allow the old lady to meet the heiress, who, I was told, had been informed of her aunt's presence. I knew it, because I had spoken to the chief Greek bodyguard, Stefanos, whom we always used and who I had introduced to

Athina. Aunt Olga Onassis left the hotel in the early hours, dejected and humiliated in her torn and worn fur coat, a reminder of better days, and went home. Many years later I learned that my intervention in bringing the case of Aunt Olga to Athina's attention, via Thierry, had results and Athina wrote to Aunt Olga paying her and her two sons, Constantine and Vassili Onassis a small monthly maintenance amount and rent in keeping with the spirit of Onassis will, payments which, according to gossip in Athens law circles was ordered by the heiress to be reduced by large increments in the near future.

    Then there was the fall in Geneva with the horse. The crowd gasped to see the heiress crash to the ground, to rise shaken, but without major injury, while her steed remained kicking among the hurdle bars, her leg broken. Carted off by crane the horse was of no further use as a competition horse for her wealthy heiress owner and the order was given. "Destroy her". Athina cried in public, touched by the loss of her best horse, but there was no operation for Camille, no convalescence, no putting out to pasture for the rest of her days after serving her mistress so well from before dawn in strenuous days of training again and again, travelling in a small division in a special animal cargo plane to the ends of the earth, to deserts, plateaus, capital city venues and country competition courses like that at Valkenswaard in Holland, close to Athina and Doda's former mansion and stables. Camille with her large eyes and loving nature had given all she had to give, and was no longer of any use. Athina turned her back on her devoted mare and the horse was lifted away to be killed.

When Athina married Doda there were objections by Thierry whom she did not invite to the wedding. Only Sandrine, her half-sister, went to Brazil and a Greek cousin whose mother told me that Athina did not supply tickets for the rest of her Greek family to go, and that because of the cost the other members of the family weren't able to attend the nuptials in Sao Paulo. How unlike Christina or Ari Onassis who would send their jet to pick up guests, even poor ones, to bring them to Scorpios, Paris or St Moritz where Villa Crystal, the famous Onassis chalet was always bustling with life and guests. Not so with Athina.

The chalet was sold, despite Athina being an expert skier and snow boarder who appeared to love the slopes when she was living with her family in Switzerland. Instead, spreading her wings, she had reached the point of living a life, with the exception of her riding, that resembled a whirlpool, sucking everything into its vortex where Athina was firmly placed. She rarely saw her siblings, Eric, Johanna and Sandrine, just an hour or so away. Yes, Thierry had arranged for a sum of money to be given to each of them from Athina's inheritance when she reached her majority, and this may have annoyed the heiress, but the amounts weren't such as to affect her financial position. Now even they, the Roussel siblings, and Gaby, who had raised her with so much love, and I had witnessed this on numerous occasions, were on the periphery of Athina's life, with Thierry out completely, and, if I understood, not to be spoken to ever again.

Inside the Onassis cocoon

There were no promises made but it was not unreasonable to expect that with the latest support I had given Athina at a pivotal moment in her life during her divorce, and with our renewed friendship there may have been a resumption of cooperation between myself and the Onassis heiress. Her sms to me again and again referred to her gratitude, as did her lawyer M in his emails and phone discussions with me.
"You will find that Athina is not ungrateful, Alexis," he said, when I was trying to convince Nicky to give up her evidence without being paid for it.

When I finally delivered the red file with the documentary evidence, proof of Doda's eight and a half years of having a paid mistress, I received an email that same day saying "You are amazing, Alexis"

Athina had her proof. It would be futile for Doda to continue demanding 30,000 Euros a month in alimony as the injured and innocent party.

I had done what I could for the heiress over the course of twenty years, undertaken to organise her family media and work closely with her lawyers when her father was in danger of being jailed in Greece, investigated and recovered the missing Scorpios shares, valued at over 150 million dollars when her administrators had declared that the island "did not belong to her", helped her father win a case when his opponents were demanding 15 million dollars from him, help that resulted in my being dragged by Athina's administrators through the criminal courts for several years, them claiming my evidence had lost them the case, before being acquitted unanimously. It all came back now. I had stood in as her and her father's witness at numerous court cases over the years and had managed to turn the tide of press and public opinion against them with daily contacts with the press and others. It had been a very long, arduous and complicated battle, much of it, such as the Scorpios shares investigation, outside my duties as press spokesman. I had done it with pleasure, only a Greek could understand what the name Onassis meant for us all, but there had been a personal cost when Athina finally got her money, with our joint efforts, and she dropped from the radar, as did her father.

She summoned me for help when she was in trouble again with her marriage split and Doda's huge alimony and other financial demands. She invited me to Holland in desperation to see what we could do with Nicky who had all the documents confirming the unknown to Athina until I informed her of the years long affair of her husband with the Belgian call girl.

Months and years of communications by phone, email and social media private messages had gone into creating a bond of trust with Nicky until she finally entrusted me with the red file filled with dozens of receipts, photos, emails, Athina Onassis

Horse Show VIP enclosure entrance validations, all fo which confirmed without doubt now that Athina was the injured party, not Doda whom Athina had walked out on.

It was a stunning record of corruption, deception, of a long clandestine affair, and the final proof for Athina to show Doda to have him back off from his exorbitant alimony and compensation demands, and for the couple to agree to a consensual (no fault) divorce where nothing of the call girl mistress scandal or of his threats to bring expert witnesses from Brazil against Athina were to be made known.

In Greece, as everyone knew, the situation for the middle class was getting desperate, a whole class of previously comfortably-off and industrious families was being financially wiped out for political and economic reasons that are too complicated to explain here.

Seeing that Athina had left the 'phone off the hook' after she received the red file, having obtained what she wanted, I decided to lay out the situation for her, explaining in detail the scope of work I had done for her, paid and unpaid, the hundred million Euro plus value of the recovery of Scorpios, which she was not aware of before I went to Holland, and so much else concerning my situation and obligations that had been forgotten or ignored, such as the offer to become the manager for Scorpios when I was summoned to meet with her administrators and lay out a management plan for the island. The promise was made, salaries discussed, and Thierry told me to wait until Athina came of age. The date came and went, as did year after year after that, with the promise of the job always open, but unfulfilled.

Now after I had brought her the red file and worked closely with her lawyers, on her request, and things finally were sorted out for Athina, it was my turn to request support.

I explained that she was not obliged to give anything, but if she did, any amount would be appreciated.

Her many written and verbal messages of thanks for the support I had given her were now followed by the request of my own. For the first and only time in 20 years I told her I needed her support.

She asked me to talk to M and to send him what I wanted in writing. His response on receiving the email was "I suggest not sending this as it will upset her and possibly jeopardize your relationship with her"!

I was flabbergasted as the messages thanking me for my support to save her from the alimony demands of Doda by proving his years' long infidelity were still fresh.

I told M to forward the request. There was no response for weeks from her to my request. At this time my wife, normally strong as a bull, was sick and was going through a series of tests to find why she was vomiting and bleeding from her intestine. I spoke to M asking what was happening with Athina. In reply he emailed me asking if I was going to "stop offering my services[5] to A" if she gave nothing!

It was a trick question. If I said yes, then it would seem like blackmail, if I said no, then she

---

[5] For which no money beyond basic expenses had been paid

would, if indeed she were the most ungrateful person on the planet, give nothing and feel no obligation either. So I said nothing would change, to allow her to take her decision without pressure. Something was strange indeed.

In the meantime my wife was positively diagnosed with a large growth in her intestine, a sample of which was sent for a biopsy, and we would know the result in a month. It looked like cancer the doctor told us, but the biopsy would be definitive. I informed M to tell Athina there was a serious issue developing and that I would appreciate Athina's answer now as the growth had been cut for the sample and time was of an essence to get to a private clinic to get quick results before the cancer spread through her system.

Nothing came for a while, a month passed and the biopsy confirmed the growth was cancerous. My wife went to hospital a week later and underwent an operation with a thirty centimeter section of her large intestine removed.

Dimitra, while being wheeled into the operating theatre gave me a worried look but was trying to be brave for my sake. My companion of forty seven years was going through the biggest challenge we had faced. We were in God's hands and in those of Professor Kouraklis, the head of the surgery wing of the hospital, a professor at the Athens University Medical School and a doctor who had spent years in Houston in an oncology surgical unit.

I wrote, reluctantly, again to M and pressed for an answer asking him to inform Athina of the latest development.

He responded that Athina "did not want to give anything". She had "a lot of things on her mind" was his explanation.

Sitting next to my companion's bed late that night in the silent dark hospital room in the eerie dim blue light, with the bubbling breathing apparatus and the silent drips going into her veins, I thought of the relief that a phone call from Athina with an offer to help would help make Dimitra more comfortable physically and help her chances of survival.

I looked at the pale stretched skin on the face of my wife as she slept under heavy sedation, struggling to make a sound from time to time when recurring pain spread across her abdomen that had been ripped open from top to bottom by a surgical scalpel to remove the cancerous section of her intestine and the surrounding tissue from her abdomen.

I suddenly felt swamped by a wave of indignation. For the attitude of Athina, for her inhumanity and total lack of compassion. Where had her soul come from, and where had it gone?

Her father Thierry had often in my presence helped people, women begging in the street, wildfire victims and Aunt Olga Onassis, with several thousand dollars when Athina had left her destitute, before resuming payments to her.

Christina had stood by her friends and staff, always generous, and had provided for them. She had also arranged for the Onassis Foundation to pay for the building of the Onassis Heart Clinic, saving thousands of lives, and grandfather Ari Onassis had given half his fortune, his skyscraper and cash to create the Onassis Foundation to help people in need, to disburse scholarships, to build hospitals and to help the public, and here the last Onassis, who had inherited half the fortune, stood totally unmoved. A Doll of Steel.

That week two of her Niarchos cousins donated a hundred and forty three new ambulances to the ailing Greek public hospital system and undertaken to cover their running expenses for eight years. To help people in need.

As a last try I decided to communicate directly with Athina, not through M who had tried to warn me in his way. Late at night in the hospital room I composed an sms to her -

"Dear Athina, I understand M explained that my most urgent support issue was that my wife Dimitra, in hospital now, has cancer and was operated on Monday. His response that u had "other things" on your mind was confusing. If you r happy to give any amount, even small, it will help greatly. If not please respect my pride and need for privacy and don't have M reply to me for you. Thank you. Alexi"

Messenger displayed two check marks on the illuminated mobile phone screen, indicating Athina had received and read the message.

I waited.

She never replied.

Neither to my request, nor to ask how my stricken companion was.

Somewhere between Switzerland, Belgium, Brazil and Holland a beautiful gilded young female butterfly had entered the Onassis cocoon, and a frigid heartless creature had emerged.

I had been close to the Onassis dynasty and stood by what I had considered its frail and vulnerable last member for close to 20 years, on and off. I was taken unawares by her indifference.

Back at my house the next day to feed the cats, shower and change into clean clothes before returning to the hospital I sat in an armchair in the unheated living room looking out of the window as I nursed a mug of strong English breakfast tea and milk in both hands. It was a habit acquired during my boarding school days in the misty chilly tea growing highlands at Kericho in British colonial Kenya where I had grown up.

Above the pine-covered mountain three kilometres away, with its landmark white-washed Orthodox convent visible like a shiny pearl in a sea of olive green, the milk-white luminous Attica sky with its watercolour strokes of pale blue wash reminded me of a similar sky on another crisp winter morning at Scorpios nineteen years previously. I must have dozed off in my armchair. Memories and images succeeded one another of the visit to Scorpios with Athina and Thierry when we went to attend the memorial service at Panagitsa chapel for the tenth anniversary of Athina's mother's death: it was the last time Athina had gone to the island. 18 years had passed since then.

And then I was interrupted by a lucid dream, those we have when we think we are awake. I saw a doll of steel standing silently in front of me. And then it started to crack open, gradually. A long black hairy tentacle came out of the fracture, and then the steel cracked wider, and another tentacle came out. Then the whole of the front steel section broke open and fell, revealing the chest cavity of the doll where there was a huge black spider staring icily at me. There was nothing else inside the doll, no heart, no light, nothing, except for that enormous black female spider. At that moment I snapped back to full consciousness, thoroughly shaken. It had been a dream, only a dream, but I knew now that for me, and Athina Onassis, after twenty years, it was

The End

Epilogue

I first saw Athina Roussel, the last surviving Onassis descendant, at her home in Lussy sur Morges in Switzerland just after her 13th birthday during what was a period of a tsunami of court cases involving her father Thierry Roussel, her Greek patrimony administrators who ran the Onassis Foundation, and a terrifying period for the family with a series of arrests of Middle Eastern operatives suspected of being involved in a scenario to kidnap the heiress and dispose of her and her father. Athina at the time was surrounded by ex Secret Air Service commando bodyguards and the family was on 24 hour standby. It was at this critical moment that Thierry Roussel invited me to Switzerland to help him with the media management regarding his criminal and other court cases in Greece. I grew close to the family, became their factotum, coordinating contacts between fifteen law offices, hiring and firing lawyers, attending strategy meetings in various countries, doing investigatory and Para-legal work and, preparing reports, trips and security. Circumstances brought us close.

I travelled with Athina and her family, stayed with them on Scorpios island, holidayed in summer at her vast Arabian nights estate in Ibiza with its eight pools, its hidden discotheque behind a man-made waterfall, shared birthday parties and dinners and went on yacht cruises in Greece and Spain with the family as well as sharing tables at family weddings and other events.

It was very early on, during a visit to Scorpios that I saw another Athina, who while only fourteen, I described as a Doll of Steel. There was something hard, immensely hard, behind the deceptive image of the timid, shy, vulnerable girl that I with my media contacts had helped to create. She became a national idol, the tragic girl who had lost her mother at three and who looked lost and vulnerable.

What Athina Onassis finally is today has been influenced by a complicated life in the centre of a whirlwind of financial issues, people wanting her money, and the undoubted traumatic experiences she went through in her formative teenage years. Later there was to be worse. After she ran off to marry her Brazilian Olympic champion the humiliating shock of how deceptive her husband had been for almost their entire eleven year marriage hit her hard. She was borderline anorexic when, after the split, she called on me for help, this time to put together the evidence from Nicky, collected in the Red File, and to deliver it to her in Holland.

She had the choice of living an open life, with all the advantages of being at the forefront of society that her fabled name and fortune offered, to engage in philanthropy as Bill Gates, the Niarchos family and so many others have done, but instead she reacted to events by withdrawing, like a female Howard Hughes, to become a recluse, without a circle of supportive friends beyond her trainers and stable staff and faithful bodyguard/chauffeur Guy Merat, spending most of her waking hours forcing pliable multi-million dollar champion horses to carry her over hurdle after hurdle from dawn to dusk, day after day, the horses forced to travel in planes and in horseboxes around the world to perform and do what is expected of them. The animals are taken from deserts to cold European venues, from the sands of Araby to London, Rio and Shanghai, receiving the attention of the best trainers and vets in state of the art stables. All this paid for by their tall slim Greek billionaire heiress owner, on condition that they never break a leg as happened to Camille in Geneva who was put to death because she would be unable to carry her mistress over another competition hurdle. For the Doll of Steel an operation on a broken leg and putting out to pasture of her faithful horses in a green field is not an option, as it was not for poor Camille.

Today that frail, shy, retiring teenager is a mature woman in her thirties, in charge of her fortune, uninterested in having to claim her destiny to be the head of the Onassis Foundation with its capacity to do good in the world to honour her family, isolated almost entirely from her Roussel family and half brother and sisters who stood by her and gave her a normal happy existence.

Athina Onassis estranged, probably for ever from, and not talking to her father, indeed a man who was interested in money and women and the good life, but he had stood by her during the court cases when the Greek administrators were claiming millions in legal fees and had sued the teenage Athina for large amounts of money. Roussel (and I was there) had sat for 42 days in a hostile court in Greece, faced with the withering comments of a prosecutor, who, life being what it is, himself was tried for felonious behaviour and sentenced to years in jail.

Roussel defended Athina's right to her grandfather's Foundation, to which she had an automatic and inalienable right to the presidency, according to the articles signed by her mother and board, but Athina had turned her back on it deciding to concentrate only on her professional athlete's life, not on good works for society, but on shaving another second, and another, off her performance round the course on show jumping competitions around the world.

Little Athina, with few, if any friends, and an obsession to keep away from people and cameras, her right to "privacy" as she describes it, but much more than that, is caught up in another situation that is not one that so easily handled.

On the one hand she shies from social contact and having a normal life while on the other she has created the Longines Athina Onassis Horse Shows, the ones that have been so closely associated with the Nicky-Doda/Braazilians scandal, where everything at this event, held in Brazil originally and now in St Tropez every May, carries her name and logo. It is Athina Onassis recluses' name and logo one sees everywhere. The loudspeakers blare out her name every few seconds, the TV announcers on her dedicated TV station at the event repeat the name 'Athina Onassis' over and over again; it is on horse blankets, posters, the website, on the prizes, on banners, everywhere, except on the venue's toilet paper, yet the hostess is never in the foreground, does not make any speeches of welcome, may not even give the prizes, refuses interviews to sports and news journalists and is in the oxymoronic position of being a recluse at a high profile event bearing her name, inviting the public to come while branding her name.

  Finally we see a billionaire who is careful with her own money, yet interested in getting even more, that of others. One only has to look at the Athina Onassis Horse Show website to see a section "Become a Sponsor", telling companies how they can get their logo on the AOHS event by giving their shareholders money to the heiress, to make her even richer.

  Athina Onassis is the opposite today of her cosmopolitan philanthropist cousins, the Niarchos brothers, who recently gave the suffering Greek medical system a gift of 143 new fully equipped ambulances and a commitment to pay their maintenance and parts costs for eight years. This followed many donations by the Niarchos family to those in need. Athina is not known for her philanthropy and indeed if she does help relatives with small amounts, as is rumoured, one can be sure that they have been warned by her lawyers that their employer has demanded of them never to mention the fact or to risk being cut off.

Athina's different path is a sad one, despite growing up in a socially active family, she has taken herself to a very lonely place, spending her time on windswept horse competition tracks and in stables with her multimillion dollar champion horses and staff for companionship. Her private life lacks the gregariousness of those in her economic bracket, or that of her brother Erik's cheerful party wandering with his circle of wealthy friends, or the quiet domestic harmony of her younger sister Sandrine, whose wedding Athina attended.

It was an uncomfortable occasion according to someone who was there for Athina to be in close physical proximity to her estranged father and her siblings with whom she has chosen to spend little, if any time, for reasons best known to her.

Athina is alone once again while Doda has moved on cheerfully after making some half-hearted efforts to get Athina back, having claimed unconvincingly his fidelity and undying love, Latin style, but he soon gave up when Nicky handed over Red File that I gave to Athina.

Doda, not a man to spin his wheels, reorganized his life in record time, found a beautiful and younger, of course, blonde Brazilian television journalist called Denise and has set off on the path to a new marriage, smiling all the way with an enamored beauty by his side, with the support of his daughter, and a nice boost to his bank account, enough to make anyone happy.

 The only major failure for Doda was his attempt to get a settlement of the magnitude that his much shrewder former father-in-law Thierry, an old and more experienced lobo in the millionaire heiress circuit, had secured from Christina. The Red File with Nicky's evidence put a stop to that and for sure saved Athina several million Euros in alimony a year.

 But Doda is a realist, and appears happy, having done well out of his marriage, become famous beyond his wildest dreams, while concurrently having enjoyed all the paid tricks that Nicky and his friends engaged in for him during the years that he had promised to be monogamous.

 Athina has been betrayed but she also had every opportunity and the tools to have forged a happier life. Her numerous bank accounts, legendary name, the public's adulation of her and her good looks gave her every advantage in the world. Instead of being attached to her Onassis legacy and its social obligations, she sold her dead mother's jewels, disposed of Scorpios, her iconic private island where those that gave her the choice and the hundreds of millions to be whatever she wanted - her mother Christina and her grandfather Aristotle Onassis - lie in silent tombs at the Panagitsa chapel on Scorpios, unvisited by the Greek heiress who goes to the ends of the world to take part in equestrian events, but never, from what is known, to kneel by the graves of her famly in prayer.

For those of us who lived, travelled, advised supported, broke bread with, and were close to the Onassis-Roussel family and Athina Onassis, in good days and bad, it has become difficult not to believe that, finally, there may be an Onassis curse that follows generation after generation, of the legendary family, like the protagonists of an ancient Greek tragedy.

Printed in Great Britain
by Amazon